Scripting Detention

Scripting Detention

*A Project in Theater
and Autoethnography
with Incarcerated Teens*

NANDITA DINESH

McFarland & Company, Inc., Publishers
Jefferson, North Carolina

Library of Congress Cataloguing-in-Publication Data

Names: Dinesh, Nandita, author.
Title: Scripting detention : a project in theater and autoethnography with incarcerated teens / Nandita Dinesh.
Description: Jefferson, North Carolina : McFarland & Company, Inc., Publishers, 2017 | Includes bibliographical references and index.
Identifiers: LCCN 2017036995 | ISBN 9781476669052 (softcover : acid free paper) ∞
Subjects: LCSH: Prison theater—United States. | Dinesh, Nandita. | Juvenile delinquents—United States.
Classification: LCC HV8861 .D56 2017 | DDC 365/.668—dc23
LC record available at https://lccn.loc.gov/2017036995

British Library cataloguing data are available

ISBN (print) 978-1-4766-6905-2
ISBN (ebook) 978-1-4766-2983-4

© 2017 Nandita Dinesh. All rights reserved

No part of this book may be reproduced or transmitted in any form or by any means, electronic or mechanical, including photocopying or recording, or by any information storage and retrieval system, without permission in writing from the publisher.

Front cover photograph © 2017 iStock

Printed in the United States of America

McFarland & Company, Inc., Publishers
  Box 611, Jefferson, North Carolina 28640
    www.mcfarlandpub.com

For all those who could not be named in this book.

Table of Contents

Introduction   1

One. Wispy Communities and George White   19

Two. Language, Carlos Sadaña and Marcos Gusmán   48

Three. Masculinity and David Villaseñor   74

Four. Psychological Differences, William Jones and Tishia Jackson   103

Five. Education and Tobiah Edwards   131

Six. The Guards   156

Conclusion   183

Epilogue   203

Appendix A: The Original Script of Lives Behind the Walls   205

Appendix B: Extracts from the Script of IFF Kashmir   214

Chapter Notes   221

Bibliography   222

Index   227

Introduction

During my doctoral work in Kashmir, between 2013 and 2015, I began to use autoethnography as a methodology with which to better frame my theatrical practice and research in times and/or places of conflict. While autoethnography was a concept I initially chose as an ethical strategy to guide my way of seeing, being in, and writing about Kashmir, it eventually emerged that autoethnography was not a choice; it was a necessity. As a non-Kashmiri theater practitioner, as a woman, and as a non-Muslim, what I represented in Kashmir was impossible to avoid: in the workshops, in the performances, and in the writing of my doctoral thesis. In each phase of the doctoral project therefore, autoethnography became an indispensable lens through which to expand my understanding of the positioning of my work (and my self) in Kashmir. As I continue to return to Kashmir, autoethnography remains a significant strategy in the performance that I am developing with a theater company in Srinagar; a performance that is inspired by Argentine playwright Griselda Gambaro's (1992) *Information for Foreigners*. *IFF Kashmir*—as I shall refer to its Kashmiri counterpart—consists of two Guides: one Kashmiri and one non-Kashmiri, who form the link in an otherwise fragmented play that occurs in different spaces of a house. The character of the non-Kashmiri Guide is crafted from my autoethnographical insights and I have come to think that this character's narratives add a complexity that moves *IFF Kashmir* just a little further away from being an appropriative initiative by an "outsider" theater director. Through the autoethnographical character of the non-Kashmiri Guide, therefore, *IFF Kashmir* is able to speak to how local narratives of war might intersect with the perspectives/experiences of outsiders who were/are trying to engage with the conflicts in the region (see Appendix B for extracts from *IFF Kashmir*). These experiences in Kashmir have made the concept of autoethnography central to how I think/write about my work as a theater practitioner-researcher in settings of conflict;

making it inevitable, perhaps, that this concept now frames how I think/write about my work within juvenile detention centers in New Mexico. It is the centrality of autoethnography that enables this book to offer a different dimension to the rich array of existing work about the use of theater/arts in contexts of incarceration (Balfour, 2004; Buchleitner, 2010; Fahy & King, 2003; McAvinchey, 2011; Thompson, 1998; Tocci, 2007; Lawston & Lucas, 2011; Shailor, 2011; Trounstine, 2004); but before embarking on my authethnographical journey vis-à-vis juvenile incarceration, this introduction seeks to clarify the particular concepts that shape my approach to this methodology: fragmentation, autoethnodrama, and the mystory.

Through my exploration of autoethnography in Kashmir, I have encountered the potential of fragmentation in a theatrical work—fragmentation that I have an aesthetic preference for implementing through the use of a promenade theater structure in which spectators move around different spaces, encountering in each space, diverse narratives about a central theme. As Annette Markham (2005:815–816) suggests, "the fragmented narrative can function as political action in many ways," to resist traditional systems of knowing and representation and to "open the space for reflexivity for" creators and performers alike. Since I do not like for my theatrical efforts to be seen as exhibiting any kind of propaganda or "message," the choice of a fragmented aesthetic design helps me "see—through disjuncture—[my] own habits of interpretation, to reveal, or at least question, taken-for-granted patterns of sense making" (Markham, 2005:815–816). Furthermore, because "fragments also tend to reveal and, therefore, make available the interstices of reading" (Markham, 2005:815–816), I have come to think that the spectator in an intentionally fragmented theatrical encounter might be forced to experience a similar disjuncture as the creators of the piece—a disjuncture in which the physical act of moving between spaces disrupts a generally taken-for-granted assumption that the performance will be experienced from a chair in an auditorium. Therefore, with such promenade-based fragmented approaches to theater making, I have found "multiplicity [to be] made more possible" and "power [to be] more distributed" (Markham 2005:815–816). Since traditional relationships between space, performer, and spectator function differently in these fragmented approaches to theater making, such performances "simultaneously make the author's particular set of arguments and allow for alternatives by revealing the practices at work in the interpretive process" (Markham, 2005:815–816). That said, while this potential for fragmentation to perform a politics of disruption has immensely benefited my work as a theater practitioner, this strategy has also been instrumental in my work as a writer. As someone who loves writing about theater just as much as I love making it; as someone who enjoys exploring theory as much as I do practice; autoethnography has provided me a methodological apparatus with which to explore novel ways of writing about what I do. My published writing to date has explored autoethnography in some form and this book is no exception; except, perhaps, in this being my most experimental effort yet.

This book is based on my work in detention centers in New Mexico, particularly an original performance that I created with incarcerated young men between September and December 2015. This prison theater project involved ten young men between the ages of 14 and 18 and consisted of a two-hour workshop once a week. By using a devised theater methodology in which the young men and I worked together as collaborators, this series of workshops resulted in the creation and performance of a piece entitled *Lives Behind the Walls* (*Lives*)—a piece that used the strategies of both the promenade and fragmentation as integral concepts. After the project ended, when reflecting on *Lives* in light of my more recent engagements in youth detention centers and my discoveries through *IFF Kashmir* I gradually came to the realization that, apart from certain aesthetic decisions surrounding the form of the performance, *Lives* did not include "my" voice. By choosing to use a devised pedagogy I had placed my own opinions, analyses, and thoughts on the backburner; *Lives* was entirely a manifestation of the young men's words, their experiences, and their stories. On the one hand, I consider this to be one of the successes of the project in that I, the outsider theater maker, was rendered invisible in the final piece. On the other hand, I have come to wonder if there might be a way for my voice to be present in *Lives* as I write about the work in retrospect. What if I were to integrate autoethnographic components—like the character of non–Kashmiri Guide in *IFF Kashmir*—to the existing content in *Lives*? Would such an approach enable me to articulate ideas that I could not while the work was enclosed within prison walls?

Before speaking to how I explore these questions throughout this book, it is important to clarify that my work within juvenile detention centers in New Mexico is not restricted to this one project. In addition to the work on *Lives*, there are other ways in which I have come to interact with the juvenile justice system in the state: I mentor and coordinate monthly interactions between young people at the detention center and young men and women from the college where I teach theater studies; I have led (and continue to lead) week-long experiential learning programs during which students from both the college and the detention center come together to more intensively work on a creative project; I help run an institute that focuses on engagements between the college and various arms of the juvenile justice system in New Mexico; I am in the early stages of conceptualizing a more holistic prison education program that the college might develop in collaboration with the detention center. I clarify these various aspects to my interactions with juvenile justice in New Mexico since I do not want my readers to consider this book as being solely based on an isolated initiative within one juvenile detention center. Rather, the autoethnographic rewriting of scenes from *Lives* forms the thread that links insights that have been gained over a two-year time frame (at the time of publishing this book).

Additionally, I must inform the reader that the identities of the young men and women, the prison officials, and the prisons in question have intentionally been kept anonymous in this book—as it was only under condition of anonymity that this writing project was approved by the detention center superintendent with whom I worked most closely. While keeping identities obscured, therefore, scenes from *Lives* frame each chapter in this book, and in each case, I use an autoethnographic strategy of the mystory (more on this later) to analyze *Lives'* processes of creation, to discuss insights from other interactions with the juvenile justice system, and to consider larger issues surrounding the detention of young people in the United States. As such, each chapter culminates in the re-writing of one scene—a new scene that integrates the existing scene from *Lives* with the voice of the Outsider (see Appendix A for the original version of *Lives*); an integration that makes the rewritten script, autoethnodrama:

> An ethnodrama, a word joining ethnography and drama, is a written play script consisting of dramatized, significant selections of narrative collected from interview transcripts, participant observation field notes, journal entries, personal memories/experiences, and/or print and media artifacts such as diaries, blogs, e-mail correspondence, television broadcasts, newspaper articles, court proceedings, and historic documents. In some cases, production companies can work improvisationally and collaboratively to devise original and interpretive texts based on authentic sources. Simply put, this is dramatizing the data [Saldaña, 2011:1213].

By bringing together strategies from autoethnography and ethnodrama the rewritten script of *Lives* combines "analysis, drama and reflection" to offer "the reader a theoretical and personal insight into experiences" that will provide them "with a more complete picture than just a research paper or just a piece of creative writing" (Moriarty, 2014:9). While these two forms of theatre making are related, in an ethnodrama, "the writer is an offstage voice but in autoethnodrama they are more present" (Moriarty, 2014:50). Autoethnodramas seek to function as texts that create "an entertainingly informative experience for an audience" (Saldaña in Moriarty, 2014:4) and Carolyn Ellis and Arthur P. Bochner (in Moriarty, 2014:48) argue that such "creative nonfictions have the ability to show the reader what is happening, rather than telling them, which is arguably a more empowering and useful research tool." As a result, autoethnodramas "aim to make experience concrete despite being necessarily 'messy' spaces where multiple voices and experiences co-exist" (Moriarty, 2014:49). These messy spaces are "rooted in and inspired by the autobiographical experiences of the researcher and the researched" and "can therefore provide a dynamic platform where the audience/reader can also challenge and debate the meaning of these lived experiences" (Moriarty, 2014:50).

Despite the potential for autoethnodramas to perform and represent complexity, however, there is no denying that the process of choosing what to include—and what to leave out—is hardly straightforward. I have struggled to curate the material in this book and every editorial choice has warranted a consideration of the ethical, political, and aesthetic repercussions of those choices. Rather than obscuring these dilemmas from my readers though, and rather than a pretense of ease in my decision making processes, my "resolution is not to shy away from these matters" (Saldaña, 2011:40). Instead I attempt to share—as transparently as possible—how I grapple with the process of content selection vis-à-vis an understanding of my responsibilities in writing this book. My first responsibility, as I see it, is to the young men that I collaborated with on *Lives*; my second responsibility is to my "personal integrity and standards of excellence" as a researcher and artist; my third responsibility is to you, the reader, who "witnesses what the first two parties have collaborated on and becomes a group of new collaborators in the [auto] ethnotheatrical event" (Saldaña, 2011:43).

Having contextualized the "theater," "prison," and "autoethnography" components to the title of this book, there is one more term that I need to introduce here: mystory. And in order to set the stage for the use of the concept in this book, I need to take a short detour back into the world of autoethnography. Deborah Reed-Danahay (in Moriarty, 2014:44) defines autoethnography as "research (graphy) that connects the personal (auto) to the cultural (ethnos), placing the self within a social context." Similarly, Corinna Brown (2013:122) proposes that autoethnography might be seen as "research, writing, story, and method that connect the autobiographical and personal to the cultural, social, and political." In this vein, approaches to autoethnography might be said to contain permutations and combinations of the common characteristics that Carolyn Ellis (in Brown, 2013:122) proposes: "action, emotion, embodiment, self-consciousness, and introspection." In speaking particularly to autoethnography that involves the creation of/participation in/intersection with forms of performance, Norman K. Denzin (2003:12) suggests that "[a]utoethnographer-performers insert their experiences into the cultural performances that they study" and extends an idea from Toni Morrison (in Denzin, 2003:20), that "the best performance autoethnographies, like the best art, are 'unquestionably political and irrevocably beautiful at the same time.'" It is Morrison's proposition that I take on as a challenge in this book: how can I write about/from *Lives* in a way that does justice to the politics involved in prison theater interventions, while simultaneously creating writing that is beautiful? Can beauty, in such writing, be found in an articulated humility when faced with a daunting array of political, ethical, and aesthetic challenges? Can beauty, in such writing, arise from an honesty that speaks lucidly—that does not seek "to simplify what is complicated or complicate what is simple" (Roy, 1999)?

Just as I have embarked on this project to more carefully understand my work within juvenile justice systems it has been said that autoethnographers often "begin projects with personal experiences that we want to understand more fully, deeply, and meaningfully" (Adams, Jones & Ellis, 2015:47). Autoethnographic representations "are artistic and analytic demonstrations of how we come to know, name, and interpret personal and cultural experience" and in these efforts we are asked to confront "the tension between insider and outsider perspectives, between social practice and social constraint" (Adams, Jones & Ellis, 2015:1–2). As such, autoethnographic accounts and analyses use "a researcher's personal experience to describe and critique cultural beliefs, practices, and experiences"; they use "careful self reflection—typically referred to as 'reflexivity'—to name and interrogate the intersections between self and society, the particular and the general, the personal and the political"; they showcase "people in the process of figuring out what to do, how to live, and the meaning of their struggles"; they balance "intellectual and methodological rigor, emotion, and creativity," and finally, autoethnographic approaches strive "for social justice and to make life better" (Adams, Jones & Ellis, 2015:1–2). There are different kinds of autoethnographies and I would particularly like to highlight four approaches to this methodology for the reader of this book: analytic, conceptual, impressionist, and expressionist autoethnographies; all of which manifest in my writing to varying degrees.

While "autoethnographies have been criticized for narcissistic self-indulgence" (Moriarty, 2014:46), I have sought to mitigate these challenges by using analytic autoethnography to make myself visible as "a full member in the research group or setting" and to develop "theoretical understandings of broader social phenomena" (Moriarty, 2014:47). Furthermore, the analytic components to my use of autoethnography in this book showcase the five key features that Anderson (in Moriarty, 2014:47–48) puts forward:

- "Complete member research status" and "Narrative visibility of the researcher's self": I make sure to highlight my own participation in, and contribution to, the moments that I analyze and reflect on. Since the collaborative nature of *Lives* meant that I shaped conversations just as much as I observed them, I try to be as honest as I can both about what I recall and about my doubts surrounding the fallacies of my memory.
- "Analytical reflexivity": where personal reflections and accounts are not taken at face value but instead, are constructed as being multi-layered and multi-dimensional. As a relative newcomer to the realm of prison theater I adopt this mode of constant reflexivity to remind the reader of the uncertainties that pervade my work.
- "Dialogue with informants beyond the self" and "Commitment to theoretical analysis": the reader will see these two elements when I address the specifics of how the mystory manifests in this book, later in this Introduction. My personal insights are always counterbalanced, nuanced, and/or opposed by different informants and while some of my informants come from the academic world and from "recognized" disciplines of study, other informants hail from the mainstream i.e., from newspaper articles, blog posts, and popular culture references that might be less "scholarly" within academic realms. While some of these informants address global questions surrounding juvenile justice and incarceration, much of the information that I have curated in this book is specifically relevant to U.S. criminal justice system—the system that most affects my young collaborators in *Lives*.

The autoethnography in this book is not only analytic though; the writing also embodies certain characteristics of its expressionist counterpart. Written primarily in first person narration, the expressionist quality to this book emerges from texts that might be called "confessional" and that seek to take the reader into my perspective of what happened during the creation and performance of *Lives* (Adams, Jones & Ellis, 2015:87–88). In the vein of "expressionist autoethnographers [who] use writing to examine and move through pain, confusion, anger, and uncertainty" (Adams, Jones & Ellis, 2015:87–88), the reader will observe many moments in which I use emotive storytelling as my mode of interpretation and analysis. From my first visit to a juvenile detention center when I returned home with tears in my eyes, to the cynicism and despair that I continue to encounter with each passing visit, emotional upheavals were/are part and parcel of this work. But in addition to the confessional and emotive tone I use to share narrative accounts about how I have been changed as a result of this work, expressionist qualities to the autoethnography in this book might also be seen in the "[c]ollaborative witnessing, which involves focusing compassionately on participants' experiences with the goal of developing and sustaining deep and committed relationships with research partners" (Adams, Jones & Ellis, 2015:87). Collaborative witnessing is important to mention since I do not see this book as being an end in itself; my relationships with the young people in the detention centers are ones on which I am still working. And as such, I am cognizant that I have to be extremely careful about how and what I write; that in seeking to theoretically and critically analyze my work in detention centers, I cannot forget to be sensitive about how my criticism is conveyed. There is criticism in this book, of course; criticisms about particular kinds of systems and laws and behaviors. And yet, I have tried to articulate those critiques with a sense of compassion: a compassion that I would not have to be so careful about, perhaps, if my work in the detention center was a one-off occurrence and if my personal relationships with administrators/guards/inmates did not have to be nurtured.

In addition to the confessional/emotive tone and collaborative witnessing, the expressionist quality to this autoethnography can also be found in the "renderings, in which the emotional lives and journeys of the researcher and participants form the crux and mood of the narrative" (Adams, Jones & Ellis, 2015:87–88). That said, while there are emotional renderings of my collaborators in this book, I always take care to contextualize my subjective interpretations of their emotional lives. As someone who grew up in India and has spent the last decade as something of a nomad, I am aware that I might be misreading/misinterpreting/misrepresenting culturally specific nuances that frame the emotional renderings that I put forth in this book. Where I am aware of a lack in my understanding, I do my best to confess to it. But what about the lacks I'm not aware of? Those, I hope the reader will forgive. My being from outside the U.S., my having different cultural frames of reference than my collaborators, my way of using English being different from the vernacular used by the young men in *Lives*—all of these were strengths in some way; strengths that I will highlight in relevant chapters. These modes of being different, however, also caused many gaps. Gaps that I hope to acknowledge, understand, and explore through the use of expressionist autoethnography.

As well as sharing characteristics that encompass analytic and expressionist autoethnographies, there is also an impressionist dimension to how I write in this book. Impressionist autoethnographies seek to "immerse readers in the sights, sounds, smells, and textures of the experience related in the account," they include "[n]arratives of space and place," and "focus on the impressions that these spaces and places make on the autoethnographer and on the reader" (Adams, Jones & Ellis, 2015:86–87). My approach to impressionism—of immersing my readers in a textured experience of juvenile detention centers—is primarily showcased through particular strategies within the rewritten scenes from *Lives*. The reader will notice that, in having to move around different rooms and different kinds of spaces, the audience member is asked to experientially see, smell, feel, hear, and taste the narratives that emerge from behind prison walls. Furthermore, in addition to this focus on creating an experience of the temporal, spatial, sensorial textures of a specific setting, the rewrites of *Lives* contain elements of impressionist autoethnographies by invoking "[i]nteractive interviews" (Adams, Jones & Ellis, 2015:87) in which characters that occupy different positions on the prison spectrum use interpersonal interaction within the frames of the theatrical performance to better represent/perform aspects to juvenile incarceration. These moments of impressionistic interactive interviews function as "[c]o-constructed narratives and collaborative autoethnographies" in which "stories [are] told by multiple narrators that pivot around a common experience, social issue, or epiphany" (Adams, Jones & Ellis, 2015:86–87)—the common social issue here being young people's experiences of incarceration in New Mexico and the U.S. I include the U.S. (in general) here, despite my work being localized to New Mexico, since narratives surrounding the criminal justice system across the country have influenced me. The reader will see evidence of this in the narratives included within the chapters.

So, while characteristics of expressionist and analytic autoethnographies can be seen in each chapter's central analyses, and impressionist elements can be seen in the rewritten scenes from *Lives* that end each chapter, there is one last approach to autoethnography—the conceptual approach—that influences all the writing in this book. Conceptual autoethnographies are said to be characterized by the use of multiple narrative voices, high levels of reflexivity, and most importantly, the implementation of strategies that "question the role and purpose of research and writing, the formality of research texts, the role of the author as artist, and the lessons that autoethnographies can offer writers and readers" (Adams, Jones & Ellis, 2015:88). Furthermore, in conceptualist texts, "interpretation and analysis are the inspiration for story; showing and interpreting are tightly coupled" and there is an emphasis on "the importance of audiences in creating and completing texts, thus making a variety of collaborative readings possible" (Adams, Jones & Ellis, 2015:88). Conceptualist autoethnographies manifest in various ways and one of these ways is said to be as"[p]erformative writing, in which the writing itself approximates—performs—the experience(s) and culture(s) being discussed" and in which there is an approach to "'writing as doing' rather than 'writing as meaning'" (Adams, Jones & Ellis, 2015:88–89). By using fragmentation, autoethnodrama and different techniques of autoethnography, therefore, I hope for this book "to do"; "to perform." Although the notion of "writing as doing" can be rather ambiguous, I will return to a consideration of this book's performativity in the conclusion: What does this book perform? What does it "do"?

Having described the four autoethnographic genres that influence my writing, it is time to return to the concept that began the discussion above: mystory. A term that is used by Denzin (1997:116) to refer to "a personal mythology, a public story, and a performance that critiques" and to build on Gregory Ulmer's (1989) proposals surrounding the term, the mystory finds two manifestations in this book. First, the concept of the mystory underpins the way in which I have rewritten scenes from *Lives* so as to take the existing script from being drama to autoethnodrama. According to Denzin (1997:116), a mystory text is "an interactive, dramatic performance [that is] presentational, not representational theater" that simultaneously "has parallels with a staged reading" while still being "performance, not text-centered interpretive events." As such, when thinking about the larger aesthetic vision for rewriting scenes from *Lives*, I adopted an approach where the "emphasis [was] on performance, presentation, and improvisation and not just a reading of the fixed text" (Denzin, 1997:116). Since "mystory is a montage," my rewrites of *Lives* combine "text, cinematic [images] and multimedia" and the rewritten scenes are "filled with sounds, music, and images taken [from my] personal history" (Denzin, 1997:116). By incorporating such strategies, I made the conscious choice to rewrite *Lives* as a performance in which the "audience coper-

Introduction

forms the text, and the writer, as narrator, functions as a guide—a commentator on what is occurring" (Denzin, 1997:116). As a result of such inspired uses of audience interaction the "same reader can read the parts of the same and different characters" in the rewritten scenes, and while each "performance is different—different readers, different meanings and interpretations; in every instance," a central story is "told and performed" (Denzin, 1997: 117). The story, in this case, is the script that was originally created for *Lives;* a story that forms the box that I experiment within; a box I simultaneously try not to change the shape of. Since mystory performances invite "each member of the audience [to bring] his or her biography and voice to the lines that are read and spoken," a "stage, per se, is not used; the wall between performers and audience disappears because all parties to the performance are also performers" (Denzin, 1997:116)—a characteristic that ties in beautifully with my own aesthetic affiliations toward a promenade form that takes place in non-traditional spaces. Finally, in addition to the breaking down of the fourth wall, the mystory-inspired rewrites of *Lives* develop characters that move away from "[s]implistic characterizations based on traditional oppositions (male-female, etc)" (Trinh in Denzin, 1997: 117); characters that move away from simplistic binary oppositions like good/bad, victim/perpetrator, and prisoner/guard.

Now, while these ideas were fascinating to me from the outset, I could not ignore their propensity for being too abstract and expansive. Eventually, therefore, I had to ask myself how such conceptual approaches to the mystory would translate into practice. How could I write mystories that would allow order and disorder to coexist? How could I ensure that performing the complexity of *Lives* through autoethnographic, messy writing would not alienate my readers by being obscure and impenetrable? How could I create a holistic form of writing that would not only contain, but complement, intentionally fragmented content? In this search for an accessible yet complex framework to craft the mystories in this book, I ultimately revisited Ulmer's proposition (in Denzin, 1997:117):

> Write a mystory bringing into relation your experience with three levels of discourse—personal (autobiography), popular (community stories, oral history or popular culture), [and] expert (disciplines of knowledge). In each case use the punctum or sting of memory to locate items significant to you.

Encountering Ulmer's three-pronged approach to structuring a mystory was an "aha" moment and immediately appealed to my desire for a structure to shape this book's messiness. Therefore, while one aspect to the mystory lies in the how scenes from *Lives* are reconceptualized and rewritten, another manifestation of the mystory can be found in my decision to structure each chapter in this book around the three levels of discourse that Ulmer suggests. As such, each chapter is composed of three kinds of mystory analyses (in addition to the rewritten text from *Lives*): personal narratives, popular narratives, and expert narratives. While the expert narratives are perhaps most "predictable" in how they are structured and written, the personal and popular narratives in each chapter are shared with the reader as creative, reflexive, and self-reflexive texts that do not sit within "conventional" academic genres. By weaving together these unstructured voices—my voice; mainstream voices; academic voices; the voices of the young people in *Lives*—in a structured way, I hope the reader will find the clarity through the messiness; the order within the disorder; the organization within the chaos.

Each chapter begins with the personal narratives: instances from my work in the detention centers that have caused me to come to particular realizations and reflections.

Example of Mystory Part One: The Personal Narratives

Until I moved to New Mexico, I had never worked in a prison setting.
I had thought about it many times,
But when I was living in India,
It didn't occur to me that such an intervention would even be possible.
Would Indian prison authorities allow an upper-middle class, South Indian woman within their walls?

> Could I even get past the bureaucracy that has, unfortunately, shaped many of my interactions with Indian government officials?
>> Was I willing to pull strings—you know, call my uncle who knows a guy who knows a guy—to be allowed access into some of India's prisons?
>>> And, of course, given my many encounters with particular strands of Indian misogyny, did I really want to work with male prisoners (note that—in my naiveté—I had only thought of adult, male prisons. I did not even consider incarcerated women or youth).

Finally, even if it was possible to get over all of these challenges, was I willing to take time/energy away from work in Kashmir?

Every time the thought of working in prisons on the Indian subcontinent entered my mind, I would just as quickly find reasons not to do the work.

Clearly, there is a lot more critical self-reflection that I need to undertake about why this has been the case.

When I moved to New Mexico in 2015, however, there suddenly seemed to be conversations about criminal justice happening all around me. Or perhaps it was just that I was paying more attention to these conversations.

When I first arrived in New Mexico as a practitioner-researcher who has mostly worked in war zones, I thought long and hard about how I would craft my theatrical interventions in this setting.

First, I thought about working on issues of immigration around the New Mexico/Mexico border.

But there seemed to be a plethora of individuals and organizations already doing wonderful work in this regard.

Then, I thought about working with theater on Native American reservations

But none of the connections that I pursued, worked out.

Finally, I thought about prisons.

Maybe because a friend was reading Michelle Alexander's (2012) *The New Jim Crow: Mass Incarceration in the Age of Colorblindness* at the time and couldn't stop talking about it.

Maybe because prisons were the only settings of conflict in New Mexico where there seemed to be both the space for, and the interest in, my work.

I can't recall exactly when I first thought of working in juvenile detention centers in New Mexico.

But I did.

And once that possibility emerged, like any applied theater practitioner has probably had to do at some point in their career, I wrote to as many people as I could find a connection to. Friends of friends of friends of friends. I pulled tens of email addresses off websites and followed up every few days until someone responded.

Serendipitously, it was around the same time that college personnel spoke to me about their existing detention center initiative and looking at this program as a possible avenue through which to learn about the juvenile justice system in New Mexico—in case my offer to conduct theater workshops as an independent artist/researcher came to naught—I jumped on board.

Some folks might consider my impetuous jump into the world of prison theater a little bit misguided.

Naïve.

Unethical even.

Perhaps it was, and is.

Just a little bit naïve.

Just a little bit unethical.

But,

The risks that come from my impetuous entry into the world of prison theater are offset by a poignancy unlike any I have encountered.

> A poignancy that is different from what I saw in northern Uganda.
>> A poignancy unlike what I encountered when working in Rwanda.
>>> A poignancy with different textures than what I experience in Kashmir.

Working in detention centers in New Mexico has been—is—one of the most poignant aspects to my life here.

* * *

The personal narratives that begin each chapter are followed by popular narratives surrounding a particular theme that has been brought to the fore through the preceding autoethnographic analyses: points of view about incarceration that might be found in "mainstream" realms. As such, these sections bring together a range of non-academic references—included as block quotations—with brief explanations about why I chose to include those particular popular narratives, how these voices relate to the personal and expert viewpoints that are showcased in a particular chapter, and ultimately, how such mainstream narratives link to particular rewrites of *Lives*. The sections containing popular narratives include excerpts/quotations from different mainstream forums—newspaper archives, movies, songs, and blog posts—and while I do not ever claim that my overview of mainstream references is extensive enough to map an entire topic, the popular narratives have been curated carefully so as to convey a diverse array of voices and opinions about a specific dimension to incarceration. All direct excerpts from mainstream sources are indented and cited, as they would be in formal academic writing, but the connections that I draw between the personal narratives and the popular voices are less formal in tone and structure.

Example of Mystory Part Two: The Popular Narratives

In mainstream media, or perhaps its more fair to say that in certain sections of mainstream media, narratives about incarceration in the U.S. are primarily framed as stinging critiques of the school to prison pipeline, the prison industrial complex, and the intersections between race, class, and incarceration. Narratives like:

> The "school-to-prison pipeline" [is] a disturbing national trend wherein children are funneled out of public schools and into the juvenile and criminal justice systems. Many of these children have learning disabilities or histories of poverty, abuse, or neglect, and would benefit from additional educational and counseling services. Instead, they are isolated, punished, and pushed out. "Zero-tolerance" policies criminalize minor infractions of school rules, while cops in schools lead to students being criminalized for behavior that should be handled inside the school [American Civil Liberties Union, 2016].
>
> The prison-industrial complex is not only a set of interest groups and institutions. It is also a state of mind. The lure of big money is corrupting the nation's criminal-justice system, replacing notions of public service with a drive for higher profits. The eagerness of elected officials to pass "tough-on-crime" legislation—combined with their unwillingness to disclose the true costs of these laws—has encouraged all sorts of financial improprieties [Schlosser, 1998].
>
> **Racial Disparities in Incarceration**
> - African Americans now constitute nearly 1 million of the total 2.3 million incarcerated population
> - African Americans are incarcerated at nearly six times the rate of whites
> - Together, African American and Hispanics comprised 58% of all prisoners in 2008, even though African Americans and Hispanics make up approximately one quarter of the U.S. population
> - According to Unlocking America, if African American and Hispanics were incarcerated at the same rates of whites, today's prison and jail populations would decline by approximately 50%
> - One in six black men had been incarcerated as of 2001. If current trends continue, one in three black males born today can expect to spend time in prison during his lifetime
> - 1 in 100 African American women are in prison
> - Nationwide, African-Americans represent 26% of juvenile arrests, 44% of youth who are detained, 46% of the youth who are judicially waived to criminal court, and 58% of the youth admitted to state prisons (Center on Juvenile and Criminal Justice) [NAACP, 2016].

Narratives that counter these critiques are harder to come by. But when they do, here are some of the views that one might encounter:

> So-called "first-offenders" are often nothing of the sort. In some cases, "first-offenders" have lengthy juvenile records that are unavailable by law to the adult criminal

justice system. These "first-offenders" are already hardened criminals. In other cases, offenders get probation for their first adult offense, and sometimes even for subsequent offenses committed while on probation.... Former Attorney General Hal Stratton of New Mexico has summed it up: "I don't know anyone that goes to prison on their first crime. By the time you go to prison, you are a pretty bad guy" [Espejo, 2002].

When social scientists control for family structure, the rates for blacks and whites are not significantly different. Broken families are most closely correlated with violent crime, regardless of race. In other words, family structure, not race, is the leading indicator of criminal behavior. There is a higher rate of crime among blacks only because black communities have higher rates of illegitimacy and family breakup [Espejo, 2002].

If having a privatized prison system means prisoners will actually serve the time they deserve, then a private prison system is ideal [Espejo, 2002].

The popular narratives in each chapter are not about espousing *one* viewpoint. They are about considering different "popular" views, opinions, and insights that are publically available and freely disseminated; voices that I delve into so as to expand my own understanding of "the mainstream."

* * *

These popular sections are followed by "expert narratives": sections that function as a more "conventional" academic discussion and use a style of writing that is similar to what has been used thus far in this Introduction, and thus no example similar to the above seems necessary. Like the popular voices, these expert discussions are woven around one particular theme that has emerged as being important from the personal analyses that begin respective chapters; the sources are intentionally multi-disciplinary and seek to highlight the ways in which scholarship is attempting to engage with particular questions surrounding incarceration. These expert narratives are, finally, followed by one rewritten segment from *Lives*.

All this being said, it is important to clarify that I do not consider one kind of narrative/text in this book to be more important than another. To me, the personal stories are as informative as the popular narratives, which in turn are as revealing as the expert voices. As a result, in some chapters I have more personal narratives to share than academic/theoretical analyses; in other chapters there are far more academic analyses than there are popular culture references. With these three integrated levels of discourse (personal, popular, and expert), an overall conceptualist approach to autoethnography (that has elements of the analytic, expressionist, and impressionist autoethnographies), and a mystory autoethnodrama that manifests as rewritten scenes from *Lives,* each chapter is crafted with the following structure:

- An epigraph from the original script of *Lives*, which functions as a prelude to the scene that will be rewritten at the end of the chapter. The original script of the entire play is available in Appendix A.
  - *Mystory Part One: The Personal Narratives*
    These sections are written with an informal tone, mostly as first-person narrative, akin to journal entries
  - *Mystory Part Two: The Popular Narratives*
    These sections bring together informal, personal ruminations and extracts from mainstream sources, which encompass a diverse array of popular opinion
  - *Mystory Part Three: The Expert Narratives*
    Academic analyses that engage with scholarship from across different disciplines in relation to the themes that have emerged as warranting attention in the personal narratives
    [All three parts to the mystory adopt relevant characteristics from analytic and expressionist autoethnographies]
  - *(A rewritten scene from* **Lives***)*
    [The rewritten script uses Denzin's mystory principles in the creation of an autoethnodrama and exhibits characteristics inherent to impressionist autoethnographies]

Having laid out the different sections to each chapter, and having put forward the concepts that shape the writing, I believe it is important to add some final points of clarification. This book does not attempt to analyze, in any detail, existing scholarship surrounding prison theater. Where particular sections warrant drawing from the rich array of works that have been mentioned in the opening paragraph of this Introduction, I do so—but the absence of these works in the remainder of this book has been a conscious choice so as to strengthen the particular aims of my autoethnographic approach. Similarly, while I draw from existing scholarship around autoethnography in this Introduction, the reader will not see these concepts tangibly reemerge in the discussions that follow—the concepts shape the writing, of course, but they are not revisited at any regular interval and this too is an intentional choice. In my quest to create an original, messy prison theater text, sources are drawn from as they fit within the "personal," "popular," and "expert" sections of each chapter, and this book has been written to serve diverse audiences: students and educators in applied and devised theater courses who are keen to see writing that inhabits spaces between theory and praxis; prison workers who hold different affiliations to the authorities that oversee/run them and who continue to see value in engaging with incarcerated youth; theater practitioners who might want to stage a less-conventional script about juvenile incarceration; writers who are keen to explore new forms to contain their content.

Finally, despite my use of this particular structure to sculpt the messiness of this book, I should acknowledge that my reader will be required "to work" in engaging with the varied and fragmented voices in these pages; "to work" both intellectually and emotionally; "to work" in a way that is different from the engagement that is demanded by a less messy text. But I hope you—the reader—will be willing to do this "work." Because in choosing to do so, I think you will gain a heightened understanding of this: that any attempt to engage with incarceration will be fraught with difficulty; that any effort to access voices that occupy barred spaces will be fractured by competing agendas; that fragmentation might be the only realistic way for a non-prisoner to represent the chimeras that exist behind prison walls.

Chapter One

Wispy Communities and George White

George White: A 15-year-old young man from Alabama, George has a strict family that forces him to go to school and expects him to get straight As. George's father was in the army, his mom is a nurse, and he is an only child. A "good" kid, George goes to the college party to meet girls. He always thought he would become a doctor or a lawyer but at the party, things change. George gets drunk on one beer, unintentionally takes 'shrooms, and starts a fire. The fire brings the police to the party and once in prison, George is really scared. He tries to stay out of prison gangs but is intimidated into joining them. Upon leaving prison, he tries to change his life but overdoses on heroin and meets with an untimely death.

Mystery Part One: The Personal Narratives

There were changes that affected my workshop every Friday and as a result, the sense of community that I was attempting to create within my devised theater workshop was often thrown amuck.

There were young men who were consistent in their attendance and those who weren't.

There were guards who were on shift one week but not the next.

There were unpredictable emergencies that occurred somewhere in the prison complex, that would have officials running in to/out of the workshop space.

Disciplinary actions.

Bad days.

Other commitments.

There were changes that affected my workshop every Friday.

And my understanding of "community" had to shift.

At first, when I saw changes in my participant group, I experimented with different pedagogical techniques.

I thought my pedagogy was the problem—so

One day I tried movement-based exercises

The next session was discussion-based

In the next session I tried to integrate video and music

And so on and so forth.

I kept varying my pedagogy so as to identify where the problem was; why I could never count on having a steady participant group.

But none of these pedagogical variations seemed to matter.

The participant group kept changing.

    And changing.

        And changing again.

So eventually, I had to acknowledge that whether or not I changed elements to my pedagogy,

There was nothing I could do about the constantly changing composition of my collaborators.

I could not control my workshops in ways that I was accustomed to.

I could not design my project with the kinds of goals that I had articulated in past work—because goals that might be easily accomplished in another context were not so simple to complete in the detention center.

For example:

> If I wanted to script a particular scene during a particular Friday, I could not assume that the young men that I had designated as the "creators" of that scene would not have a mandatory counseling session (that they had not known about a week prior).

> If I wanted to work on one particular actor's monologue during a particular Friday, I could not assume that the young man would not be called away for a mandatory wrestling club meeting (that he had not known about a week prior).

This constant unpredictability within a criminal justice system that is designed to be painstakingly predictable is an irony that is not lost on me.

Within these constant changes, I did the best I could to make the workshop as collaborative as possible and to ensure that every participant had a say in the final performance that the group created. During one of the early workshop sessions, I facilitated a discussion (with whoever was present that day) and asked the young men to suggest possible themes/ideas that they wanted to explore for their final performance. The ideas abounded:

"We should talk about a party"

"We should show something about rival gangs in a prison"

"We should perform something about the experiences of young people in prison"

"What about doing something around anti-gang interventions?"

"Could we create a performance from the lyrics of a song?"

"Oh, if we can base the play on a song, can we not also base it on a movie?"

As I said, the ideas abounded.

After a time of discussing each of these ideas and the benefits and challenges of each one, K put his hand up and said that he had found a way to combine all his peers' ideas into one story:

A group of young people goes to a party. There are many illegal goings-on at this party and high on drugs, one of the young partygoers (George White) accidentally starts a fire. The police are called as a result of the fire and all the young partygoers are arrested. Once in prison the young people form two different prison gangs that constantly get into fights with each other, and during one of these fights, one of the gang leaders is murdered. [Eventually the story changed a bit: the two rival gangs would attempt a reconciliation and discontented with his gang leader's desire to make peace, one of the gang's second-in-command would murder his friend].

While K had certainly found a way to weave together many of the ideas put forth by his peers, I intervened upon hearing the complex storyline:

"Less is more,"

I suggested to the young men,

"Sometimes, it might be better to take a focused theme or topic and develop it as best we can; rather than picking up a story that is complicated and is one that we might not be able to do justice to."

"Yeah, and don't you think,"

N added to my concerns,

"that we're just gonna show people exactly what they think happens in prisons? I mean, if our families are going to be watching this performance and they see, like, they see us beating each other up and shit.... That's what people think happens in prisons, anyway."

Despite these words of caution from N and myself, however, in the anonymous vote that we held at the end of the ideation discussion, it was K's idea that was voted in with a significant majority.

Was this because K's suggestion made most of the young men happy by incorporating as many of their ideas as possible?

Sure, maybe this was part of the reason.

On the other hand though, there was an interesting dynamic that emerged during that process of voting—a dynamic in which the unassuming and quiet K emerged as a leader amongst the group. While there were other more vociferous members in the workshop who I would have assumed to be leaders because of their ability to articulate and intimidate (like N), it was the unassuming K who had the votes behind him; votes that even my words of caution did not impact.

K's status was not limited to the ideation process and his prominence within the unit was again brought to my attention later on, when observing how his contributions were remembered by his peers even when K had been paroled and was no longer part of the project.

Despite this first instance in which K emerged as an unexpected leader though, and despite the independence that the young men displayed in choosing the content for their final performance, the sessions that followed the ideation discussion gave me far more control over *Lives* than I desired.

The week after the group voted and the plot had been chosen, when I returned to the prison, I was met with a very different situation. I was told that the young men had gotten into a "rush" with the staff in the preceding days: a fight had broken out between the inmates and the guards when the young men did not want to turn off the television in their common room and return to their cells at a prescribed hour of the night. This had occurred earlier in the week and therefore, on Friday, when I arrived at the detention center for my usual session, I was told that I could only work with the young men in two smaller groups. As a result, my plan for the day—of creating character profiles with the entire group listening to each other's ideas—had to be executed under very different conditions.

Instead of working in the common area that lay in a large space between the young men's cells, where we had worked in sessions past, I was directed to a smaller room and told to wait for the first of the two groups into which the young men had been divided. In the first group, only two of the five young people who were to attend, showed up. The other three participants, I was told, "didn't feel up to it" and one of the young men who did not attend, I later realized, had been given the added punishment of having to have his hands and legs chained every time he left his cell (for his role in the "rush"). As a result, T and N were the only two participants in the first group and their distracted states of mind were palpable. In hushed voices, between moments that involved creating their character profiles, T and N told me about the "rush" and about the different degrees of punishment that had been meted out to each of them as a result of the unit's behavior.

> Once T and N left, the second group arrived with more young men in attendance; four out of the five individuals in that group attended the session. K was in this second group and the more jovial atmosphere between the youth suggested that these young men had not been as implicated in the rush as their peers in the first group.
>
> > It was during this session that I began to notice a perceptible shift in K's mode of participation. The previously quiet and observant young man had suddenly become more playful and unable to concentrate in our sessions; I think this coincided with the time during which K was officially informed about his date of release. Who could blame him for not being able to concentrate on the workshop anymore?
>
> Amidst many giggles and laughter therefore, the second group also came up with their character profiles and I was told on my way out that my next session would also have to be carried out in the same, divided, manner.

The following Friday then, forewarned about having to work in two groups, I went in with all the character profiles written out (these profiles are the epigraphs that begin each chapter), so that both groups could see what their peers had come up with the previous Friday. I also went in with an idea for the structure of the script (Table 1) and with diagrams that gave the young men a few different options for how to stage the piece (Table 2).

Table 1: Handout with my suggested structure for the script

Scene 1: The party (ensemble scene)
Scene 2: Monologue 1
Scene 3: The arrest (ensemble scene)

Scene 4: Monologue 2
Scene 5: Entry into the prison (ensemble scene)
Scene 6: Monologue 3
Scene 7: The formation of the gangs (ensemble scene)
Scene 8: Monologue 4
Scene 9: The formation of the gangs (continued; ensemble scene)
Scene 10: Monologues 5 and 6
Scene 11: The fight (ensemble scene)
Scene 12: Monologue 7

Table 2: Handout with choices for spatial configurations

1. Proscenium

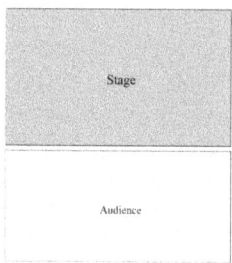

2. Three quarter round/Thrust

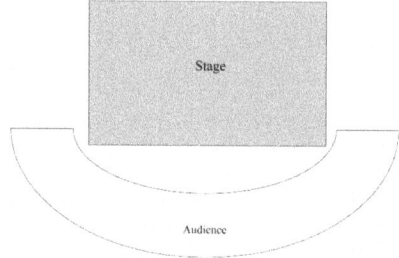

3. Theater in the round

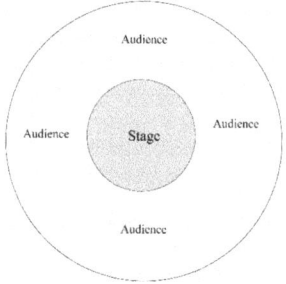

    4. Promenade theater
       Each scene takes place in a different location and the audience must walk from one place to the other as part of the action.
    5. Scattered seating
       Spectators are seated in a (seemingly) random fashion.

Two of the most important days in the creation of *Lives* therefore,
Days that involved the creation of the character profiles, the structure of the script, and the audience configuration,
Were days that had the young men working with me in two different groups.

   While each young man was asked to vote for the audience arrangement they preferred and was welcomed to disagree with and/or edit the script structure that I had set out, given that I was working with a December timeline for the performance, I felt the pressure to take on more control over the decision-making process than I otherwise would have in a devised theater context. Therefore, while both groups of young men agreed with the structure that I suggested in Table 1, I must admit that their acceptance of my suggestion might have had a lot to do with their being divided into two groups. Had we discussed the monologue-scene structure in the full group, and had all the young men heard each other's reasons for voting for the promenade as compared to the proscenium, it is entirely possible that different decisions might have been made.
   Or perhaps, no decisions would have been made at all.

Ultimately though, while I did have more control than the young men at this stage in the creative process, the aesthetic shape of *Lives* kept evolving when we all started working together again.

In this chapter and the ones that follow, the reader will notice the many changes that manifested

   Between the structure in Table 1 and the final structure of *Lives*.
      Between the script that was written and that which was performed.
         Between the character profiles that were generated initially and the final characterization that emerged.

Sometimes these differences were minimal, at other times, the changes were significant.

For instance, three actors chose—the Friday before the final performance—not to perform their scenes at all.

The control that I had in shaping the structure of the script, therefore, was temporary

Fleeting

"Wispy"

It was a control that I was happy to hand over to the young men when we were all able to work together again.

...

K took on the character of George White and every time he played this character during our rehearsals, K could not read his lines without breaking out into uncontrollable laughter. I never did understand the reasons behind K's mirth or why the idea of a father yelling at his son was so humorous to him.

> Was it because the father-son situation depicted in the scene was either too close to, or too far from, K's reality?
>
> Was K giggling because he was a teenager having a good time?
>
> Or was K giggling because he could count down the days until he would be released from prison?

K was paroled before I had the chance to ask him these questions and two weeks after his departure, when J joined the unit, it was only natural that J took on George White's role. To my surprise and chagrin, however, the other young men in the unit constantly compared J's work with what, to me, was an idealized version of K's performance.

> "Man, K could really play this character ... what are we going to do with J?"

I heard on many an occasion.

And between J's peers' palpable skepticism of his skills and his late entry into *Lives*, it was no surprise that J's final performance of George White's monologue fell far short of what was originally envisioned.

...

   ...

      ...

The constant changes to the workshop environment

The way in which the creation of the script contained different manifestations of "status"

These are the two concepts that shaped my rewrites of George White's scene.

Mystory Part Two: The Popular Narratives

The prison "community" is tenuous in many ways. It is tenuous in terms of its constantly shifting nature; an inconsistency that I have described in the previous section. And while I have described the shifting composition of the participants and mentioned the changes in security personnel, there is another shifting population whose presence I have not mentioned yet. A presence that augments the tenuous quality of community that exists in detention centers. The presence of prison volunteers.

Given the obvious reasons behind my being drawn to this volunteer perspective, the popular culture narratives in this section of mystory include differing (mainstream) viewpoints from/about volunteers who work within prison settings. Volunteers, like myself, who engage with prison populations in varied initiatives and whose presence adds an additional element of unpredictability within the already evanescent community that exists. Volunteers come, volunteers go. And with our entries and exits, we contribute toward creating a culture of incarceration that, for all its measures of control, is completely unpredictable. So, what are some of the popular narratives that surround prison volunteers?

First, there exist the descriptions that surround why/how prisons recruit volunteers and in looking through publically available archives, this seems to be the general rhetoric espoused by prisons that look to engage volunteers from outside their walls:

> You can make a difference. Services and programs offered by Bureau staff can be supplemented by citizen volunteers, thereby supporting community reentry efforts and promoting institution safety. When inmates transition from our institutions to half-way houses, they must readjust to life in the community and find employment. Through faith-based and community/neighborhood organization partnerships, volunteers play an important part in making a positive difference in their lives. As mentors, they provide strong guidance to the inmates and help them to promote accountability. You can assist in meeting the needs of the inmate population by providing a variety of services in different skill areas and/or specific types of programs such as:
>
> **Skill Areas**
> - Academic
> - Vocational/Career
> - Interpersonal
> - Wellness
> - Mental Health
> - Cognitive
> - Character
> - Leisure
> - Daily Living

Types of Programs
- Vocational training
- Alcoholics Anonymous
- Narcotics Anonymous
- Tutoring
- Leisure-time activities
- Spiritual counseling
- Religious services
- Marriage and family issues
- Preparing/participating in mock job fairs

Make a difference. Contact the facility closest to you and speak with the local Reentry Affairs Coordinator today [Federal Bureau of Prisons, n.d.].

And sure enough, reflecting the same diversity as the prisons that request their services, there is an entire spectrum of possibilities for those who want to voluntarily engage with their incarcerated counterparts.

There are religious/spiritual volunteers who seek to "make a difference" in the lives of inmates through some form of proselytizing:

WOULD YOU LIKE TO VOLUNTEER WITH PRISON FELLOWSHIP?

If you have a passion for sharing the Gospel and serving others, we invite you to consider taking the love and truth of Jesus Christ behind prison walls. Whether your interests lie in prison ministry, advocacy, or family reconciliation, Prison Fellowship will partner with you towards making a difference in the lives of prisoners, their families, and their communities. We encourage you to look through the volunteer opportunities listed below and prayerfully consider embracing Jesus' call to "remember the prisoner" by becoming a certified Prison Fellowship volunteer [Prison Fellowship, 2016].

Then, there are the non-religious prison volunteers who—in a very generic (and problematic) way—just want to "do good." I include myself in this category:

I tried to treat each inmate I encountered as an individual. I miss my weekly interactions with inmates. I miss feeling like I'm doing work that is important, appreciated, and has a profound, direct impact on underrepresented individuals. Recently, I had the opportunity to speak with a NJ Department of Corrections administrator who told me that he believes the future of the criminal justice reform work lies in young people. I agree. We have to start speaking out about these injustices because by the time change is able to be made, we are the ones who will be funding and creating the opportunities. I encourage more people (young and old), to find ways to get involved. Be an inspiration [Arbogast, 2013].

There are the subversive volunteers:

I don't believe in prisons. After working as a volunteer in the state prisons for mote than thirty years, I don't believe the American prison system as we know it should exist. The American prison system is not only about a corrupt system, but a corrupting one. It corrupts those who are employed by it and those who are incarcerated in it. It corrupts the contractors who build the prisons and the [...] It even corrupts the do-gooders like me who try to cut down the recidivism rate and make prison a little less of a hellhole for the people who are forced to live in it. In order to continue our work, we must become subversive and devious [Shelton, 2007].

And the volunteers who are in it for their own nefarious purposes:

Texas prison records name 133 employees, contractors and volunteers indicted on sex charges in cases involving prisoners between 2000 and 2014. Of those convicted, nine were sentenced to serve time in jail. The vast majority of the rest received a type of probation called deferred adjudication, a plea deal where a defendant's convictions are cleared from their record after court conditions are met [The Marshall Project, 2015; emphasis mine].

While the subversive and abusive narratives are not as mainstream as the narratives that speak about the act of volunteering within contexts of incarceration in life-affirming ways, delving into the popular narratives about this subject revealed a murky dimension that became intriguing as I rewrote George White's scene.... The murkiness, for me, arose from how difficult it is to encounter publically available archives that critique prison volunteers. For example, I am yet to come across a forum in which prison volunteers' work has been criticized or problematized by prison officials and/or former prisoners. And the absence of this critical voice is precisely what makes the whole realm of volunteerism seem more contentious than anything else. How can there be such a deafening silence when it comes to talking about the ethics of volunteering in prisons? Sure, there might be academics and researchers who talk about the ethical questions, but where are the voices of the prison guards/officials and the prisoners in critically reflecting on the work of volunteers? How can so much of what exists in the public domain be shaped solely be "feel good" viewpoints of what it means to engage with incarcerated populations?

Because discourses that critique prison volunteer work are hard to encounter, I drew from other kinds of critiques surrounding volunteerism or "voluntourism" to add a layer of complexity to my rewrites of George White's scene. And in looking for appropriate, popular, material I revisited scathing critiques about outsider interventionists in a "service-learning" or "service industry" context. The reader will no doubt, like me, be able to apply the risks and concerns espoused below to the prison context:

There exists the argument that some returned volunteers have gained insight into the damage they have done to others—and thus become more mature people. Yet it is less frequently stated that most of them are ridiculously proud of their "summer sacrifices." Perhaps there is also something to the argument that young men should be promiscuous for awhile in order to find out that sexual love is most beautiful in a monogamous relationship. Or that the best way to leave LSD alone is to try it for awhile—or even that the best way of understanding that your help in the ghetto is neither needed nor wanted is to try, and fail. I do not agree with this argument. The damage which volunteers do willy-nilly is too high a price for the belated insight that they shouldn't have been volunteers in the first place. [...] If you insist on working with the poor, if this is your vocation, then at least work among the poor who can tell you to go to hell. It is incredibly unfair for you to impose yourselves on a village where you are so linguistically deaf and dumb that you don't even understand what you are doing, or what people think of you. And it is profoundly damaging to yourselves when you define something that you want to do as "good," a "sacrifice" and "help" [Illich, 1968].

When we volunteer in prisons, prisoners are in no position to tell us to "go to hell."

Prison administrators do have this power, but for those of us who manage to get clearance from prison officials, we (literally) have a captive audience.

An audience that cannot point out our biases and hypocrisies.

An audience that might face repercussions for not attending our workshops.

An audience that cannot tell us to "go to hell."

So, can it ever be ethical to volunteer in prisons?

...

These diverse, popular narratives about volunteering tie in with my personal reflections about community and status, which emerged from working with K.

How can these different dimensions that surround volunteers' impact on prison communities be showcased autoethnodramatically?

This is one of the central questions that I seek to address in the rewritten scene at the end of this chapter.

Mystory Part Three: The Expert Narratives

As mentioned earlier, one of the most challenging elements to deal with during the creation and performance of *Lives* was the transient nature of the group that participated in the workshop. The first participant I lost was X, a young man who I had identified as a potential co-director because of his enthusiastic participation in the initial sessions. X was transferred to a different unit in the detention center after two weeks of my knowing him, because of "disciplinary issues," and I never saw him again. Then, a month before the final performance, R—another participative young man who always seemed engaged and interested—was released on parole. Soon after R's release, K was also paroled and with K's departure from the detention center we lost both the person who had come up with the plot for *Lives* and the actor who was to play the role of George White in the first scene of the performance. To complicate matters even further, in addition to X, R, and K's departures, the other young men's attendance at my workshop sessions was not always guaranteed either. One or two youth would inevitably be absent because of other activities that they were required to attend (therapy or wrestling club, for instance), others would not attend due to various forms of disciplinary probation, which meant that were not allowed to leave their cells except to go to school in the mornings, and a couple of the young men occasionally did not come to my workshops because they were having "bad days" and did not feel up to it. Given this constantly shifting participant group therefore, one of the primary concepts that have come to frame my experience in *Lives* is that of "transience."

Devised theater workshops are usually centered on principles of collaborative creation and this approach to creating theater seeks to foster a sense of "community" amongst co-creators and facilitators. So, how could I deal with my constantly shifting participant group while also attempting to create a sense of "community" that would enable the creation of a cohesive piece of theater? My prior projects as a theater maker in contexts of conflict have involved a meditation upon the notion of community in two ways. First, pedagogically, I have come to utilize particular strategies that create the conditions for a healthy and respectful camaraderie amongst my co-creators and myself. In this camaraderie my collaborators are invited not only to work together in conceptualizing, creating, and performing a piece that stems from their own ideas; they are also asked to become a community in which no idea is shot down without consideration and to function as an ensemble where constructive criticism and debate are encouraged. Second, from a logistical standpoint, a sense of community in my prior devised theater workshops has come from always working with a committed and consistent participant group. Until this experience in *Lives*, whenever I have entered a new context in which to work, my only requirement has been that my workshop be composed of collaborators who are interested in the theater and who can commit to attending every workshop session. There are no other qualifications or requirements that I impose on the composition of the group. Clearly my approach to, and understanding of, "community" had to be reframed extensively due to the transient nature of my participant group in *Lives*.

In thinking about how to achieve an understanding of "community" in a juvenile detention center, I have found it useful to consider what Gary Alan Fine and Lisa-Jo van den Scott (2011:1319) called "wispy communities" i.e., "social ties that exist within evanescent, limited micropublics—worlds of action that are temporary, limited in time and space, and have the potential of being displaced by more insistent identities." Extrapolating upon this term, the authors argue that in such wispy communities "relations are frequently intense, but after their conclusion relations slip into latent memory, available to be retrieved under proper circumstances" (Fine & Scott, 2011:1319). While Fine and Scott apply their idea of wispy communities to events and gatherings that are composed of individuals who come together temporarily around a focal point, I have come to consider the applicability of this term, "wispy," to the community that I found (not) to occur during the creation and performance of *Lives*. The term seems particularly applicably since *Lives*' co-creators, as young men in a detention center, found themselves working together on a devised theater project not out of choice: they were there working together simply because of a (forced) shared circumstance, incarceration. Furthermore, while I had been told that the young men from the unit who were not interested in theater could opt-out of my workshop, later conversations with guards revealed that this was not necessarily how the participants understood the situation. In internal communication that had been disseminated amongst prison officials, my workshop had been presented (I was told by the unit guards) as being mandatory for all the young men in that unit. *Lives* was made up of a "wispy" community precisely because of these tenuous connections that brought all us together—of the young men happening to be incarcerated in the same unit and of them believing, for whatever reason, that they *had* to partake in my workshop.

Fine and Scott use Benedict Anderson's (1983) proposal of an "imagined community" as their point of departure, a proposal in which Anderson seeks to "explain how states could generate the idea of moral and cultural belonging among the populations under their control" (Fine & Scott, 2011:1320). While it might not be easily apparent, I have come to find certain relevance in looking at a juvenile detention center as an imagined community that is wispy because of how it is bounded by time and space. The young men in the New Mexican juvenile detention center found themselves in the same space/time as a result of very different actions: actions that were linked only in their all being outside the purview of the law, and even then, to varying degrees. However, within the context of the devised theater workshop, and in other programed activities that take place as part of their lives in prison, these young men were asked to work together; to collaborate; to co-create; to function as a "team"; despite the wispiness that brings/holds them together. Drawing again from Fine and Scott (2011:1321), wispy communities "though temporally and morally bounded" are said to "have a behavioral reality" in which the "gathering is real, although the identity that is embedded is neither continuing nor insistent and exists primarily in latent memory to be activated when appropriate." The young men that I worked with in the detention center therefore, were confined within a temporally and morally bounded environment that was composed of rigorous behavioral realities: their coming together in that prison, in that unit, was all too real and required them to conduct themselves with a (sometimes, forced) spirit of collaboration.

That being said, it is also important to acknowledge an important distinguishing factor between how Fine and Scott use the notion of a wispy community and how I apply the term to a detention center: a difference that relates to the (im) permanence of identities. While Fine and Scott argue that identities that are created as a result of wispy communities are not continuing or insistent, the identities of incarcerated young men as "prisoners"—while (conceptually) intended to be transient, in that these identities are supposed to be discarded upon the prisoner's parole/release from the detention center—are not always ephemeral. Given the generally high recidivism rates in the United States (U.S.) in general and in New Mexico in particular, it is actually more than likely that many formerly imprisoned young men will find themselves back in contexts of incarceration, making their identities as "prisoners" and "offenders" potentially long-term affiliations. In such cases, obviously, the wispy community of a juvenile detention center does not manifest only as a latent memory but becomes more firmly encoded into the young men's presents and futures. Furthermore, apart from recidivism being a cause that leads to the "prisoner" identity being intransient for many of these youth, the lived experience of being incarcerated could also become deeply embedded within the young people's repertoires (and those of their families and communities) such that even those individuals who do *not* get rearrested upon their release, might very well become stuck with the identity of "ex-offender" once they leave the prison context. Here the wispy detention center community is not temporary or non-insistent, rather, the "prisoner" identity continues to be an active component of how ex-offenders are identified/identify themselves outside the prison context. While the transience of identities remains an underlying difference in how I use "wispy" in comparison with Fine and Scott's use of the term, I believe there remains a strong resonance between the underlying implications of "wispiness" and the kinds of the ties that seemed to underscore the manifestation of community in *Lives*.

In addition to community, as mentioned in the personal narratives at the beginning of this chapter, attempting to understand the reasoning behind the young men's vote about the theme/story of *Lives* has also led me to consider the notion of status: how does leadership emerge in the wispy and imagined community that exists within the walls of a prison? It has been said that in prisons, "status may be either ascribed or achieved": ascribed status "is generally formulated in advance by cultural definition, and signifies some characteristic feature, such as age, race, intelligence, or family background of the inmate" and achieved status "is acquired by the individual inmate because of choice, special ability, or unique achievement" (Caldwell, 1956:653). Furthermore, in analyzing how status manifests in prisons, data has been collected to indicate the following influential factors: "(1) the personality traits of prison leaders, (2) the methods of gaining leader status, (3) the tenure of the leader and, (4) the general nature of leadership among prisoners and its effect in the prison community" (Clemmer, 1938:862). It has also been said that status in prison contexts may be achieved through the consideration of factors such as "previous criminal record, observance of the 'prisoners' code,' personality, educational status, work placement within the prison, type of custody, informal group membership, type of visitors, and type of political connections with the outside world" (Caldwell, 1956:653). So, was K's leadership status during *Lives* achieved or ascribed? What made K be seen as a unanimous leader within the context of the detention center, more so than even the facilitator of the workshop? I do not mean this to sound like a petulant "Why didn't the boys listen to me?" but rather, as a question that demonstrates my curiosity at what emerged during that vote about the theme/story for our final performance. As a teacher and a theater facilitator over the last decade, I have come to realize the power of suggestion. That simply being in the position of the person coordinating a workshop can allow the questions one poses to be considered more seriously, for better or for worse. So, when I cautioned the boys against picking a plot that was extremely complicated—like K's story—even though I was delighted that they made their own decision, I began to wonder why my words seemed to have less force in that environment. Was it because the young men consciously desired the freedom to choose what they wanted to do, without an authority figure telling them what would work best? Were they testing me, to see if I was indeed as open to collaboration and their opinions as I made myself out to be? Or was it that K's idea was the most popular one simply because it combined everything that the young men said, thus increasing the likelihood that there would be less tension amongst them once I left after my workshop? Or was it that K had achieved a leadership position in the group because he was leaving the center soon? Or had K proved his creativity and intelligence in other activities, thus leading his peers to believe that his suggestion would be the best one? In thinking about the many reasons why *Lives* was chosen as the final performance, I have come to wonder if the simplest answer might indeed be the most appropriate one: K's idea was chosen because it was the most diplomatic option; it was the option that would cause least friction; it was the option that would not test or break the connections between a group of young men who had been asked to collaborate simply because they occupied the same physical and temporal space of the prison.

I am aware that I ask more questions than provide answers in the preceding discussion but there is no other honest way in which I can articulate these insights that I have taken away from *Lives:* insights around transience, community, status, and leadership. The questions that have emerged from my retrospective analyses of *Lives* are ones that I continue to grapple with; questions that I seek to give a theatrical voice to as I rewrite George White's section within the play. In this vein, through the rewritten scene below, I seek to draw in the questions that have been highlighted in the three parts to the mystory in this chapter: the personal, the popular, and the expert. In so doing I generate a new scene in which George White's part within *Lives* is not only about a young boy who gets thrown into prison for accidentally starting a fire at a party and who sees college as his way of escaping his overbearing father. Rather, I want to think about this young man's story for how it might be interpreted in the larger context of outsiders (like myself) engaging in prisons: what might these outsiders read as subtext in George's story? How can I include all the multi-dimensionality that underscored the creative process into one particular scene that was created by one specific young man? And in giving dramatic shape to the nuances and layers within the creation of George White's voice, how can I also do justice to what K wanted to say with/through this character? In my exploration of these questions the reader will notice some small, and some major, shifts in my conceptualization of the original text from *Lives* that can be found in the Appendix. That said, I believe that the discussions above will help frame the rewrites for my readers, I also consciously choose *not* to more explicitly explain why and how my thinking around "transience," for example, manifests in a particular aesthetic strategy in the rewritten scene below. Instead, I invite the reader to draw those connections for themselves and to find their own links between the different parts to the mystory and the rewritten scene that follows.

Rewriting George White

SCENE ONE

There are a maximum of twenty audience members that can be accommodated at each performance. The spectators arrive at the entrance of a real prison or a building that has been designed to look like a prison. When each spectator enters, s/he is met by GUARD 1 and GUARD 2 and is handed a label that has either GROUP 1 or GROUP 2 written on it. There should be equal numbers of spectators in each group. As they enter, the audience members have to go through a metal detector and on the other side of the detector, they are asked to hand over any cell phones or bags or coats that they are carrying with them to a guard who is stationed in a cubicle with cubby holes.

The first space that the audience members enter is a waiting room: a room that has reading material (brochures, magazines, etc.) that talk about the steps that are being taken to rehabilitate juvenile offenders. It is recommended that while the material be drawn from real-world juvenile justice systems, that there be no mention of a particular country or state or region on the reading materials. What is important in this piece is not that the performance is set in the U.S. or in Norway or in India; what is important is the generation of a more holistic critical reflection around what juvenile incarceration entails. In this vein, wherever contextual information has been drawn on in this script, it has been footnoted and the reader will note that the material is relevant to the U.S. (in general) and New Mexico (in particular). However, directors of this script are welcome to edit/adapt the contextual information in ways that more carefully reflect the juvenile justice laws in the specific setting in which the piece is being performed.

The OUTSIDER enters with the audience members and always moves with them. This actor can join either GROUP 1 or GROUP 2.

In order to underscore the gender dynamics in prison contexts, it is suggested that GUARD 1 be identified as male and GUARD 2 be identified as female. While some clues are provided within the script about how the gender dynamics might be played out between the two characters, directors are also welcome to nuance the GUARDs' relationship as per their particular vision and the context of the play's implementation.

Once all the audience members have arrived and are seated:

GUARD 1: So, you're the people who want to listen to the kids' stories, huh? All right; but before we begin this experience you have got to understand something. This is our show. You follow our instructions. We will tell you what to do. We will tell you where to go. If you don't want to listen to us, you can leave right now. Anyone want to leave?

A pause to see if any of the audience members want to leave.

GUARD 2: First, all those who have been given badges saying "Group 2" need to follow me. All those who have badges saying "Group 1" need to follow my colleague (*points to GUARD 1*). While we will be going to the same places, I am Group 2's leader—he is Group 1's leader. You always have to follow the instructions given by the leader of your group. Is that clear?

Audience members are given a few moments to divide themselves into their respective groups. Once they are in their groups—

GUARD 1: Today you will witness the stories of some young people: what brought them here; what they do now that they are here. They will tell you things, things about us, even. Whether or not you choose to believe them, well, that's up to you.

GUARD 2: You do not get the luxury of just sitting back and being silent though. Before every story that you hear, before every space that you visit, we will give you specific instructions on how you need to conduct yourselves in that space. Remember, this is a prison. You can't just do what you like in here.

GUARD 1: On our first stop, we will be meeting a young man named George White. Now, before we go to meet George, each of you needs to take one of these pieces of paper from us.

GUARD 1 hands out a piece of paper to each of the members in GROUP 1 while GUARD 2 does the same for GROUP 2. The content included on the piece of paper will become clear in the following scene.

GUARD 1: Group 1. Please read the first line on your piece of paper. Aloud. Together.

GROUP 1 is given time to read their line. GUARD 1 has them do it over until they are reading in unison.

GUARD 2: Group 2. Same thing. Please read the first time on your piece of paper. Aloud. Together.

GROUP 2 is given time to read their line. GUARD 2 has them do it over until they are reading in unison.

GUARD 1: Good. A little bit faster now. Group 1—go.
GUARD 2: Group 2. Go.

The GUARDs continue with this till the audience members get into a rhythm of following the GUARDs orders.

GUARD 1: Excellent. All you have to do is keep following our instructions as you did just now and this experience will move forward successfully. The better you follow what we ask of you, the more smoothly this will go.
GUARD 2: Please keep the piece of paper carefully until we collect it from you. Each copy is numbered and will need to be accounted for upon its return. We will need all of them back. You never know what these young people will do with things that are left lying around. On a similar note: never give anything to the inmates. Make sure you leave with everything on you. If you leave behind an earring, they could pick a lock with it. If you give of them a piece of chewing gum, they can use it to jam some of the electric doors. Do not give them anything. Do not leave anything behind.
GUARD 1: Now please form single lines behind your group's leader. Those of you in GROUP 1 please form a single line behind me. GROUP 2, please form a line behind my colleague. Unless indicated otherwise, you need to walk behind us in your lines. Is that clear?
GUARD 2: Wait, do we have the code of conduct forms signed yet?
GUARD 1: Shit, I knew we were forgetting something.

The GUARDs take out a sheaf of papers that can either be fictional or drawn from existing documentation about documents that need to be signed by volunteers. These are consent forms on which the spectators must agree to a host of different requirements. Something like this:

VOLUNTEER
Code of Conduct Agreement

This agreement is made and entered into by and between the "Agency" and the "Volunteer" and is effective as of the date set forth below upon which it is executed the parties involved. As per this document the Volunteer agrees that:

1. They will not share or divulge, with any individual or organization, any confidential information that is provided to, or developed by, the Volunteer within Agency premises
2. They will not give, or take any items from, inmates unless prior approval has been sought from Agency officials
3. They will not get involved in the personal affairs of any prisoner
4. They will not use vocabulary or hand signs that promote gang culture
5. They will be accompanied by an Agency official at all times
6. They will not ask a prisoner why they have been incarcerated
7. They will wear modest clothing
8. They will not promise things that cannot be followed through on

The Volunteer shall defend, indemnify and hold harmless the Agency from all actions, proceeding, claims, demands, costs, damages, attorneys' fees and all other liabilities and expenses of any kind from any source which may arise out of the performance of this Agreement.

Signature: _____
Name: _____
Date: _____

If audience members ask questions about the content in the form, the GUARDs can provide answers to the best of their abilities. If some audience members are particularly difficult or challenging, they can always be asked to leave the performance space.

Once all audience members have signed the forms and the documents have been collected:

GUARD 2: Now please form single lines behind your group's leader. Those of you in GROUP 2 please form a single line behind me. GROUP 1, please form a line behind my colleague. Unless indicated otherwise, you need to walk behind us in your lines. Is that clear?

Transition

GUARD 1 and GUARD 2 get the audience members to stand in single lines behind each of them and once there is order in how the audience members are standing, the GUARDs lead the spectators to the next location. While leading the spectators the GUARDS occasionally look over their shoulder and make sure that the line is straight and that people are not talking to each other while in the line. If people are standing out of line or speaking/laughing, the GUARDs stop the lines and silence those who are "misbehaving."

The GUARDs take the spectators to the first cell, where GEORGE WHITE's scene has been staged.

Scene Two

When the GUARDs and the audience enter this room, GROUP 1 is given seats on one side of the space, while GROUP 2 is seated on another side. It doesn't really matter if the two groups are facing one another or not, as long there is an obvious spatial demarcation between the two groups.

GEORGE's section of the room is covered in books. Thick books. Thin books. Old books. New books. While GEORGE speaks, the OUTSIDER is making paper cutouts of people holding hands.

GUARD 1: Ah yes, I'm supposed to help out in this one.

GUARD 1 puts on a costume piece to show that he has changed character. GEORGE is sitting on the floor. There is a piece of paper on the floor beside him. GUARD 1 (FATHER) walks around GEORGE in silence for a few beats.

FATHER: B. You've brought home a B? I've given my life to serve this country and you've brought home a B? Answer me.

FATHER repeats these lines over and over till he is screaming at the top of his voice. Finally.

GEORGE: SHUT UP.

Pause.
FATHER discards the costume piece and becomes the GUARD 1 again. GEORGE watches him make the change and then speaks.

GEORGE: College was supposed to be my salvation. It was supposed to be my escape ... from him. I was going to go to college and thought

I would become a doctor or a lawyer. Well, he thought I should become a doctor or a lawyer. He's my dad, man. He has given his life to serve this country.... I owe him.... I thought I owed him.

Lights change. GEORGE and OUTSIDER freeze in position. Whether or not they are able to hear the voices of the groups is left to the discretion of the director.

GUARD 1: Group 1. Please read the first line on the paper given to you. Read it in unison.
GROUP 1: We will transform our communities.[1]

At any point in the call and response that occurs in this scene, the GUARDs can ask audience members to repeat themselves should their voices not emerge in unison or in a manner that suits the GUARDs' preferences.

GUARD 1: Second line.
GROUP 1: We will demonstrate to all people that they are beloved.[2]
GUARD 2: Group 2. Please read the first line on the paper given to you. Read it in unison.
GROUP 2: We will not be voluntourists.
GUARD 2: Second line.
GROUP 2: We will not be voluntourists.
GUARD 1: Group 1. Third line.
GROUP 1: We believe that when serving the most vulnerable, an authentic spiritual transformation happens—for both giver and receiver.[3]
GUARD 2: Group 2. Third line.
GROUP 2: Volunteering can cause real harm. Acknowledge the truth that amateurs often don't have much to offer.[4]

Lights change. Focus shifts to the OUTSIDER. As the OUTSIDER speaks, GEORGE begins to read a book. He starts slow, reads faster at some points, studying, memorizing, and rocking himself while he doing so. As GEORGE reads, the GUARD begins to interrogate the OUTSIDER.

GUARD 2: Why do you want to work in a prison?
OUTSIDER: Well, I just ... you know. For a long time, I've been working in contexts that are really privileged. Working with young people who are already seen as being the cream of the crop. Young people who have had opportunities handed to them. Young people who ... who have had all the breaks. Don't get me wrong; I love the kids I work with. They are smart and talented and curious and I love work-

ing with them. But somehow ... somehow I cannot help but wonder if working with them is less necessary in the grand scheme of things. Less useful. The kids that I work with already have the privileges, you know? They already have the opportunities. Even without the best teachers, they will be ok because they have extensive support systems to catch them when they fall. But with these young men ... it's different.

GUARD 2: So what you're saying is that, you want to sleep better at night by working with these kids? The kids that no one else wants to work with?

OUTSIDER: Yes. No. Look, what I mean is—there is a part of this quest that is incredibly selfish. I realize that. I realize that working with "criminals" is going to beef up my resume. That it will make me sound like ... like a "badass" at dinner parties; like I'm doing "God's work" for people who believe in that kind of thing. And I cannot deny that I ... that I would ... you know ... enjoy being seen as "noble." I cannot deny that. But apart from the part of me that wants to work with these young men because of a perverse desire to engage with the "kinds" of people that I otherwise would not get the chance to interact with; apart from the part of me that wants to do this work for the selfish goals of ... of ... for the delusions of grandeur that it might give me, I also just.... I believe that this kind of work can help. You know? I just want to help.

GUARD 2: So if—

OUTSIDER: No wait, I'd like to just say a little bit more. Please, if I may. I ... look, you can't expect someone who has been a victim to these young men's crimes to be able to see the importance of working with them. You cannot expect the people they have robbed from, or shot at, or assaulted, to think that there is anything redemptive about them. I cannot imagine that I would want to work with them had I ever been at the receiving end of whatever action they committed in order to get here. The reason that I want to work with these young men is because I've been lucky. I've not been victim to these young men's acts of crime. I've not seen people I love fall victim to their actions. I can engage with these young men, I can *want* to engage with these young men, precisely because I have not had to face the consequences of their actions in a personal way. In my body. On my body. I have not had to face the impact of their actions. So, I can work with them and believe that something different is possible because of what I do.

Pause.

GUARD 2: You do know they're not all criminals, right?

OUTSIDER: They're in jail so…

GUARD 2: Where are you from?

OUTSIDER: Not from here.

GUARD 2: Look, I don't know what it's like where you're from but here, it's not quite so cut and dry. Not every one in here is a criminal. Some of them are here because—well, let's just say that the odds are stacked against them.

OUTSIDER: But they must have done something, right?

GUARD 2: Sure, they've done something. A lot of people have done something. Not everyone gets locked up.

OUTSIDER: I don't know if I understand what you're telling me. You're part of this system—surely you must believe that they deserve to be here…?

GUARD 2: I have a baby on the way. Two older kids who go to private school because the public schools where I live aren't the best. This is my job. Someone's got to do it.

Lights change. OUTSIDER and GEORGE freeze in position.

GUARD 1: Group 1. Please read the fourth line in unison.

GROUP 1: You can make a difference. Volunteers play an important part in making a positive difference in inmates' lives.[5]

GUARD 2: Group 2. Please read the fourth line in unison.

GROUP 2: Are you sure you are not doing more harm than good? Something is not always better than nothing.

GUARD 1: Group 1, next line.

GROUP 1: If you have a passion for sharing the Gospel and serving others, we invite you to consider taking the love and truth of Jesus Christ behind prison walls.[6]

GUARD 2: Group 2, next line.

GROUP 2: Prisons were very often founded by religious leaders who wanted to reform the lawbreaker. Even today, religious programming is easily the most common and pervasive form of correctional rehabilitation available to prisoners.[7]

Lights change. Change in focus to GEORGE. While GEORGE speaks, the OUTSIDER tears the paper cutouts that s/he has painstakingly made into small bits and blows them into the air.

GEORGE: He told me once that when he was off fighting, that he saved the lives of one of the men in his company. The guy couldn't hold a gun, my dad said, and in the middle of gunfire he—this guy in my father's squad—froze. So my dad leapt into action and saved that kid's life. He saved his life and to this day, my dad speaks about this guy he saved. How he's like a son to him. A son. A son who froze in the heat of battle. A son he saved and forgave and loved. A son from whom imperfections were accepted.... He comes to our house once a week, this coward that my dad had to save. And they sit in the garden, drink their beers, and talk about the good old days. My dad looks at him and he smiles. My dad can smile...

Lights change. OUTSIDER and GEORGE freeze in position.

GUARD 1: Group 1, please read the sixth line in unison.
GROUP 1: We have learned from each other.
GUARD 2: Group 2, please read the sixth line in unison.
GROUP 2: I don't know if I did anything.
GUARD 1: Next line.
GROUP 1: I am more empathetic.
GUARD 2: Next line.
GROUP 2: I hope I didn't make things worse.
GUARD 1: Next line.
GROUP 1: I have been a positive role model.

Lights change. Change in focus to the OUTSIDER. While the OUTSIDER speaks, GEORGE slowly and steadily builds a fort with the books. A strong, tall, imposing fort is created with the books. GEORGE climbs over the books and gets inside the fort.

GUARD 1: What if I told you that I believe you; that you can work with these young men.... But there are some rules and you'll have to abide by them.
OUTSIDER: Sure.
GUARD 1: You cannot bring any electronic equipment into the center with you. No phones. No cameras. No laptops.
OUTSIDER: Of course.
GUARD 1: You cannot use handshakes and forms of language that might be related to gang culture.
OUTSIDER: I'm not sure I understand what that entails.
GUARD 1: Those are the rules. You cannot use handshakes and forms of language that might be related to gang culture.

OUTSIDER: I heard you, sir. It's just, I don't know what language or handshakes might be related to gang culture.

GUARD 1: Look, it's what the policy is. Just agree not to use handshakes or forms of language that might be related to gang culture and its all good.

OUTSIDER: Right, sure. I agree,

GUARD 1: If you bring in any pens or pencils you have to count them when you take 'em in and when you take 'em out. They can use them as shivs.

OUTSIDER: Oh right. Yes, of course. I'll count them.

GUARD 1: Please do not give them any chewing gum if you happen to have any on you. They can use them to jam the doors and try to escape.

OUTSIDER: Sure.

Pause.

GUARD 1: You cannot give the inmates any item from outside these walls without checking with us first.

OUTSIDER: So I can't bring in food for them sometimes?

GUARD 1: It depends.

OUTSIDER: On what?

GUARD 1: On the person in charge.

OUTSIDER: Ok. Can I ask: how many kids will I be working with?

GUARD 1: Clients. We call them clients. Not kids.

OUTSIDER: Right. How many clients will I be working with?

GUARD 1: Ten, maybe less. Maybe more. You've got to be flexible.

OUTSIDER: Flexible?

GUARD 1: Clients come, clients go. We can't guarantee whom you'll be working with.

OUTSIDER: So how do I plan my sessions if...?

GUARD 1: You'll just have to be flexible.

OUTSIDER: Ok, I'll be flexible. That's fine. I can be flexible.

GUARD 1: Never be alone with any of them. You don't know what they're capable of.

OUTSIDER: Sure.

GUARD 1: Look, between you and me, they are just kids and at the end of the day, we have a lot of hope for them. We just need to, you know...

OUTSIDER: Follow the rules?

GUARD: Yes.

OUTSIDER: Yes.

Lights change. OUTSIDER and GEORGE freeze in position.

GUARD 1: Group 1. Last line.
GROUP 1: We can change them.
GUARD 2: Group 2. Last line.
GROUP 2: We're doing more harm than good.
GUARD 1: Repeat.

GUARDs 1 and 2 have the audience members say the last line back and forth quickly and multiple times before stopping the call and response.

Lights change. Change in focus to GEORGE. While GEORGE speaks, the OUTSIDER makes paper cutouts again but this time, the figures in the chain are of different sizes.

GEORGE: College was supposed to be my salvation, man. That party, all I wanted was to go there and meet someone nice. I'd never been on a date and I just wanted to meet someone nice. But shit just happened. I didn't mean to drink that beer. I didn't mean to take those 'shrooms. It just happened so quickly and before I knew it, the whole place was in flames.

GUARD 1: George, what have I told you about blaming others for your actions?

GEORGE: I didn't mean to, Mr. H. I just wanted to—

GUARD 1: I know what you were trying to do. You remember what we talked about?

GEORGE: Yes, sir.

GUARD 1: That's right. Look, I think you've told these people enough and I'm going to take them to meet the others now. All right ladies and gentlemen, let's move on to the next location. I think this one has told you everything he has to say. You *(to the OUTSIDER)—*

OUTSIDER: I would like to stay—

GUARD 1: You need a guard with you at all times and we're the only ones on duty right now so you'll have to come along. *(Turns to GEORGE)* You need a restroom break before we go, sir?

GEORGE shakes his head in the affirmative. The GUARD unlocks a door on one side of the room. This door is attached to a structure that is designed to look like a restroom—however the restroom's walls are created with a material that, through the use of lighting, will allow the audience to see GEORGE's shadow while he is inside the structure.

GEORGE walks into the structure. The audience members watch GEORGE's shadow, and hear him, relieving his bladder. They hear him, and see his shadow, flushing the toilet. They hear him, and see his shadow, washing his hands. GEORGE comes out of the structure looking bashful at having had a room full of strangers listen to the sounds of his body.

GUARD 1 locks the door to the restroom structure and then requests the audience to get into two single lines again, behind the two guards. The OUTSIDER leaves with the spectators. The GUARDs lead the two lines out of the room.

Once the audience members are all outside the room, the GUARD locks GEORGE into that space.

CHAPTER TWO

Language, Carlos Sadaña and Marcos Gusmán

Carlos Sadaña: Carlos is 18 years old and is from California. His family is lenient and although he sometimes got in trouble during his early adolescence for smoking marijuana/going out with girls/getting drunk, his family did not force him to do anything he didn't want to. He is arrested with everyone else in the party and once in prison, he stays to himself. But when people start messing with him, he becomes a gang-leader so that he can get benefits from the guards. He gets killed by one of his own gang members when he attempts to reconcile with the other gang.

Marcos Gusmán: Marcos and Carlos grew up in the same neighborhood and are childhood friends. Unlike Carlos, Marcos often got in serious trouble and upon finally ending up in prison; he is Carlos' second-hand in the gang that is formed. When Carlos attempts to make peace with a rival gang, it is Marcos who kills him.

Mystory Part One: The Personal Narratives

It was clear from my first session with the young men that "theater" was not a term that all of them understood. While one or two members of the group immediately displayed some recognition of the word, there were many blank stares and confused gazes that confronted me. In order to address this, I recall presenting the group with an extremely simplistic definition of the term: I believe I asked them to consider theater to be a "live" version of a medium like film, since the young men had access to movies even within the detention center.

With this very rudimentary definition established, I designed the first two workshop sessions to include very basic exercises: theater games that I borrowed from Augusto Boal's (1985) repertoire, basic storytelling activities that I designed, and videos that showcased particular elements to theater making. For example, in one session I decided to show the participants *Five Truths* (2011)—a series of videos from Katie Mitchell's installation in the United Kingdom—which puts forth five different interpretations of Ophelia's famous "mad scene" from *Hamlet*. Each of these five interpretations is framed around the theories of Antonin Artaud, Bertolt Brecht, Peter Brook, Jerzy Grotowski, and Konstantin Stanislavski respectively, and recreates Ophelia's scene (in each video) by using elements of theater of cruelty, epic theater, ritualistic underpinnings, poor theater, and realism. Using this particular video series was a choice that I made so as to demonstrate to the young men how the same story, the same scene, could be told in a myriad different ways based on the intention of the person conceptualizing the narrative. Through this, I hoped that the participants would come away with a slightly better understanding of storytelling: that not all stories have to be linear; that not all "telling" requires the usage of words; that one story could become another based on how it is told.

I began this session by asking the group to see if they could decipher the intention behind each different recreation of Ophelia's scene and as such, after each video, I paused and facilitated a short discussion about what the young men thought the objective of that specific interpretation was. Then, I used this discussion as a springboard from which to present the youth with more information about each particular approach to theater making in *Five Truths*.

"I didn't know people actually thought about this stuff in theater,"

N said,

"You mean this sort of stuff is why I come out from movies feeling differently each time?"

"She's tripping, man,"

R said about Ophelia;

"she's acting like she's on 'shrooms."

A final discussion after the five videos was subsequently followed by a storytelling exercise in which I asked each of the young men to write down five things they wanted the world to know about them. Once they had their ideas written down, I asked them to think about how they would like to speak those five things to an audience (the rest of the group) so as to create a short monologue of sorts. While the group found it relatively simple to write down what they wanted the world to know about them, I realized that the terminology that I had used to described the next part of the exercise—terminology that had worked in my prior workshops with theater-familiar participants; terminology like monologues, storytelling, and intention—were not terms that were readily understood by all the young men in the group. And as a result, this particular exercise did not go as well as I had hoped.

I realized that I would have to adjust my pedagogy quickly and begin each exercise with the assumption that someone in the group would have absolutely no idea what I was talking about. But the challenge with this was predictable: how effective could my defining concepts "in theory" be, when many of the young men did not know what those ideas meant in practical terms, i.e., when many of them had never seen a live theatrical performance or read a single script?

Furthermore, given the time constraints of my work in the detention center and the logistical constraints of taking in a laptop/video every time I went in (laptops cannot be brought in without prior permission), how would I present the theories and terms in a way that both made sense to, and was able to effectively engage, this participant group?

Ultimately, since the young men seemed to prefer "doing" to discussing, I realized that my usual workshop design of starting with an exploration of general theater concepts through discussion/theater games and later building toward a final performance would need to be flipped. As such, I began working with the group on a concept for their final performance from the third session itself—using the specific performance as the point of reference from which to introduce the young men to more general ideas from the theater.

Just as much as my use of terminology seemed like a foreign language to the young men in the detention center, the challenge also worked the other way. The participants often used particular turns of phrase in English that I had no familiarity with. Phrases like "that's tight," or "he was the pull out," or "he's the OG," were phrases/statements that I needed the young men to translate for me. In fact, I kept a running dictionary where I would record unfamiliar phrases/statements that were used in each workshop, so that I could remember them for the next time that I visited the detention center. The young men seemed to be more amused than anything else, that despite my facility with English, I could not understand some of the things that they said.

When they got to know me better though, during yet another occasion when I did not understand something that one of them said,

"You're racist, miss,"

L commented before breaking out into gales of laughter.

While I too saw my lack of understanding as a source of amusement, L's off-hand comment forced me to identify a more serious undertone within my inability to understand some of the ways in which the young men wielded English. Although I do not think "racist" is the right term to denote what L was implying, he had unwittingly made an important observation: my knowledge of United States' (U.S.) usages of English is defined by interactions within specific kinds of settings; perhaps, even, by interactions within a specific socio-economic class. My years of higher education in the U.S. have given me a fluency in academic, formal, and some informal uses of English in the region; I am also familiar with the English that is used in mainstream movies and television shows. But the "dialect"—if I might call it that—that was being used by the young people in *Lives* was not one that I had any experience with. And although this insight is not surprising in retrospect, it caught me completely off guard in the moment. I had naïvely assumed when I began this project that my skills in English and Spanish would be sufficient in addressing most language-based complexities that would emerge in a New Mexican detention center, at least in terms of negotiating verbal communication. But instead, between the young men's lack of knowledge about theatrical vocabulary and my own ignorance about some of their uses of English, we found ourselves in the midst of many (often comedic) miscommunications.

Apart from these more obvious linguistic misinterpretations, there were other aspects to the use of language that the young people and I had to negotiate with each other. For instance, the first time one of the young men said, "fuck," there was a moment of silence in the room. The young men looked at me, and then they looked at the guards, who were also looking at me. In a context where the use of language is strictly monitored and controlled, I realized that everyone in the room was expecting me to chastise the person who had used "the f word."
I did not.
For better or for worse, the use of "the f word" is not an act that I find to be particularly problematic, even in more formal classroom settings—and once the young men caught on to my attitude, of course, the swearing occurred far more often.

However, I never found these instances of swearing to be violent toward anyone in particular; rather, the swearing was used mostly as an adjective with which to punctuate the young men's stories and statements. That said, my particular position on such uses of language within a workshop setting was not a popular view in the prison context (to be honest, it is not a popular view in many contexts) and the headmistress of the school that was housed at the prison complex—the school that all the boys attended—told me in no uncertain terms that she thought the youth's use of language was tied to their criminality.

While I politely agreed to disagree with her in that instance, I was surprised to learn on the day of the final performance of *Lives* that the headmistress had decided not to give the young men academic credit for their performance (as had been previously agreed) because of the use of "the f word" in some instances in the play. When my discomfiture with the last-minute communication and the lack of transparency of this decision became visible, another prison official—higher up on the chain of command than the headmistress—agreed to go back to giving the young men credit for their work *if* they would refrain from swearing in their final show. And since the headmistress herself would not be present for the final performance, this official said that they could be a little "flexible" vis-à-vis how much swearing was too much swearing for academic credit. The use of language in *Lives*, therefore, remained a point of contention up until a few minutes before the young men went on stage and when I mentioned the officials' condition to the group, the young men decided that they would curtail their already limited (I thought) use of explicit language in the show; they wanted the academic credit.

I remain unsure to this day if the credit was actually given to them as promised since I do not believe my pedagogy ever met with the approval of the headmistress of their school.

In addition to how the young men wielded language in terms of whether or not they swore during the workshops or *Lives*, my own questions around language and criminality emerged in a very different way when the participants told me that they wanted a hip hop musical score to accompany their performance. I have to admit to the reader—as I did to the young men—that hip hop is a genre that I do not know anything about. In fact, I consider my musical knowledge, in general, to be quite limited and I often receive expressions of horror when I admit to enjoying Bollywood musical numbers.... I think the assumption is that a practicing artist like myself would have more "discerning" musical tastes. But growing up in southern India had certainly not given me much exposure to hip hop and even though I did much of my later schooling in the U.S., hip hop is not a genre that I spent any time on. When the young men said they wanted to use hip hop extensively in *Lives* though, I had to do my homework, and much to the amusement of those around me (who were aware of my musical proclivities or lack thereof), I spent a weekend listening to songs performed by artists that I had never heard of before: Lil Cuete, Akon, Twin Beredaz, and many more. I was given a long list of songs to listen to—the young men had made a list for me when I shared my ignorance of the genre with them—and in listening to their suggested pieces, I became quite conflicted.

While there were clearly very important and relevant socio-political themes being addressed in almost all of the songs that the young men recommended, the ubiquitous use of the "b" and "n" words were immensely problematic for me. So, I took this concern to the detention center the next time I visited and discussed it with the group.

I could be flexible about most things,

I told them,

but language that objectified/demeaned women or other minorities, or language that glorified the use of violence (against women, in particular) was where I drew the line.

The young men giggled at first—both at my ignorance of the genre and at the nature of my concerns—but despite their amusement, they decided to accommodate my request and worked with me to shortlist the songs that we could all agree on.

To be fair, they had to accommodate me (whether or not they wanted to) because in that context, I had all the power to ban the use of hip hop in the piece.

But despite that tangible power imbalance, the young people were graceful about their accommodation of my concerns and did not demonstrate even a little bit of resistance; they seemed to "get it."

However, even though we resolved the issue amongst our little group in terms of the performance itself, I had to ask myself a not-so-comfortable question: would I have had the same degree of discomfort with the language in the songs if they were being listened to by students in the privileged college in which I also teach? Or was it the use of violent musical imagery in a prison context that was particularly disconcerting to me? Was I embodying an unconscious bias, which assumed that my non-incarcerated students had the good judgment to separate musical lyrics from real-life actions, while my incarcerated students did not? And if in fact I did have this bias, what was I going to do about it? Perhaps it was the headmistress' words coming back to haunt me, but I began to wonder about links between the language in the music that we listen to and the way that we behave.

As evidenced by the discussion above, the process of *Lives* was underscored by various questions and ideas surrounding language: the links between language, discipline, and surveillance; the connections between music, language, and criminality; the foreign-ness of artistic language; the nexus between culture, personal background, and the prison. In thinking about how to use these experiences in rewriting T and Q's scene then, there were a number of questions that framed my conceptualization.

How could I include material about the complexities surrounding the young men's use of language—both personally and in terms of the languages they preferred in/of music?

> How could I dramatically shape what those linguistic choices revealed (if anything at all) about particular individuals' present and past behaviors?

>> Was there a place in the scene where I could allude to the politics surrounding which language is spoken within prisons?

These interweaving questions have most come to frame the ways in which Carlos Sadaña & Marcos Gusmán's scene has been rewritten.

Mystory Part Two: The Popular Narratives

I do not completely disregard the point of view espoused by the headmistress of the school. Has the use of language, in speech and/or music, been linked to forms of delinquency? What does our use of language say about who we will become? In curating the popular narratives that would shape my rewrites of Carlos Sadaña & Marcos Gusmán's scene therefore, I began a search for different points of view on the subject of language and criminality. I began by looking at the concerns that language—in communication; in music—adversely impacts young people. And here is the narrative that seems to dominate that particular area of the mainstream view:

> A concern to many interested in the development and growth of teenagers is the negative and destructive themes of some kinds of music (rock, heavy metal, hip-hop, etc.), including best-selling albums promoted by major recording companies.

The following themes, which are featured prominently in some lyrics, can be particularly troublesome:
- Drugs and alcohol abuse that is glamorized
- Suicide as an "alternative" or "solution"
- Graphic violence
- Sex which focuses on control, sadism, masochism, incest, children devaluing women, and violence toward women

Music is not usually a danger for a teenager whose life is balanced and healthy. But if a teenager is persistently preoccupied with music that has seriously destructive themes, and there are changes in behavior such as isolation, depression, alcohol or other drug abuse, evaluation by a qualified mental health professional should be considered [Appalachian State University, n.d.].

These views about the use of language have gone so far as shaping how particular groups/organizations present and identify delinquency:

SIGNS OF DELINQUENCY
- Irresponsibility
- Extreme moodiness
- Lying
- Destructiveness
- Hanging out with the "wrong" friends at the "wrong" types of places
- Stealing
- Truancy
- Violent temper
- Drug/alcohol use
- Child coming home late
- **Swearing**
- Complaints from others [Kansas Children's Service League, n.d.; emphasis my own].

Given some of these existing mainstream narratives therefore, certain educators (unlike me) agree with this particular positioning and speak about ways in which they address these issues amongst "at-risk" youth in their classrooms. "At risk": a term that is, in and of itself, extremely complex:

FORMAL & CASUAL LANGUAGE
I teach at-risk high school students the difference between formal language and casual language. I explain that formal language is the language of the work world. I explain that I expect them to practice formal language in my class [...] When they slip, I simply ask them to find a better way to express their thought. They have no trouble following this practice most of the time.

STREET TALK V. SCHOOL TALK
I have worked with "ghetto" kids, military kids, and kids from high-income neighborhoods. With all of them, I demand respect and I act as a role model for the stu-

dents. I let them know that the language they are using in my classroom is just "practice" for when they go off to college or the work force.

If they say "yeah," I say, "I'm sorry, didn't you mean 'yes'?" After a few weeks, they get it and I see them catching themselves. If they tell you that it's "street talk," let them know that there is a difference between school and the street. I usually get the students by asking "You wouldn't say that in church, would you?" And they understand [National Education Association, n.d.].

However, just as there exist these popular narratives on how the use of language is linked to delinquency, there are also views that suggest quite the opposite:

Those who are liberal in their use of swear words are not the lazy and uneducated individuals they are often made out to be, a new study claims. In fact, a well-stocked vocabulary of swear words is actually a healthy indicator of other verbal abilities [Cowburn, 2015].

And of course, between the voices that condone and condemn particular uses of language, there are popular narratives that occupy the space in-between the opposite ends of the spectrum. Such in-between voices highlight the fact that, it is never language in isolation that is linked to delinquency; rather, it is an intersection between the use of language and the ways in which a particular person might be targeted by it:

Results published in the journal *Child Development* show that parents' hostility toward their teens increases their children's risk of delinquency and risky behavior. The surveys revealed that when harsh verbal discipline is used during early adolescence, teens are more likely to suffer detrimental health outcomes later in life. Teens who were screamed or cursed at by 13 years old were found to suffer more depressive symptoms between ages 13 and 14 than students who were not disciplined this way. These participants were also more likely to display bad behavior in school, lie to their parents, steal, and fight [Borreli, 2013].

While the narratives above speak to the use of language in its spoken form, there are other positions that emerge when specifically considering the popular narratives that chronicle concerns about language in music. These viewpoints ask us to consider the complex socio-political relationships and realities that shape music that, for some, is problematically related to crime—I limit myself particularly to hip hop in my consideration of these narratives because this was the genre of preference among the young men in *Lives*:

The mid–1990s were a particularly active period for the hip-hop agenda. In 1994, C. Delores Tucker told a Senate panel that the hip-hop generation, "coaxed by gangster rap," would "trigger a crime wave of epidemic proportions that we have never seen the likes of." And then added, "Regardless of the number of jails built, it will not be enough." In his book *Can't Stop Won't Stop*, author Jeff Chang traces the evolution of the hip hop activist movement noting that it was initially mostly grass roots and locally focused. But as movements against the prison-industrial complex and police brutality emerged simultaneous to movements against corporate globalization, many young hip hop activists began to organize nationally. As hip hop has become a globalized art form, hip hop's progressive, activist agenda has traveled with it around the world. Organizers in Paris, Cape Town, Sweden, New Zealand Chile and in countless other countries have employed the tools of hip hop to work for change in communities, empower youth and give voice to unchecked issues. While gangster rap has been blamed by cultural critics for triggering crime waves, hip hop activism has stood up against the prison industrial complex, addressed environmental racism (many went on to encompass green politics) and corrupt systems that cause poverty around the world [Wikipedia, 2016].

And within the context of prisons themselves, in views that counter those that were offered by the headmistress during *Lives*, there are the projects and initiatives that seek to possibly subvert, and potentially reinvent, controversial cultural forms into avenues of learning, creativity, and imagination:

> The Hip Hop Poetry Project provides intensive performance arts programming—classes, performances, and workshops—during public school breaks at St. Louis City Juvenile Detention Center; we hold one in the spring and one in the summer. Our goal is to have each young person in the institution spend every day of the project in constructive, creative activities. This project provides workshops in poetry writing and performance, design and dance. The student poetry is shared through a concluding performance, CD, and an anthology [Prison Performing Arts, 2015].

In rewriting Carlos and Marcos' scenes, therefore, it was my personal encounters with the use of language and the abovementioned popular narratives about the use of language in communication and in music that most drew my attention. That said, apart from the concern about the links between language, music, and delinquency, what became a pertinent question to consider was this: how are individuals affected when their use of language is controlled; limited; censored?

In the context of a detention center, where—I hope—the larger goal is to reintegrate young men back into their communities and societies, how does the curtailment of language impede the ability for these very same youth to understand the power behind their words?

How does censoring language distance young people from the notion that how we use language can also be empowering, and political, and life affirming?

By creating binaries between the language of the criminal and the non-criminal; of the delinquent and the non-delinquent;

couldn't it be easily argued that the same questions that we encounter when considering post-colonial uses of colonial languages also exists in contexts of incarceration?

In any context where how one uses language is controlled through the use of force—either historically, or in the present—how does an individual begin to shape their linguistic identity?

And in a context like the U.S., where biases surrounding race and class further complicate the demographic composition of prisons, don't we begin to see glimmers of re-colonization; of the neo-colonial?

How do these layered concerns about language become interwoven into an autoethnodrama?

How can I rewrite Marcos and Carlos' scene in a way that honors the original text but also brings in these personal and popular dimensions to the use language vis-à-vis criminality?

Mystory Part Three: The Expert Narratives

T and Q immediately mentioned their Latino heritage in their introductions to me and once they realized that I could speak Spanish, there was an instant camaraderie that seemed to develop between us. T and Q would often mutter things under their breath in a language that they knew few in the room would understand; a language that somehow connected the three of us within the tenuous context of that detention center. As an applied theater practitioner-researcher, the dynamics of language is always on my radar, wherever I may work. Am I working in my first language and if not, am I being careful enough with the words that I use? Is the language that the workshop is being conducted in, also the languages in which all group members are comfortable? Are we all working in a "colonial" language and if so, what does that language reveal about power dynamics that are present within the context in question? How does the language of the theater resonate with (or not) the setting in which the work is being conducted? Language is always complex terrain in theater work that occurs in community settings and working in the detention center was no different. However, like any other context, there were specific nuances to questions around language that emerged because of the prison environment: the foreign-ness of theatrical terminology; the links between language, discipline, and surveillance; the connections between music, language, and criminality; the nexus between culture, personal background, and the prison. It was these nebulous and multifaceted concepts that then shaped how I reinterpreted T and Q's scene, and the discussion that follows will put forth scholarly explorations vis-à-vis the complexities of language manifested.

In investigating this question further I came to encounter a variety of perspectives on the intersections between musical choices and individuals' behavior. Susan Gardstrom (1999) suggests that "the relationship between exposure to so called "controversial" musical genres and antisocial or aggressive behavior appears to fall into four distinct camps." The first category that Gardstrom (1999:210) proposes is the "reflection-rejection" hypothesis where it is purported that "music, no matter what the genre or source, is neither good nor bad; it is simply a reflection of societal values, issues, and responses and can be rejected as a potential threat." The second category is attributed to social learning theory, which "asserts that individuals' antisocial, aggressive responses are shaped by early experiences with parents and other significant adults" (Gardstrom, 1999:211) i.e., our musical choices are independent of our behaviors because our behavior is ultimately shaped by the learning that occurs when we are young. The third camp, "drive reduction theory," suggests, "that music can serve as a conduit for the expression of difficult feelings such as anxiety, anger, or hostility" (Gardstrom, 1999:212). And finally, Gardstrom (1999:212) puts forward the "[e]xcitation-transfer" possibility, which presumes "that physiological states (regardless of their source or cause) transfer to subsequent situations and intensify postexposure emotional states." From her own work within juvenile detention centers, Gardstrom (in Selfhout et al., 2008:438) states that, generally speaking, "juvenile delinquents consider their preference for deviant music to mirror reality, rather than cause their deviant behavior" i.e., the reflection-rejection hypothesis is what seems most applicable in the juvenile detention center context.

While my immediate inclination is to agree with Gardstrom, it is important to mention that there seem to be just as many studies that offer contradictory insights and suggest that "a preference for music styles with antisocial content activates antisocial schemas [...] may in turn lead to actual antisocial behavior" (Selfhout et al., 2008:437). Additionally, studies are said to have revealed that "exposure to heavy metal and hip-hop music and music videos may increase the prevalence of several externalizing problems [...] For example, Johnson et al (in Selfhout et al.,

2008:437) found that males exposed to violent rap music videos expressed more acceptance of the use of violence than those who had seen nonviolent videos or no videos at all." Therefore, while I cannot state with absolute certainty where on this spectrum of opinions the young men in *Lives* fell, it did seem—from the ways in which they reacted to/engaged with music—that the reflection-rejection scenario was what remained most applicable for them. The young men appeared to see music as a mirror of their realities and since *Lives* was supposed to reflect their experiences, it was important to them that the performance include "their" music. There were no occurrences that gave me reason to suspect that the young men saw their music as having played some part in the actions that caused them to be incarcerated. That said, while I find much interest in exploring this area of musical language and behavior, it is important to clarify that do I not seek to address this issue as a question that needs an answer. Rather, what is interesting to me (within the context of this writing project) is how these political and ethical dimensions to language in music might be interwoven within a rewrite of T and Q's scene—two participants who were among the most vocal about the presence of hip hop in *Lives*.

Just as music played an important part in T and Q's work in *Lives* so did another dimension to language: verbal descriptions of, allusions to, acts of violence. This was particularly relevant to Q who was the only person in the group that was comfortable articulating his thoughts about physical violence. It was hard to tell if this comfort came from Q's desire to "shock" whoever was listening to him, or if it indicated his early indoctrination into a "Culture of Violence" that reflected Q's "conviction that the world is a dangerous place, where the best way to ensure survival is to be vigilant and ever prepared to take the offensive" (Funk et al, 1999:1129). I remain unsure about his intentions since Q's discerning gaze seemed to want to watch his audience's reaction to graphic verbal descriptions of violence and yet, I wondered if it was his previous "chronic exposure to violence" that had possibly triggered a "desensitization process which limits the emotional impact of subsequent exposure to violence"; a desensitization that is said to "increase one's tendency to endorse proviolence attitudes" (Funk et al, 1999:1132). In either case, Q—while initially unsure about participating in *Lives*—decided that he would perform only once I told him that he did not have to write out his monologue but could choose to make it a piece of structured improvisation. Q wanted the liberty to improvise and to be able to talk about his own life experiences, as he often told me, using the mask of his character. As such, the details of Q's monologue would always change just a little bit and he would be more or less graphic about the violence that he talked about based on the responses he read on his spectators' faces—Q was immensely skilled at reading a room! While there were always some changes to Q's monologues though, the aspects that did not change were the episodes in which he would speak about shooting at a police officer and about killing his (character's) father. Although the monologues were to be "fictional," in that I told the young men that I would never ask them where they got the material from, Q came to me at the end of one session and said, "When I get out of here, I'm going to kill that m*****f****r," referring to his own father. Unsure how to respond, unsure whether or not I should even attempt an engagement with his statement, I stayed silent. Clearly Q's talking about physical violence as Marcos Gusmán had multiple, personal layers to it.

Like Q, T also told me from the outset that his character—Carlos Sadaña—was influenced by his personal experiences. Using no mention of physical violence in his monologue though, T spoke to me about his mother and how her more liberal approach to discipline was something that he really appreciated and admired—an appreciation that he incorporated into his monologue in *Lives*. Thus, when thinking about how to highlight the multidimensionality to T's scene, given how much his mother's granting him independence at a young age seemed to matter to him, I looked into literature that surrounds the notion of "parental autonomy" and the links that have been made between this approach to child-rearing and the future behavior of children. Investigating existing literature in this particular realm highlighted one particularly interesting study: a study by Efrat Sher-Censor, Ross D. Parke, and Scott Coltrane (2011) that looks into the manifestation/outcomes of parental autonomy within Mexican-American immigrant families; a study that immediately caught my attention given what T had told me about his Mexican heritage. This study suggests that that "[p]arental autonomy promoting could be particularly important for Mexican American early adolescents, who may face a challenge of integrating Latino familial values with a developmental need for autonomy endorsed by the European American host culture" (Sher-Censor, Parke, & Coltrane, 2011:674). This autonomy, it has been suggested, "could be relatively pronounced in parent–son relationships as a preparation for the son's traditional future role as family provider and authority figure in traditionally hierarchical Mexican American families" (Sher-Censor, Parke, & Coltrane, 2011:675). Could it be then, that T's description of his relationship with his mother was somehow indicative of his family's particular immigrant experience? Could it be that T's appreciation for the autonomy afforded him by his mother was intertwined, somehow, with an affirmation of his cultural heritage? Furthermore, could the autonomy that T spoke about, be linked to the young man's air of self-assuredness? Sher-Censor, Parke, and Coltrane (2011:688) suggest that young people's "perceptions of more maternal and paternal autonomy promoting were related to their higher self-worth [...] adolescents could feel more worthy, especially as the gap between loyalty to the family and respect for the parents and the developmental need for autonomy is smaller." Could it be that T's way of carrying himself spoke to a relatively high sense of self-worth? For instance, even when some of the rehearsal sessions became utterly chaotic with all the young men talking over each other, T would stay silent; very rarely losing his cool and even when he did, saying very little to get his point across. T always just wanted to get the work done and while he remained unsure until the very end about whether or not he would be capable of performing in front of an audience, T was steadfast in his attendance and commitment to the workshops. While I might never know the answer to my musings around the links between T's self-assuredness, the parental autonomy that he spoke of, and his identification with his Mexican heritage, an interesting juxtaposition emerged for me between these aspects to T's creative process and his reticence to speak his monologue in Spanish. In fact, none of the three Spanish speakers in the group (T, Q, or L) chose to speak in Spanish despite my constantly inviting them to do so. I often wondered if this was because the young men were forbidden from using languages that their guards did not speak. Although this rule (if it even was one) was never explicitly mentioned in my presence, there was something about the way in which T, Q, L, and myself were watched by the guards when we conversed in Spanish that makes me consider this possibility.

The links between language, discipline, and surveillance, the connections between music, language, and criminality, the foreign-ness of artistic language, the nexus between culture, personal background, and the prison, my personal encounters with miscommunication in the detention center, popular narratives surrounding language and delinquency, and existing scholarship that speaks to larger disciplinary questions about language and criminality, are all ideas that have come to shape the aesthetic choices that I have made in the rewritten scene that follows.

Rewriting Carlos Sadaña and Marcos Gusmán

Transition

The two groups of audience members are lined up against two different walls in a passageway between the previous space and the next. The GUARDs collect the papers that have been given to the audience members. If any audience members have forgotten their papers inside GEORGE's space, a big show of frustration is made by one of the GUARDs who then unlocks GEORGE's room again and goes back in to get the papers left by the audience. The GUARDs visibly count the papers that are given back to them and make sure everything has been returned.

GUARD 1: Ok. Now you have an idea of how things work.
GUARD 2: In the next space that we will visit, things are going to work slightly differently.
GUARD 1: Pay attention to the projections that you will see in front of you. Follow the instructions on them.

The GUARDs take the audience to the next classroom, for CARLOS' and MARCOS' monologue.

Scene Three

Similarly to the previous space, the audience members are arranged in two different areas such that GROUP 1 is only able to see one screen, while GROUP 2 only has visibility access to another. The screens show different images to both groups and it is imperative that the projections are clear enough for the audience to be able to follow along.

The OUTSIDER walks toward a wall in the room that is covered with words on pieces of paper or wood or some other material. What is important is that only one individual word is written on each piece of material: imagine something like the poetry magnets that decorate many a refrigerator, enabling the onlooker to rearrange the words into new phrases and sentences. The words that are used should not be random, though. Perhaps they could be taken from the prisoner's rulebook, of how inmates are supposed to behave while incarcerated. Perhaps they could be in multiple languages i.e., the languages that inhabit the prison in question (Spanish, dialects of English, Navajo, whatever is most contextually relevant). Perhaps the words could take from poems or stories that have been written by previously incarcerated contributors. Perhaps they are the laws that shape juvenile justice in the country/region.

The OUTSIDER walks toward this wall, almost entranced by the words. S/he rearranges the words constantly, trying to find hidden combinations that would transform the words into something more, or rather, into something different. MARCOS and CARLOS do not pay much attention to what the OUTSIDER is doing until indicated later in the scene. Similarly, the OUTSIDER is seemingly oblivious to the conversation between CARLOS, MARCOS, and the audience that is happening at the same time.

GUARD 1: All right, folks. Settle down. Now, this client has something creative that he would like to do with all of you. He has discussed his idea with us and we have approved it, but if any of you are uncomfortable with participating in his "activity," you are very welcome to stay silent. Sir, would you like to begin this with what we discussed?

MARCOS: Of course, Mr. H. So y'all are here and before Carlitos and I tell you a little bit about ourselves, I'm gonna teach you a few lines of my favorite song, yeah? I'm going to sing a line and you gotta repeat it after me. Could we get the music, sir?

GUARD walks over to turn on the music.

GUARD 1: As you can see, we like to encourage our inmates to be creative and this one here, well; this young man really likes music and wanted to a chance to do this activity with you all. I hope you will participate. It might seem strange what he's asking you to do, but remember; this is what we're all here for, right? We're here to encourage these young people to try and change things up for themselves.

The GUARD turns on the music. The lines below are sung first by MARCOS and the audience is invited to repeat the words after him. The lyrics are from MARCOS's favorite song: Lil Cuete's (2010) "So you wanna be a gangster."
MARCOS *sings the first line from the song.*
Audience repeats.
MARCOS *sings the second line from the song.*
Audience repeats.
MARCOS *sings the third line from the song.*
Audience repeats.
This call and response continues for as long as is deemed necessary.
While the call and response happens, CARLOS is scrutinizing the audience members. Once the call and response has gotten into a rhythm, MARCOS stops the activity. MARCOS is a charming, charismatic young man and if audience members don't participate, he uses his conversational skills to get them involved.

Two. Language, Carlos Sadaña and Marcos Gusmán

MARCOS: All right, all right. Thank you all for doing this. I love this song, man. I love it. Carlitos, you want to talk to them first, guey? Or should I?

CARLOS: I'll go first ... so ... you all want to hear my story, huh? It's not going to be what you expect. It's not a story about a helpless boy who needs your pity. It's not the story about a boy whose family did him wrong. Far from it.... In fact, I think I want to start by telling you about Maria, my first love. Maria sat next to me in Spanish class and man, that girl was fine. Hair like ... like brown silk. Eyes that could see right through you. And her boo—shit, sorry I was told not to talk about her booty.

CARLOS and MARCOS laugh at his inadvertent blurt.

CARLOS: Anyway, the first time Maria looked at me, man, I couldn't speak. I just couldn't find the words.... And the first person I talked to about Maria, was my mother. My mamá is a cool lady. Yeah she yelled at me sometimes when she caught me drunk or stoned or something, but she is a cool lady. You know the coolest thing about her? She's my friend. Not many people can talk to their moms about being in love and shit but for me, my mother was the first person I went to. And then this shit went down.... You know something though, even when all this crazy shit happened and I ended up in here, my mamá didn't give up on me, man. Sure, she was angry at first but not for very long. Sometimes I don't understand why she isn't real mad at me for getting myself in this mess.... I tried to stay under the radar when I first came to this joint, you know? I tried to stay to myself. All I wanted to do was serve my time and get back home. To my mamá. To Maria. But if people mess with you, you got to stand up for yourself ... that's what my mother taught me.

CARLOS begins to speak rapidly.

CARLOS: Mi mamá es.... Mi mamá es increíble. Ella es mi mejor amiga y me ha enseñado como sobrevivir en circunstancias que parecen imposibles. Ella me ha enseñado como pensar por mi mismo—claro mis decisiones no han sido perfectas y por lo tanto estoy en esta mierda, pero mi situación no es la culpa de ella.[1]

GUARD 2: Could you speak in a language that we all understand please?

Pause. CARLOS glares at GUARD 2.

CARLOS: ...I know what you all think. Mexican boy, single mother, its no wonder that he ended up in here. But this shit ain't got nothing to do with my mom. She taught me to make my own decisions and I fucked up. That's all. I fucked up.

GUARD 2: Watch your language, please.

CARLOS smiles.

CARLOS: Fine. I *messed* up. But now that I'm here, I always remember how she taught me to stand up for myself. To fight for what I want. I tried to stay to myself in here, man. To keep my head down and stay out of trouble. Hell, I wanted to serve my time and get out of this joint as quick as I could. But ... they wouldn't leave me alone. So I had to do what I had to do. And now, I run this bitch.

MARCOS: Hey hey hey, now. *We* run this bitch, bro!

Lights change. Projections come on. CARLOS and MARCOS freeze.

GUARD 2: It has been said, by someone named Osho, that there isn't a word in the English vocabulary that is as diverse as the word FUCK.[2] Groups. Please pay attention to the screens and read what is written there.

SCREEN 2 projects the lines allocated to GROUP 2. SCREEN 1 projects lines allocated to GROUP 1.

SCREEN 2: Ignorance:
SCREEN 1: Fucked if I know.
SCREEN 2: Trouble:
SCREEN 1: I guess I am fucked now!
SCREEN 2: Fraud:
SCREEN 1: I got fucked at the used car lot.
SCREEN 2: Aggression:
SCREEN 1: Fuck you!
SCREEN 2: Displeasure:
SCREEN 1: What the fuck is going on here?
SCREEN 2: Difficulty:
SCREEN 1: I can't understand this fucking job.
SCREEN 2: Incompetence:
SCREEN 1: He is a fuck-off.
SCREEN 2: Suspicion:
SCREEN 1: What the fuck are you doing?
SCREEN 2: Enjoyment:

SCREEN 1: I had a fucking good time.
SCREEN 2: Request:
SCREEN 1: Get the fuck out of here.
SCREEN 2: Hostility:
SCREEN 1: I'm going to knock your fucking head off.
SCREEN 2: Greeting:
SCREEN 1: How the fuck are you?
SCREEN 2: Apathy:
SCREEN 1: Who gives a fuck?
SCREEN 2: Innovation:
SCREEN 1: Get a bigger fucking hammer.
SCREEN 2: Surprise:
SCREEN 1: Fuck! You scared the shit out of me!
SCREEN 2: Anxiety:
SCREEN 1: Today is really fucked.

Lights change. Focus on MARCOS.

MARCOS: So, its my turn now to tell you a 'lil something about myself. Carlos and I, we grew up together, man. Same neighborhood, same school, same everything. But my family, nothing like his.... This one day, I walked into my house and I see my dad on top of my mom. She's screaming and he's just going at her, man. So you know what I did? I went to the kitchen, grabbed the closest knife that I could find, and cut his throat.

MARCOS mimes cutting his throat with his knife, making an appropriate sound. As he does so, he looks at the audience, assessing their responses. He makes eye contact with the spectator who looks most uncomfortable before continuing.

MARCOS: The blood flowed everywhere. The walls, the sheets, they were covered with blood. Then I took his body, cut it up into little bits, and fed it to the pigs we had outside. Those damn pigs, man, they'll eat anything...
GUARD 1: I think they've heard—
MARCOS: Yeah yeah, I'll move on.... I've been getting into trouble as long as I can remember. I usually get away with it too. I even got away with shooting at this cop while I was robbing a jewelry store. All of that I get away with and then what finally brings me in here is a dumb ass party. I'm telling you, man, if I ever get my hands on that stupid kid who started the fire—that George something or the other—

he's gonna be in big trouble…. Can you believe that shit though, man? I kill my dad, shoot at a cop, and finally, after all of that, what gets me to prison is a fire that someone else started. That's bullshit, you know? But anyway, like Carlos said, now that we're in here, we gotta make the best of it. That's why Carlos and I … we run this bitch…

MARCOS looks at GUARD 2 and smiles. GUARD 2 turns to the audience while CARLOS and MARCOS begin to look at the OUTSIDER.

GUARD 2: I don't what he's trying to imply, ladies and gentlemen. As I said, these young people say things. Sometimes they make up all these elaborate stories. We can't always believe them. You know the joke about the lawyer who goes into a prison, right? Anyone know that joke? There's this old joke about a lawyer who says that he's never met one guilty person in prison. Hah. Every one in here will tell you that they're innocent.

MARCOS: Hey, hey you. What are you doing? Hey. Hello? You with the words! HEY!

The OUTSIDER comes out of their trance with the words and finally looks at MARCOS and CARLOS.

OUTSIDER: Me? I umm…. I'm just rearranging these words.
CARLOS: You're rearranging the words.
OUTSIDER: Yes.
CARLOS: Why?
OUTSIDER: Why?
CARLOS: Yes, why are you rearranging the words?
OUTSIDER: To see what comes up.
MARCOS: To see what comes up?
OUTSIDER: Yes.
CARLOS: Why?
OUTSIDER: Why?
MARCOS: Oh for God's sake, yes. Why are you doing that?
OUTSIDER: For … just for the heck of it I suppose. Don't you think it's fascinating how just rearranging some words in a sentence can change its entire shape? How putting words together differently can take something from being threatening to being loving? That just the shifting around of a few simple words can change the entire meaning of a sentence? Don't you think it's fascinating?

Pause.

MARCOS: Not really, no.
CARLOS: Fascinating is a bit of a stretch…
GUARD 1: Gentlemen watch your tones, please.
OUTSIDER: No, no. It's ok. I suppose it is a bit … hard to understand.
MARCOS: What are you doing here anyway?
GUARD 2: Hey, watch how you speak to our visitor.
OUTSIDER: No, no. It's fine. I'm just here to … spend some time with you all. To … to … you know, see what we can learn from each other.
CARLOS: Learn what?
OUTSIDER: Whatever skill each of us has to share. I'm hoping that we can all create something together. A work of art, perhaps.
MARCOS: What's that?
OUTSIDER: What's what?
MARCOS: What's a work of art?
OUTSIDER: I umm … look, well, that's a long discussion and philosophers have been debating the answer to that question for centuries. But in a very simplistic sense, a poem, a story, a performance, a film, a song, they're all works of art. I'm hoping that we'll get to create something like that together—something creative.
CARLOS: Why?
OUTSIDER: Why?
MARCOS: Are we going to get credit for this? I'll do it if they'll give me credit for it—I'm just one credit short of my GED.
OUTSIDER: I… I don't know, to be honest. I can—
MARCOS: Hey, Mr. H. Can we get credit for this thing?
GUARD 1: It might be possible.
OUTSIDER: What would I have to do so that they can get credit?
GUARD 2: We can talk about that later. You shouldn't do this only for the credit though. Think of it as an amazing opportunity you have been given to learn from someone new.

GUARD 2 turns to the OUTSIDER.

GUARD 2: Why don't you try something with them? Give them an idea of what they can expect from their time with you?
OUTSIDER: Sure, that's a great idea. Let's start with something simple. I would like you to tell me… tell me five things you want the world to know about you.

Pause.

MARCOS: Five things we want—
CARLOS: Why don't you start and show us what you mean?
OUTSIDER: Umm … ok. Ok, so…. I want the world to know that I work hard for what I want; that I am passionate and determined and if there is something that I truly believe is right, I'm going to do my best to make it happen. I want the world to know that I am an idealist and that I really believe that the things that are so horribly wrong in the world around us can change for the better. I want the world to know that I am just as much a cynic though—that it is difficult for me to witness the complex structures of inequality and injustice that prevail all around us and to continue to believe that we will ever find a light at the end of the tunnel. I want the world to know where I am from because who I am is so defined—for better or for worse—by the place I was born in and the family I was born into. And finally, I want the world to know that I am artist. That I am driven by this incomprehensible hope that beauty can be found in the darkest and strangest of places.

Pause.

MARCOS: Damn, son, that's tight.
OUTSIDER: Tight is a good thing?

MARCOS laughs out loud. CARLOS is bored out of his mind.

MARCOS: Yes, tight is a good thing.
OUTSIDER: Would one of you like to try it out? What about you?

OUTSIDER looks at MARCOS.

MARCOS: Me? I … umm…. I just would want…. I would want the world to know one thing, I guess. I would want the world to know that I'm pretty.
OUTSIDER: Ok … why do you want the world to know that?
MARCOS: Because most Chicano men are not pretty, you know. So the world should know that about me.[3]
OUTSIDER: Ok, tell me more. When did you realize that being pretty was important to you? Could you develop that into a monologue?
MARCOS: What's a monologue?
OUTSIDER: It's … you know what? Forget about the monologue. Just tell me more…. What must someone do to achieve prettiness?
MARCOS: You know, you can become pretty by going off drugs.

Silence.

OUTSIDER: Right.... I suppose that is true, isn't it.... What about you, Carlos? Would you like to give this exercise a shot?
CARLOS: I'm good, thanks.
OUTSIDER: Are you sure? It could be fun?
CARLOS: I'm sure. I'm fine.
MARCOS: It's not that bad, man.
CARLOS: I said I'm fine, guey.
GUARD 2: You should give it a try, Mr. Sadaña.
CARLOS: Fuck this, man. I can't do this shit.
GUARD 2: Watch your language, son.
OUTSIDER: No, it's ok—
GUARD 2: He needs to watch his language.
OUTSIDER: I don't mind, really. He doesn't have to—
GUARD 2: I do. Watch your language inmate, or you're done for the day.

Silence. CARLOS and GUARD 2 stare at each other.

CARLOS: I guess I'm fucking done for the day then.

CARLOS steps forward as if to hit GUARD 2. Immediately, GUARD 1 steps in between them and adopts an almost protective stance to cover the female GUARD 2.

GUARD 1: All right, let's go. You know the drill. *(Turns to GUARD 2)* Make sure you file an incident log about this.
GUARD 2: I can do—
GUARD 1: No, leave this to me. It's going to be hard to control this one.

GUARD 1 takes CARLOS out of the room while the OUTSIDER and MARCOS watch them leave. GUARD 2 moves over to a writing pad that has been nailed to the wall or placed on a table and makes an entry as if to document the incident.

OUTSIDER: I'm sorry about what happened to your friend. I hope I didn't cause any trouble.
MARCOS: It's all good, man. It's not your fault. He's just having a bad day is all.
OUTSIDER: Why?
MARCOS: Why is he having a bad day

The OUTSIDER nods.

MARCOS: We're in jail. We have many bad days.

Pause.

MARCOS: So this is what you do for a living, huh? Make this art stuff with people like us?
OUTSIDER: That's part of it, yes.
MARCOS: What's the other part?
OUTSIDER: Just that you know, I work with different kinds of people; not just—
MARCOS: Not just some crazy ass prisoners?
OUTSIDER: No, that's not what—
MARCOS: I'm just playing with you…. Let me ask you something. Do you make money doing this?
OUTSIDER: Well, I'm no millionaire but yes, I make a living from this work.
MARCOS: Really? I didn't know you could do that…
OUTSIDER: Yes, yes you can…. What do you think you'll do when you get out of here?
MARCOS: Oh, I'm gonna join the army.
OUTSIDER: Really? The army…. Why?
MARCOS: I can't go back to my family, man. If I go back I'll just end up killing someone.
OUTSIDER: That's why you want to join the army?
MARCOS: That and … well, it's going to be nice to have a schedule. I'm used to that now.
OUTSIDER: Right.
MARCOS: But mostly, it is because I don't want to go home.

GUARD 1 walks back in.

GUARD 1: Has this one has been behaving himself?
GUARD 2: He's been fine.
MARCOS: Hey, Mr. H, can we all do the song again?
GUARD 1: Ladies and gentlemen, raise your hands if you would like to sing again?

If a majority of the audience members want to do the call and response again, it is performed again. If not, it isn't.

OUTSIDER: Thank you. I'll be back soon.
MARCOS: Sure. We'll see.
GUARD 1: Back to your bed please, inmate.

MARCOS goes back to his mattress and lays down. CARLOS' bed is conspicuously empty.

GUARD 2: All right ladies and gentlemen let's go on out of here now. Please follow us in your lines. You know the drill.

The GUARDs lead the audience out of the room and lock the door. The OUTSIDER leaves with the spectators. As the audience leaves, MARCOS comes to a glass pane/window near the door and waves at the audience with a huge smile on his face.

CHAPTER THREE

Masculinity and David Villaseñor

David Villaseñor: David is 18 years old and is from California. His dad was never around and his mom always had to work. Because of the family's financial troubles, David started to "run the street," began to rob houses, and earned a lot of money by selling drugs. A martial arts fighter, David always carried a gun and knew a lot of people. A girl gets him to go to the college party and once in prison, he's a "savage." He becomes a gang-leader. He has many tattoos and also gets many benefits from the guards. David succeeds once he leaves the prison.[1]

Mystory Part One: The Personal Narratives

The first time I saw N was when I was being given a tour of the detention center, on a visit that preceded the beginning of my workshops.

The deputy superintendent of the center had asked for a meeting to iron out the logistics of the project and as part of this conversation, offered to take me to the school that is housed on the premises.

Once in the school building,

upon realizing that there was a dance class in session,

the deputy superintendent took me to the classroom to have a look.

N got my attention because of his tattoos.

The sight of a tattooed young man,

in a prison uniform,

attempting to learn ballet,

Three. Masculinity and David Villaseñor

was an image that…

an image that struck me for the many contrasts it showcased.

The "tough" inmate, in an all male environment, twirling on his tippy toes and breaking into smiles—this was not an image that I expected to see.

This image of N became my first glimpse into what came to be an interesting, and unexpected, series of encounters vis-à-vis gender within the prison context:

> the very stereotypical ways in which my initial expectations were framed going into the project;
>> the ways in which my stereotypical opinions began to be questioned, reaffirmed, or nuanced because of my interactions with the young men and their guards;
>>> the differences between the young men I was working with in *Lives* and young female inmates that I worked with in a different project (a project that I shall describe later);
>>>> an occasion in which I had the opportunity to witness adult male prisoners in interactions with their families.

It is these varied experiences of gender, and the autoethnographic insights that they catalyzed, which frame how I rewrite N's scene; the scene with David Villaseñor.

…

"Can I step out?"

The question that the young women needed to ask if they were going to step outside of their cells and into the common area.

"Do you need to use the restroom?"

A structured restroom break that was provided to the young men before our workshops.

"Don't spit while you're walking. Don't drag your feet"

A common refrain when the young men were marched in a single file from their unit to the space where we had our final rehearsals of *Lives*.

"You need to roll down your pants, son,"

a guard tells N before we start one of our rehearsals.

"They are rolled down,"

N argues, pointing at the fold that has his pant legs sitting above his sneakers.

"Not enough, they're not. Roll them down please."

> "Really, man?"
> N asks again.

"Yes. Do it now please."
The guard repeats himself and turns away.

> N rolls his eyes.
> "Fuck you,"
> he mouths silently.

You need permission to step out of your room.
You need permission to perform bodily functions.
You need permission to speak while walking.

One must ask: what kind of rehabilitation is possible when people are taught/told/forced to obey orders instead of thinking for themselves?

> What kind of "change" is possible when you're (re) conditioned to believe that you can get away with anything, as long as no one's looking?
>> What kind of decriminalized citizenry can such a process of "justice" create?

After one of my first sessions at the detention center, after a particularly arduous day of watching the young men's every movement and word being disciplined and punished, I spoke with a friend.

> "It must be so emasculating for them,"
> I told her.
> "To be made so powerless in a situation; especially in front of a stranger like me."

"Emasculating?"
she replied.
"Or dehumanizing?"

In the face of being absolutely powerless in banal, everyday tasks like relieving one's bladder, surely it becomes understandable why many of the young men kept getting into trouble with prison officials?

> Surely it becomes easy to see why they keep finding/inventing different ways to act out/protest against their "masters"?

Some of the youth mouthed off to the guards

> > Others found physical release through sports or fights with each other
> > > Others hurt their own bodies with tools they fashioned out of pencils and pens and anything else that could be found
> > > > Each of these ways was a possible performance to enact power—to perform masculinity—in response to a justice system that does its best to remove any semblance of self-control or self-regulation.

Now, I must state that I understand—theoretically and intellectually—why some of these mechanisms of discipline and control have been put in place in a prison system that is designed with particular objectives in mind.

> Objectives of control.
> > Of surveillance.
> > > Of disciplining the criminal out of the man.

But being as much an educator as much as I am a researcher-practitioner, it is also so very evident to me that the more powerless you make someone, the more they will look for ways to "act out" and to assert themselves. How could they not? Doesn't everyone know that the best way to get a person, especially a young person—to do something—is to tell them *not* to do it?

N embodied all of the abovementioned behaviors.

He often challenged the guards, his fellow inmates, and his teachers.

And sure enough, N's performances of his fearlessness and protest got him into a lot of trouble.

I recall an instance in which I ran into the headmistress of the school after a particularly productive session in which N and X (when he was still in the unit) had contributed many good ideas:

"So how were the boys in class today?"

She asked.

She looked exhausted.

Frustrated.

Maybe a bit sad?

> > "They were lovely. I think N and X particularly have a lot of potential"
> > > I replied,
> > "Maybe the two of them can actually help direct the final performance."

She smirked.

"What?"

"Are we talking about the same young men?"

she asked me.

"The unit had a rough day in school today"

"They were throwing erasers at their teachers"

"And then they insulted their teachers with all the choicest insults that they had up their sleeve"

"Those two you mentioned … they were the worst"

Pause.

"Well, they only see me for two hours a week…"

I replied.

"Perhaps, I'm bound to see better behavior on average?"

"It's also the honeymoon phase, right?"

"Who knows, I might have to cry on your shoulder sometime soon"

She smirked again.

Maybe it was a smile.

I could never tell with her.

On my long walk and train ride home that day, I kept asking myself: these nice young men throwing erasers at their teachers? It can't be. They're so … lovely. So kind. So respectful. I mean, they were so polite that they cringed when I asked them to call me "Nandita" instead of calling me "Miss" or "Ma'am." These young men were throwing erasers at, and being rude to, their teachers? I couldn't fathom it.

It was almost a knee-jerk response for me to blame their teachers.

> Maybe the teachers were creating a power hierarchy that the young men couldn't stand?
>
>> Maybe the teachers were policing them too much, disciplining their body language, their spoken language, and their languages of themselves?

I had to take pause though.

> I had to wonder if I only saw the good side because I was temporary and they could not take me for granted in the same way they do their other teachers.

Three. Masculinity and David Villaseñor

> I had to think about the darkness in some of these young men's pasts—what had brought them to the detention center in the first place—and wonder what they might be capable of.
>
>> I had to wonder if it had nothing to do with the behavior of their teachers and if I had just gotten lucky in my interactions with them...

I don't know the answer to this one yet.

I hope it's not just dumb luck,

although I'm sure there is some element of luck to it.

I hope that some of the rapport that I was able to establish with the young men had to do with my pedagogy.

> I hope that the smile on their faces when they see me was earned.
>
>> I hope the sincerity that I sensed in my interactions with them stemmed from something I did, rather than from simply their fascination with the newest toy on the block.

...

When I returned to the detention center a few months after *Lives*, on a weeklong project with students from the college that I also work at in New Mexico (more on the college and the project later), N was not allowed to participate. Participation in this project was contingent upon "Stage 4 status," I was told by the unit supervisor; the label "Stage 4" implying that the young men in question were showing "good" progress and were less likely to misbehave in their work with me.

The "Stage 4s" were the "good" prisoners...

I do not mean for that statement to sound as facetious as it does.

Or maybe I do.

Anyway, on the final day of this project between my students from the college and the young men in the detention center, the incarcerated youth (most of whom had also been part of *Lives*) wanted to make a "Jailhouse Spread" for us—us being myself and the students from the college. The first dish that they prepared was a mish mash of Cheetos, doritos, ramen, and other fried salty substances that were crushed together in a big garbage bag, before being doused with boiling hot water that was heated in the microwave, which was housed in the unit's common room. This fuchsia colored entrée was followed by dessert: again a mish mash of Kit-Kats, moon pies, and various other kinds of chocolaty/sugary goodness that were crumbled together in a microwaveable bowl and then nuked for a few minutes until all that remained was a congealed mound of mouthwateringly delicious, sugar-filled, ingredients. The Stage 4 boys and the students from my college ate this "spread" in a room that had glass walls—glass partitions that separated the feasting group from the common room in which the rest of the unit—the non–Stage 4s—sat doing their homework. In agreement with the unit supervisor that, Stage 4s or not, the other young men in the unit should also be able to avail of the "Jailhouse Spread," albeit not the convivial atmosphere in the glass-walled room, I took N his plate of food and asked him how he had been doing since *Lives*.

"I'm fine, miss,"

he said.

"I wish I had done more though…"

"It was a great opportunity and I should have done more"

—words that sounded as if they had been told to him
by one of the supervisors of his behavior.

"It's fine,"
I replied
"We all have those times when we wish we had done better"
"Don't worry about it"

N gazed fixedly at the exercise book in front of him…

I got the sense that the conversation was over.

"All right, man. I'll see you later,"
I said.
Turning to head back into the glass-walled room.

N continued gazing down at his book

He didn't make eye contact

He didn't seem to want to say anything

"Miss you, miss."

He muttered under his breath as I walked away.

I walked back into the glass-walled room with tears in my eyes.
N said he missed me.
And it felt like a victory.

Perhaps I am way too sentimental for my own good.

…

DIGRESSION 1

The college that I work at in New Mexico has community engagement initiatives in place with the detention center. And as part of this initiative, young people from the college—who are between 16 and 19 years of age and come from over 70 countries—visit their peers at the detention facility through differently structured programs. At their core, these initiatives are centered on the potential of peer-to-peer interaction.

Juvenile detention centers (generally) do not allow their inmates to receive visits from anyone except biological family

Many incarcerated young people do not get to interact with non-sibling peers from outside the prison walls (though, I believe, exceptions are sometimes made for significant others)

However, for a variety of reasons

The officials running this detention center have agreed to put an arrangement in place for our students to visit their prisoners.

I think it is the national diversity of the student body that makes visits from the college a "selling point" for the prison officials

That somehow, our young students—who are the same age as/younger than the youth in the detention center—

Can become "mentors" of sorts.

While I am not convinced about the potential for mentorship

There is no denying that there is something "special" that takes place in these interactions between the college students and the young men and women who are housed in different single-sex units within the same detention center campus.

When I first came to the college, therefore,

Even before *Lives* took place,

I was introduced to these interaction programs and requested to be a faculty presence on the activity.

And given my (problematic) desire to work in prisons,

I agreed and worked on the college's initiatives while also doing my own work through *Lives*.

I was told that the college's initiatives in the past involved the interaction between both male and female students and their respective counterparts at the detention center.

> I was told that the initiative with the young men had been discontinued because those programs did not—as visibly—demonstrate positive outcomes, as did the interactions that occurred between female students at the college and young women prisoners.

> I was told that, while the young women were quick to establish rapports and often wrote letters to each other between their once-a-month interactions, the young men were not been able to get the same kind of connection going.

However, since I had not witnessed these occurrences myself—the above-mentioned events had occurred before my employment at the college began—I wondered if things would be different given the relationship that I had established with the young men through *Lives*. So, I decided to lead a weeklong experiential education project in March 2016, in which young men from *Lives* worked with young male students from the college, in a short and intensive creative writing project.

Given what I had been told about past initiatives, I expected the project between the boys to be ... challenging.

I realize, in retrospect, that my expectations of difficulty stemmed not only from what had been said to happen in the past,

> My expectations of difficulty stemmed from an assumption that it was hegemonic constructions of masculinity that made the young men have a more difficult time interacting with each other than the young women.

I realize—now—that this concern was a manifestation of my own gender-based biases than anything else.

I framed the weeklong project as being structured around creative writing, rather than theater, since I was not sure how the two groups would work with each other—

And somehow, working on writing seemed to be more "benign" than asking the two groups of young men to perform in front of each other (should they not get along).

As such, every day of that weeklong project was designed to include two hours of collaborative, creative writing exercises that I would facilitate.

However, on the very first day of the project, both groups of youth asked me if they could spend an hour playing a sport instead.

So, I altered the schedule and one hour of writing was followed by one hour of either basketball, or American football, or soccer.

On the first day of the project, the two groups of young men played basketball in teams that were defined by their institutions: one team with the boys from the college; one team with the boys from the detention center. The young men seemed to use this first session as a way to check out each other's skills and by the second day, something had shifted.

On the second day the young men did not want to play on separate teams and instead, decided to play in mixed groups.

I remember wondering if their playing on opposing teams on the first day was some kind of rite of passage: where both groups of youth needed to be sure about the "other" side before they were willing to play for the same team.

Quite unlike the girls who worked in mixed groups from the outset, the young men took a little bit more time in making that leap.

Regardless of why this happened—I cannot make an informed guess about this—seeing the young men in the detention center working with their peers from the college was revealing for the very different dynamic that emerged from when I worked with them alone during *Lives*.

For example, as soon as the youth in the detention center knew that they would get to play sports with young people their age, even those amongst them that did not really want to do any creative writing made sure to participate in the one hour of writing exercises—quite unlike the situation I had with *Lives* where the young men had no issues with missing a session if they didn't feel up to it.

Furthermore, in the presence of the young men from the college, there seemed to be less of a need for the youth from the detention center to assert themselves as adults, or as "men"—as sometimes occurred in my work with them on *Lives*. Instead, the young men simply "hung out" with their peers from the college and no further demonstration of their masculinity or adulthood seemed to be necessary...

...

"All they want to do is make them play sports,"
the prison's deputy superintendent said to me one day.

And certainly, there seemed to be a physical activity bias/interest that was more present in the boys' detention center. With the girls, sports were hardly ever mentioned in conversations: what came up more often were art projects and singing and relationships with family and (past) lovers and children. But with the young men, physical activity—wrestling, basketball, football, working out—were often popular conversation topics.

"We should rec them before your sessions,"
the unit supervisor once told me.

"Rec" being the term used to denote strenuous
physical activity, I learned.

"That way they'll be more focused during your workshops"

The young men were seen; it seemed—by the prison officials; by the juvenile justice system itself, perhaps—as being more in need of physical exertion than their female counterparts.

The young men were seen as, or saw themselves as, having "aggressions" that could only be worked out through sport or strenuous physical activity.

Not so with the young women.

The young women did not seem to be viewed as having the same kind of "aggression."

The young women did not need to be "rec-ed" as often

They seemed to be viewed as being less aggressive.

Less "dangerous."

Of course, I have no statistics to back me up here—of whether or not there are more physical altercations between male rather than female inmates in that particular detention center; of whether or not the young men came in thinking of themselves as needing to be "worked out" in order to concentrate, or if that was a behavioral pattern than they learned in the prison context.

But in my observations of how much physical activity was stressed upon for the young men in comparison to the young women, I could not help but question how policies of incarceration—explicitly or implicitly—further hegemonic constructions of masculinity and femininity.

That there is not just the concept of a good citizen

That there is a difference between being a good male citizen and a good female citizen.

I suppose this shouldn't surprise me. After all,

> [i]deas about gender have shaped prisons, literally and figuratively, from their very first appearance as institutions of social control. Nineteenth-century reformers made women's presumed inherent difference from men the primary basis of their case for separate institutions for women, run exclusively by female staff. In a similar way, ideas about masculinity played a role in the architecture and styles of discipline advocated in early men's prisons. In a more general sense, the role of the total institution as a societal microcosm, as a small society in itself, means that gendering processes that may be diffuse or hidden in more open organizations may be easier to identify in this closed institutional context [Britton, 2003:3].

…

DIGRESSION 2

An additional, personal dimension to my perception of masculinity in the prison context emerged when I visited an adult prison for the first time, as part of an event that was organized by a not-for-profit organization in New Mexico. Partly constructed around bringing Christianity into the prison system, this particular organization organizes (what it calls) "family days" in adult prisons in the region. On these days, families of adult offenders—and the inmates themselves—are offered a series of activities over the course of a day: a sprinkling of spiritual songs and readings, storytelling exercises, the sharing of food, and time for structured conversation. While there are many ways in which I could talk about my experience at the family day that morning, there was one particular moment that stood out.

Two inmates joined the event later than the others. They looked "tough": tall, heavyset, muscular, tattooed, with an air of nonchalance at the activities that were being conducted. For the initial part of the event, these two men looked utterly uncomfortable and completely out of place in the face of the "feel good" activities that were being conducted. All this changed though, when the father of one of the inmates and the grandmother of the other, reached the event.

Suddenly, the men seemed more "gentle," less "macho"...

They smiled.

They chatted away.

They smiled.

I don't know if my reading of these men's behavior was influenced by what I expected to see

Or if in fact they did "soften" in some way in the presence of family.

Regardless of the reason though,

One of the insights I came with that day was how the presence of family in the context of an adult male prison could neutralize the hyper masculinity of that space.

In the presence of their wives, girlfriends, children, parents, and grandparents—the way in which the men carried themselves shifted ever so slightly.

A shift that has to make one wonder if isolating people from their families (in most cases, of course, not all) could in fact be detrimental to the rehabilitative goals of the justice system.

In watching the changed body language and behavior of the men in the presence of their families, I came away with one more insight into the potential impact of prison structures on performances of gender.

...

DIGRESSION 3

When talking about gender within the prison context, one cannot (of course) forget the roles of the male guards who supervise male prisoners.

Going into this project I expected something like what I had seen on Prison Break (the television series)—power hungry guards who would be out to punish the young men they guarded. And while there was certainly some (in my perception) unnecessary disciplining of the youth, many of the times, I was surprised by what I witnessed.

The senior most guard of the unit—Mr. H—was someone whom many of the young men seemed to have adopted as a type of father figure. For instance, the week before Thanksgiving, I walked in on a conversation where Mr. H was telling the young people about the food that he was going to bring them from his home to share on the holiday.

On another occasion, I saw out of the corner of my eye, one of the young men resting his head on the shoulder of a guard standing next to him.

On a third occasion, I saw the young men playing basketball with one of the guards on duty—with no reservations (it seemed) about their hierarchical relationship.

I mention these instances from many others since these were occasions in which I had no reason to suspect that the acts of kindness were being performed for my benefit. Instead, these were moments that occurred on the periphery of the workshop. Moments, which I just happened to be privy to.

In addition to how masculinity was/ was not performed by the young men in the detention center therefore, there are some intersections to consider in terms of gender-based interactions with the adult men who guard the institution itself. More on this in Chapter Six.

...

...

...

Three. Masculinity and David Villaseñor

In light of the digressions above, I want to go back to N and especially his unpredictable/erratic reactions at different moments during *Lives*.

N was initially one of the participants who was most interested in the workshop and who attended every single session.

When conceptualizing how he would develop David's monologue, N was also the only one who wanted to tell that story through dance. N was learning different dance genres in school and wanted to experiment with contemporary dance, he said. I was thrilled to hear about N's desire to bring the medium of dance into *Lives,* especially excited when he told me that he was going to talk to his dance teachers about helping him choreograph the piece.

But something happened in the midst of the process, and suddenly, N did not want to dance any more.

He asked me to write a monologue for him instead, a structure that he could improvise around—which I did—based on the character that he had created for David.

N was initially excited about the monologue and continued to attend all the rehearsals—despite his nerves at rehearsing his piece in front of his peers.

But, during the final rehearsal for the performance (my second to last workshop session, the last session being the performance itself), N decided that he did not want to act any more. He said that the performance was "shit" and that he did not want to perform in front of other people. And since I was adamant that I would not force any of the young men to participate, I lost N as an actor a week before the performance.

While I would have used that occurrence, in a more traditional educational context, to understand why my student was behaving that way, time was not a luxury I had at the detention center.

I did not see N for the next week

I did not get to understand why he had changed his mind.

All I got to experience was his—and David's—ultimate absence from the performance

And just as he said when I saw him months later,

N came up to me immediately after the performance and told me that he would do better next time; that he wished he had acted.

Why did N change his mind that day?

Why did he not perform despite his interest in, and commitment to, the project?

Was it because he was afraid of "failing" in front of peers who were otherwise intimidated by him?

Was it because he was afraid of "failing" in front of guards that he often stood up to?

Would a perceived "failure" have changed the image that he had created for himself within the confines of the detention center?

Rewriting David's scene therefore, involved an amalgamation of all the abovementioned (admittedly fragmented) concepts and reflections. First, in terms of incorporating an element of improvisation in which audience members' biographies would be interwoven in unpredictable ways, I decided to frame the interactive component around a question that is likely to elicit different responses based on the lived experience of each individual spectator—the question being: what is a "real" man? By using this question as the point of departure from which to revisit David's scene, I began to choose aesthetic strategies through which I could bring in the stereotypes propagated by popular media images of masculinity in prisons, with the surprises that underscored my interactions with gender in this detention center. Therefore, while David's original characterization, as the reader will see in the original script of *Lives* in the Appendix A, was far more predictable in how masculinity was framed—or rather, in how masculinity was left unquestioned—my goal in bringing in the Outsider's voice in this scene was to present some of the grey zones that also influence performances of gender in prison contexts.

Could there be a way to show David's character with all the masculinity that N wanted in it, but to also simultaneously show the spectators that this "manhood" was far from being a simple issue?

> Could there be ways to represent the various forces—some of which were out of his control—that came to shape David's understanding of what it means to be a "man"?

Mystory Part Two: The Popular Narratives

Popular narratives about masculinity in prisons have been articulated in many ways and one of these viewpoints is based on how the notion of "hegemonic masculinity" pervades the settings of total institutions:

Power, avoidance of femininity, avoiding expressions of emotion. These are some of the attributes of what psychologists call "hegemonic masculinity." There is perhaps nowhere it is more prominently on display than all-male prisons. "It's often very often split for the men in prison. The mask they have to put on when they're outside interacting with other men really conforms very heavily to the extreme, quite traditional versions of masculinity but often, underneath that, there's a struggle." But prison can be the place where this can change [Sommers, 2015].

Speaking to this potential for change, the realm of the popular also contains narratives that speak to how prisons—simultaneously—can be spaces where notions of masculinity are challenged or changed: "This can be having children of his own, a romantic relationship or, in some prisoners' cases, undergoing drug or alcohol treatment or literacy classes" (Sommers, 2015). Within these constructions/rejections of hegemonic masculinity, popular narratives also bring up poignant questions around non-consensual sex. Around the ways in which non-consensual sex between prison inmates has become a mainstream narrative—especially in movies and television series—of how masculinity is asserted and stripped away in the prison context.

> It's the punchline of countless jokes, the socially accepted way of casually discussing a violent and horrifying act. "Don't drop the soap," someone might say with tongue firmly planted in cheek. "Don't you know what they do to pretty boys like you?" asks every stereotypical cop in every bad crime show. So what is gay sex really like in prison? In a recent first-person essay titled A Gentleman's Guide To Sex In Prison, writer and former 10-year inmate Daniel Genis breaks it down in fascinating detail. Here's what he has to say about man on man action in lockdown: "I can speak only for myself, but in my own time in the New York State system, I rarely saw or even heard about non-consensual sex between men. Perhaps I was just very lucky" [Sommers, 2015].

These dominant ideas of masculinity are not isolated to prisons of course, and mainstream viewpoints bear witness to different settings in which representations of masculinity might need to be questioned and/or nuanced:

> From the outlaw cowboy in American history to the hypermasculine thug of gangster rap, violent masculinity is an enduring symbol of American manhood itself. Such violence has become so pervasive—not just in popular culture forms such as music, movies and video games, but also in military culture and sports—that many Americans have become desensitized to it, supporting violent culture through consumerism, even unwittingly.
>
> What's the solution? [...] filmmaker Byron Hurt mentions that getting "men to take a hard look at [them]selves" might be one way to reach beyond the limits of stereotypical masculinity. "We're in this box," he says, "and in order to be in that box, you have to be strong, you have to be tough, you have to have a lot of girls,

you gotta have money, you have to be a player or a pimp, know you gotta to be in control, you have to dominate other men, other people, you know if you are not any of those things, then you know people call you soft or weak or a pussy or a chump or a faggot and nobody wants to be any of those things. So everybody stays inside the box." Through introspection and an opportunity to engage in dialogue around what masculinity means, young men and boys could find ways to move outside of the box [PBS, n.d.].

The questions that Hurt proposes are above are not in isolation and are, in fact, queries that are being explored in various settings through various strategies:

Do you think American men—and maybe men elsewhere in the world—are confused about what it means to be a man? A professor at Stony Brook University does, and he has founded a Center for the Study of Men and Masculinities to study the problem. *What does "being a man" mean to you? Why?* Michael Kimmel stood in front of a classroom in bluejeans and a blazer with a pen to a whiteboard. "What does it mean," the 64-year-old sociology professor asked the group, most of them undergraduates, "to be a good man?" The students looked puzzled. "Let's say it was said at your funeral, 'He was a good man,'" Dr. Kimmel explained. "What does that mean to you?"

"Caring," a male student in the front said. "Putting other's needs before yours," another young man said. "Honest," a third said. Dr. Kimmel listed each term under the heading Good Man, then turned back to the group. "Now," he said, "tell me what it means to be a real man." This time, the students reacted more quickly. "Take charge; be authoritative," said James, a sophomore. "Take risks," said Amanda, a sociology graduate student. "It means suppressing any kind of weakness," another offered. "I think for me being a real man meant talk like a man," said a young man who'd grown up in Turkey. "Walk like a man. Never cry" [Schulten, 2015; emphasis in original].

That said, considering gender—in isolation—is not entirely revealing; what is often more informative are the intersections between gender and race, culture, and/or socio-economic background. Furthermore, given that the racial and socio-economic composition of U.S. prisons have been discussed and debated immensely in recent years, how can intersectional narratives of masculinity be considered in contexts of incarceration? Thinking about this particular question prompted me to investigate how different minority communities in the U.S. problematize masculinity within their particular groups. Could such narratives help better an understanding about the politics of masculinity in a justice system that is notorious for its racial profiling?

The pressure to conform to white male patriarchal standards of manhood as protector, disciplinarian, and provider are representative of such a dilemma for Black males. Despite the unconscious internalization and acceptance of the white male patriarchal standards, inequities in education and employment and limited access to educational opportunities prevent the expression of these behaviors [Nedhari, 2009].

One result of the machismo is that young [Latino] males may not want to ask the questions necessary to be successful in school, the researchers said. Ponjuan and Saenz aren't the only scholars that see the machismo as an educational roadblock. Dr. Gilberto Q. Conchas, an associate professor of education at the University of California–Irvine, said machismo among Latino males shapes their social ambitions as well as their academic performance [...] "Persisting and doing well in school is often seen being at odds with masculinity," Conchas said. But talk to young Latinos and they say that there are positives that come with machismo that they are reluctant to abandon. Chief among them is the devotion to family and the obligation to provide for the family, dedication and values that are admired in most cultures [Newman, n.d.].

For Asian American men, their stereotypical emasculation deeply impacts self-conception. For some, the uplift of Asian American male gender and sexual identity is among the most critical political priorities for Asian Americans. Most Asian American activists—myself included—embrace efforts to redefine Asian American masculinity as part of a holistic approach to challenging anti–Asian stereotypes. Yet, rarely does our community dissect what we mean when we talk about masculinity, and the tactics that we take to empower Asian American men in reclamation of it [Jenn, 2014].

South Asian American men are not usually depicted as ideal American men. They struggle against popular representations as either threatening terrorists or geeky, effeminate computer geniuses. To combat such stereotypes, some use sports as a means of performing a distinctly American masculinity. *Desi Hoop Dreams* focuses on South Asian-only basketball leagues common in most major U.S. and Canadian cities, to show that basketball, for these South Asian American players is not simply a whimsical hobby, but a means to navigate and express their identities in 21st century America. [...] And though they draw on black cultural styles, they carefully set themselves off from African American players, who are deemed "too aggressive." Accordingly, the same categories of their own marginalization—masculinity, race, class, and sexuality—are those through which South Asian American men exclude women, queer masculinities, and working-class masculinities, along with other racialized masculinities, in their effort to lay claim to cultural citizenship [Thangaraj, 2015].

The notion of "traditional" Muslim masculinity has been juxtaposed with liberal interpretations of what it means to be a man. As Muslim men, we want freedom of expression and liberty for our women, but both might end where the honor of our families and the integrity of our faith begin. We have not yet found a comfortable middle ground between the real world pressures of modern day societies and the need to assert a form of cultural authenticity(ies). Competition, not just between different images of the masculine, but also between men themselves seems to lie at the heart of Muslim masculinity today [Darwish, 2009].

When there are obvious trends in arrest rates—when people of particular racial and socio-economic backgrounds find themselves incarcerated at a higher rate than others—we must ask how incarceration subsequently affects the perceptions and performances of gender within those particular groups.

    Is it those who are more likely to perform their masculinity in specific ways that are more likely to find themselves at the risk of imprisonment?

        Or is it the prison environment that creates a particular approach to, and performance of, masculinity?

            Is it a particular kind of man who finds himself in prison?

                Or is it the prison that creates a particular kind of man?

There are various ways in which existing voices in popular culture speak to constructions of masculinity within and outside prison settings and these constructions intersect with race, sexual orientation, class, and many other factors. Considering the performativity of gender within the prison context therefore, is not any more or less complicated than considering gendered ways of being outside prison walls.

    So, how might these popular narratives about gender (particularly masculinity) come into conversation with my personal narratives from within the prison context?

        How can these discussions that highlight both the stereotypes and the intersections of masculinity and race/heritage/culture become part of David's scene?

            Is there also a place to autoethnodramatically bring in questions about the feminine, although my interactions with the young women's detention center was far less intense than my work with the young men?

                How can I get my audiences to reflect on the gendered nature of prisons, on the place for gender in prisons, through rewriting David's scene?

Mystory Part Three: The Expert Narratives

> Brother, I smoke, I snort, I've begged since I was a little baby, I've washed car windows, shined shoes, killed, robbed.... I'm not a child. I'm a sujeito-homem [man-subject]"—Lins in Drybread, 2014:754

    In entering the prison context, I would be lying if I said that I went in without extremely gendered biases—biases that have come from watching one too many prison movie and television show. After all, it has been noted that "the ways that we think about the prison are deeply gendered and reflect an exaggerated version of life in men's institutions," one in which "real men" compete for physical dominance over each other (Britton, 2003:2). Given the sheer number of "cultural ideologies surrounding the prison," for many, "the generic prison is a men's institution, a site in which brutal inmates and sadistic guards perpetually battle" each other for power (Britton, 2003:13). These cultural ideologies are particularly evident when we look at the "number of cultural representations of men's prisons versus those of women's prisons" where in a search done on the Internet Movie Database, "by mid–2002, there had been 91 'women's prison' movies (or TV series) released, as compared with 657 'prison' films" (Britton, 2003:13). Not only is it interesting to note the quantitative difference in the number of films that are produced about male versus female prisons, it is also pertinent to highlight that "the content of these fictional representations differs dramatically" (Britton, 2003:13). Furthermore, while representations about men's prisons in the aforementioned study were generally found to center on physical violence, the comparatively fewer representations of women's institutions were said to revolve around sexuality.

Not immune to the cultural ideologies that such popular culture representations perpetuate—and not immune to the baggage that comes from my own lived experiences vis-à-vis gender—I started my work on *Lives* being hyper aware of the "maleness" of the setting that I was entering. And although I anticipated that the reality of gender dynamics within the detention center would be more complex than the notions that media representations had left me with, I began *Lives* with many ill-informed questions: Would I see gruff young men who would act out against a female workshop facilitator? Would I encounter male guards who would attempt to undermine me because of my gender? Would I, because of the young men's lack of contact with women, find them looking at me with a lascivious gaze? These questions arose from very simplistic understandings of prison-based gender dynamics that my experiences with media had left me with: that young men in prison are always violent and that I needed to be careful.

Immediately after my first workshop though, I knew that I had to try to "understand gender" in the detention center by going "beyond gender" and as a result, I made efforts to separate my view of the young men's masculinity from being defined in opposition to my femininity (Goodey, 1997:403). Instead, I attempted to understand the group's gender dynamics both in relation to the young men's identity markers—like class, race, sexual orientation, status within the group—and in conjunction with the setting of the prison itself. That said, exploring such an intersectionality without being privy to information about the young men's pasts was extremely limiting and I had to "be content with brief glimpses into [the] boys' lives over a few weeks/months" (Goodey, 1997:405). In so doing, I began to look for frameworks that would help me hone my observations and there was one particular proposal that I found helpful in framing my autoethnographic analyses: the idea that, given the limitations of time and money, what "research can look for are shared experiences of fear and fearlessness which can begin to divulge the meaning of what it is to become a 'fearless' male" (Goodey, 1997:405). Using Goodey's proposal as a point of departure, I began to look at "performances of fear and fearlessness" as a frame through which to better understand gender in the detention center and I must clarify here that the performances that I refer to are not only in relation to the young men and their male guards; I also include the fear and fearlessness that influenced my actions/responses as a young woman working in a male-dominated space. What did my fear/fearlessness while entering the prison context say about the performativity of my gender? How did these fears, or lack thereof, subsequently influence the rapport I developed with the young men? How were the young men's performances of their fears and fearlessness affected by the presence of a young, female theater practitioner like myself? How would the male guards counter the young men's performances of fearlessness in my presence? Questions such as these have come to define my rewrites of David Villaseñor's scene.

When I saw N during my first workshop session, I would be dishonest if I did not admit to my (slight) fear of what his physicality represented vis-à-vis my knowledge of prison masculinity from popular culture. I knew that tattoos were associated with gang cultures and that they hold much significance in the prison context. And yet, without the tools to read N's tattoos, I had no way in which to understand what story his ink was telling me. N also carried himself with the air of a natural leader: he would always speak up with this ideas, he came up to me during the first workshop to tell me that he was interested in the arts, and judging by others' body language when N said something, he seemed to be someone that the others in the unit would not—unless absolutely necessary—get into any arguments with. N also spoke very loudly about the crime that had got him incarcerated: "Haven't you seen it on the news, miss?" he asked me once. And when I told him that I had not seen anything about his crime on the news, N—without revealing any specifics—spoke about his crime in a way that communicated his "fearlessness" of a situation that many others would fear. Was N testing to see if mentioning the sensationalism of his crime would make me fear him? Were N's tone and demeanor when speaking of his past actions a performance of his hegemonic masculinity in a context in which he was "emasculated" constantly?

Scholarship suggests that in "its extreme, 'fearlessness' can be expressed as physical aggression among working-class boys in their attempt to assert their masculinity" in comparison to, "middle-class boys" who have more opportunities "to project their masculine hegemony through different channels, such as academic success" (Goodey, 1997:410). If I were to replace the term "working-class" with "incarcerated" and "middle class" with "non-incarcerated"—though the class based distinctions provided might indeed demonstrate links to rates of incarceration—could I attribute N's (seeming) attitude toward his crime and toward the guards as being parallel phenomena? This is to say, did N work with strategies of aggression and of sensationalizing of his crime because there were no other avenues present for him (within the prison context) to display his independence and fortitude? If, as some scholars suggest, "varieties of youth crime serve as a suitable resource for doing masculinity when other resources are unavailable" (Goodey, 1997:410), could N's ways of talking about his crime and his habit of acting out with the guards and teachers be representative of his not having other avenues through which to perform his masculinity? Was it because other ways of being a man were inaccessible to N in his life outside the prison that he got into a life of crime in the first place; a pattern of aggressive behavior that continued behind the walls? Although such "socially structured circumstances" are not always "a constricting and negative process," it must be considered that "[c]rimes in the street also pose an opening for the expression of" masculinity and "as a reflection of having to prove one's fearlessness as a man" (Goodey, 1997:410). Furthermore, given the link that has been suggested in existing scholarship between performances of masculinity, class, and the opportunities present in one's environment, could the concept of "masculine protest" (Goodey, 1997:404) become relevant in better understanding N's mode of asserting himself? Masculine protest, it has been said, is a form of protesting against individuals and situations so as to compensate for an "experience of powerlessness; a protest displayed in aggression" (Goodey, 1997:404). This is to say that "the growing boy [might put] together a tense, freaky façade, making a claim to power where there are no real resources for power" (Goodey, 1997:404); an idea that becomes useful because "it brings the social, in the form of gendered powerlessness, into an understanding of the individual's resultant protest" (Goodey, 1997:404). Was N's behavior ultimately a form of masculine protest; a way for him to perform his protest and his fearlessness?

In addition to the notion of masculine protest, Kristen Drybread's analyses of masculinity in a Brazilian juvenile detention center also provide an interesting lens through which to reflect on gender within prisons. From her research in Brazilian juvenile detention centers, Drybread speaks to finding that "bodies, sexuality, and femininity were relatively unimportant to inmate definitions of manhood" and that understanding masculinity within a juvenile justice context "inevitably requires theoretical engagement with a complex system in which issues including age, class, race, and rank are also at work" (Drybread, 2014:754). By challenging the assumption that "male prisoners, no matter their age, are always already men" Drybread points out that "the unstable social and legal status of juvenile offenders (who are not quite men and not quite children) might have for the acts of violence or the performances of masculinity they undertake while incarcerated" (Drybread, 2014:755–766). Drybread's suggestions propel me to ask if the ways in which the detention center demands, "that inmates act like children" bolsters "the centrality of violence to inmates' understandings and experiences of masculinity" (Drybread, 2014:760). Was masculine protest the only way N could distance himself from being a "child"? Can performances of fear/fearlessness be underpinned by the male juvenile offenders' precarious position between childhood, adolescence, and adulthood? And how does this liminal, not-adult-not-child, space that is occupied by young male offenders nuance an understanding of masculine protest under incarceration? These stimulating questions have come to influence my rewrites of David Villaseñor's scene.

I realize that while I have considered masculinity from different personal, popular, and theoretical dimensions in the discussions above, I have been unable to provide a similarly multi-dimensional conversation about manifestations of femininity, androgynies, or other genders within the prison context. Although I have made occasional comparisons between the young men and young women at the detention center, I have not done justice to the nuances of these differences and how they might manifest especially for juvenile offenders. After all, if prisons can be said to create a particular kind of man, can the same not be said about incarceration creating a particular kind of woman? If yes, what is the hegemonic construction of femininity that exists in the prison setting and how might these constructions be challenged? If no, what are the points of connection and fracture between the ways in which performances of different genders are encoded within facets of the criminal justice system? These are questions that are incredibly interesting to me but, given the far less frequent interactions that I have had with young, incarcerated women, these are not analyses that I can do as much justice to; hence the focus on masculinity in this chapter.

The rewritten scene below takes the thoughts on masculinity and gender that have been discussed in the sections above and weaves them together in an autoethnodramatic retelling of David Villaseñor. From the personal narratives I particularly highlight the ways in which my own preconceived notions about hyper masculinity were challenged. From the popular narratives, I have been inspired to consider an aesthetic framework through which audience members and performers might collaboratively engage in discussions about what it means to be a man; a real man. From the last section on expert narratives, what interests me most for the autoethnodrama is the concept of "masculine protest" for those who are caught between being child and being man; for those who are man-subjects.

Rewriting David Villaseñor

Transition

The GROUPs enter a passageway en route to the next space. Audience members are lined up on different sides of the aisle.

GUARD 1: Thank you for your participation in there. It's so wonderful how well you are all following the directions.
GUARD 2: So, now. Something different.

The GUARDs give small pieces of paper and pens to each of the audience members. GROUP 1's papers have this question on them: "What does it mean to be a man?" GROUP 2's papers have this question: "What does it mean to be a real man?" Audience members are given a few moments to write down their responses. The GUARDs walk around and help, as needed, if some spectators are struggling. Once everyone has written something, the GUARDs painstakingly collect all the pens.

GUARD 1: In your lines again, please. Follow us.

The group moves to the next room, for DAVID's scene.

Scene Four

The audience sits in different sections, in their groups. There are projections on each of the walls; projections that show mainstream media portrayals of masculinity in prisons. Perhaps selected scenes from a series like Prison Break *in which men with tattoos meander in a prison yard in gangs. The projection plays without audio until the images change.*

On the floor, on one side of the room, are photographs. Pictures of tattoos that have different kinds of relevance: gang tattoos, tribal tattoos. There are also pictures that showcase different kinds of masculinity and femininity: pictures that portray more mainstream and conventional gender tropes and those that don't. The OUTSIDER walks over to the pictures while the audience is settling in, and begins to look at them carefully.

As the scene is being established, DAVID greets the audience members individually—shaking their hands and making small talk.

> GUARD 2: All right all right, that's enough. Get on with what you have to tell them. This one's a smooth talker … got to be careful with the likes of him.
>
> DAVID: What do you mean, man? They got to be careful with the likes of me. The LIKES OF ME? What the hell is that supposed to mean? They got to be careful with the likes of me. You certainly weren't being careful when…
>
> GUARD 1: THAT'S ENOUGH. Get on with what you have to say or I'm taking them to the next place.
>
> *Silence. DAVID and GUARD 1 stare at each other.*
>
> *Lights change and focus is on the OUTSIDER. As the OUTSIDER speaks about different prison tattoos, the name of the tattoo and an image are projected where the previous video was being screened.*[2]
>
> GUARD 1: Both groups. Please read the name of the image that is at the top of the screen.
>
> GROUPS 1 & 2: 1488.
>
> OUTSIDER: Fourteen represents fourteen words that are quoted by Nazi leader David Lane: "We must secure the existence of our people and a future for White Children." The 88 is shorthand for the 8th letter of the alphabet twice, HH, which represents Heil Hitler.
>
> GROUPS 1 & 2: The Cobweb.
>
> OUTSIDER: Cobwebs typically represent a lengthy term in prison. The symbolism is associated with spiders trapping prey; or criminals trapped behind bars.

GROUPS 1 & 2: The Teardrop.
OUTSIDER: It could mean a lengthy prison sentence or that the wearer has committed murder. If the teardrop is just an outline, it can symbolize an attempted murder. It can also mean that one of the inmate's friends was murdered and that they are seeking revenge.
GROUPS 1 & 2: The Three Dots.
OUTSIDER: The three dots represent "mi vida loca," or "my crazy life." It's not associated with any particular gang, but with the gang lifestyle itself.
GROUPS 1 & 2: The Five Dots.
OUTSIDER: Also known as the quincunx, the four dots on the outside represent four walls, with the fifth on the inside representing the prisoner.
GROUPS 1 & 2: The EWMN.
OUTSIDER: Evil, Wicked, Mean, Nasty. These letters simply represent the general disposition of some prison inmates.

Lights change.

DAVID: He talks to me like I'm a savage or something.... Maybe I am though. Maybe he's right. I used to run my streets, man. I knew people. People knew me. I used to run my streets, man. Let me show you all something.

DAVID does a martial arts sequence.

DAVID: You know what that is?
OUTSIDER: Not really, no.
DAVID: That's martial arts, man. I had to learn that shit real young. Got to be able to defend yourself when you're running the streets.
OUTSIDER: Why you were running the streets?
DAVID: Why does anyone run the streets, man? I needed the cash. You've heard the story before. Boy's father abandons his family. Mom has to work ridiculous hours to make ends meet but she still can't of course. She still can barely bring home any money. So young boy has to do what he can to take care of things at home. You all have heard that story before. Ain't nothing different about mine.
GUARD 2: All right then, I'll just have these nice people move—
DAVID: I'm not done. Just because my story ain't different, it doesn't mean it shouldn't be heard.... When I get out of here, I'm gonna change things up. I'm going to have the kind of life where I never

have to come to a place like this again. I'm going to change my life. I'M GOING TO CHANGE MY LIFE...

OUTSIDER: How?

Lights change.

GUARD 1: What does it mean to be a man? You, what have you written?

GUARD 1 points to different members of GROUP 1 and has them read out what they wrote down on the pieces of paper during the transition preceding this scene.

Lights change.

DAVID: Do you want me to give you a tattoo?

OUTSIDER: *(Looks nervously at the GUARDs)* I didn't think that was allowed in here.

DAVID: Don't worry; it's not a real tattoo. I asked them for permission.

GUARD 1: Yes, please go ahead.

OUTSIDER: In that case, sure, it would be great if you could give me a tattoo.

DAVID: All right. So tell, me. Tattoos have to be about something that represents you. The essence of you. What do you want your tattoo to say about you?

OUTSIDER: I have no idea.

DAVID: Come on. Look, let me give you an example. You see this one here, on my neck? Like vines? It was to represent how I felt at home. The ... suffocation. It was what would have gotten me in here even if that George kid had never started the fire.... What represents you?

OUTSIDER: In this moment, perhaps what most defines me is ... is searching for something. Not that I always know what I'm searching for.

DAVID: A search.... Hmmm.... Anyone have ideas about what could symbolize that?

DAVID asks the audience for ideas. Takes the idea. Starts drawing on the OUTSIDER's arm or face or neck. While DAVID is doing this, lights change.

GUARD 2: What does it mean to be a real man? You, what have you written?

Three. Masculinity and David Villaseñor

GUARD 2 *points to different members of GROUP 2 and has them read out what they wrote down on the pieces of paper during the transition preceding this scene.*

Lights change.

DAVID: There we go. Done. Mr. H—do you have a mirror?

GUARD 1 *steps forward with a mirror and shows the OUTSIDER their tattoo. DAVID is transfixed by the mirror. Lights change. GUARD 1 and the OUTSIDER freeze. The projected images—which is still of the last tattoo—changes to mirrors. There are mirrors everywhere. DAVID looks at the mirrors on the screen. He looks at the mirror being held by GUARD 1. He takes the mirror out of the hands of the GUARD and smashes it on the ground. There are shards of glass everywhere. DAVID picks up a sharp piece of broken glass and begins to carve a shape onto his body—how this moment is staged is up to the director but it is a moment that needs to make the audience wince. As DAVID carves a tattoo on some part of his body, he winces and repeats: "Man Up." Once he is done giving himself a tattoo, DAVID finds another mirror under his mattress and places it in the hands of GUARD 1. Lights change.*

GUARD 1 *and the OUTSIDER unfreeze and do not seem to notice the broken glass, the blood from DAVID's impromptu tattoo, or any other changes that have occurred.*

OUTSIDER: Thank you. I love it.
GUARD 1: Ready to move on?
OUTSIDER: I just have one last question—

GUARD 1 *nods.*

OUTSIDER: You said you're going to change your life when you leave here, David. What do you think you want to do?
DAVID: We've been learning dance in school.
OUTSIDER: You think you might want to be a dancer?!

DAVID *smiles.*

OUTSIDER: Would you like to show us some of your moves?

DAVID *starts to perform a sequence that he has learned in school. It should be a sequence that presents an interesting contrast with the setting; with DAVID's tattoos. He is incredibly self-conscious though and while his grace and talent are visible for all to see, he keeps stopping and starting. Initially, he giggles when he makes a mistake and has to restart the sequence.*

But gradually, he begins to get more and more frustrated at making mistakes in front of the audience. His frustration builds up so much that when he makes a mistake one more time, he loses his cool entirely and throws something—whatever is closest to him—across the room.

> DAVID: Fuck this shit, man. I can't do this anymore.

Lights change. The GUARDS chain DAVID up. His hands and feet are bound together. The way in which the chains are placed is almost ritualistic in nature. The OUTSIDER watches. DAVID looks at the OUTSIDER from time to time, while he is being chained, but there is nothing he can to do prevent the guards from binding him. Once his chains are put on, the GUARDs step away from him.

DAVID walks over to his mattress in his chains—walking slowly, because his gait is hampered by the chains—and sits down, with his back to everyone.

> GUARD 2: I think we should move on, ladies and gentlemen. He's—well, it's best to leave him alone when he's in a mood like this.
>
> GUARD 1: Please pick up all your pieces of paper and walk out in single lines, in your groups please.

The OUTSIDER walks with the audience members and they exit the room. The GUARDs lock the door.

Chapter Four

Psychological Differences,[1] William Jones and Tishia Jackson

William Jones: William is 18 and is from Memphis, Tennessee. He has everything given to him as the oldest child in a rich family. On the night of the college party, William steals his parent's car keys and takes his friends out for a ride. He is extremely spoiled. In prison, he shaves his hair off because everyone makes fun of him and he joins a gang for protection. People befriend William for his money and he is attracted to large women. He falls in love with Tishia Jackson in prison; they get married upon their release and do well.

Tishia Jackson: Tishia is a 16-year old African American woman who shoplifts twinkies. Her love interest is William Jones. She is from Galvinston, Texas and she has faced a lot of discrimination. Because of the discrimination she faced and because of anger issues in her family, Tishia eats an excessive amount of twinkies, as a coping mechanism. In prison, she is frustrated because she doesn't get enough food. No one messes with Tishia though, after she beats up a deaf inmate. She joins the same gang as William Jones, where they fall in love. Once released, she marries William and they live a long and happy life together.

Mystory Part One: The Personal Narratives

M and Z—William and Tishia—were…
Well, there was something about both of them that is hard to pin down.

M was, in many ways, the "model" prisoner.

He seemed to always be respectful towards those in authority and in my workshops

He was—from the get go—one of the most disciplined members who consistently remained as such.

And yet, there was something about the way in which M adhered to the prison rules, when so many of his peers were protesting in different ways, which just seemed…

Different.

>Later, in conversations with prison officials, when we were discussing who amongst the group was participating the most, "Oh I'm sure M is one of them," the deputy superintendent said. And yet only providing nothing but a tight-lipped smile to my enthusiastic, "Oh yes, he's a great kid."
>
>There also seemed to be a strange dynamic in place between M and the other young men in the unit. He seemed to be laughed at quite often.
>
>I first thought that this might be a function of him being one of the youngest members the group.
>
>And then I wondered if it was because M sometimes adopted an affect that seemed… disingenuous, somehow.
>
>Let me explain this a little more: it seemed to me, from off-the-cuff statements that were made by the young men and the prison officials, that M was from a well-to-do background (unlike many of his peers). But, when it was time to write something down or to perform a piece, M adopted vernacular that didn't seem to roll off his tongue quite so easily as with the others. And when M used this vernacular, the others in the group would snigger and smirk.
>
>M was aware of his peers' response and most of the time, he would ignore then and continue—with utmost confidence—with whatever task he was in the midst of. Sometimes, though, sometimes M would lose his cool, say, "Fuck this," and stop working. At which point all his peers would try to cajole him into working again. Sometimes M would get back to work, sometimes he wouldn't.

There were many indicators that led me to wonder why M had a strained relationship with the other young men in his unit

>Was it because he came from a very different socio-economic background than many of the others?

Four. Psychological Differences, William Jone and Tishia Jackson

> Was it because M had a very different crime story—a story that shaped the behaviors that he seemed to take on in prison—so as to be included within a group of his peers that had very different lived experiences?
>
>> Was it just that his counseling sessions always happened on Fridays or did M seem to need more "help" than others in the group?

And was M's need for "help" the reason behind his fraught relationships with the rest of his unit?

I found out about M's crime many months after *Lives* ended, when I returned to the detention center with my students from the college for the weeklong project that was mentioned in Chapter Three. Until then, I thought of M as nothing but the most exemplary participant.

Always interested.

Almost always the first to raise his hand when I asked a question.

On that sunny spring afternoon, during a creative writing exercise, I asked M how he was doing.

> "I'm appealing for early release. I hope it'll work out."

Later that same afternoon, standing next to the unit supervisor while the students were playing American football:

"I hear M is appealing for an early release?"

> "Yes, he is."
>
> Pause.
>
> "It's not going to work though."

"It'll only happen if the people he's harmed are ok with his early release"

> "And they are not going to be ok with it."
>
> Silence.

The unit supervisor then went on to paint me a picture of M's crime, in very vague terms. But through his veiled statements, it soon became obvious what he had done. It soon became obvious why the young man was incarcerated. And why he would never get early parole.

Leaving the prison that day, sitting on Albuquerque's public bus system, I was surrounded by the college students' banter. They were talking about the football game—some of them were playing American football for the first time—they were chattering away about what they were going to cook for dinner—they were laughing at inane observations they were making about other people on the bus.

Unlike other days though,

When I was able to banter with the students despite the weight of the detention center that I always seem to carry with me for hours after I leave,

On this day,

On this day that I found out what M had done,

All I did was stare out the window.

The day that I found out why M was in prison…

One of the biggest challenges of working in a detention center, for me, is learning how to balance an acknowledgment of the crimes that have been committed by my young collaborators with the simultaneous recognition that the criminal in question, is a child.

A child who,

as we are taught across cultures,

is meant to embody hope.

> To represent the future.
>> To symbolize change.

Until the day I found out about M's crime, I thought I was doing quite well at walking that tightrope

I thought I was doing quite well at balancing my perceptions of/attitude toward the young man who had committed a crime with my fondness for the same young man who was still a child, capable of embodying hope.

But on the day that I was told about M's crime,

My balance went off kilter.

My ability to revel in the "grey zones" of human nature

> An ability that has enabled me with engage with individuals who are positioned across various spectrums of victimhood and perpetration
>> This ability that I have always been proud of
>>> It was frazzled.
>>> Challenged.
>>> Shoved off kilter.

The day that I found out about M's crime.

Back in the manufactured heat of the rented accommodation that I was sharing with the college students, in the privacy of my room,

Four. Psychological Differences, William Jone and Tishia Jackson

I began to do internet searches for M's name.
And sure enough,
I found numerous online reports about what he had done.
About his crime.
About what he had done.
A crime that....
A crime that had affected an entire community.
M's was not a "petty crime."
M's crime was far from being the result of his being mired in structural inequalities caused by race and class (it seemed)
M was privileged (it seemed)
M had had a stable family life (it seemed)
As far as the warning signs for delinquency go, M seemed to have shown none.
And yet.
He did what he did.
He.
    Did.
        What.
            He.
                Did.
And there was/is no way I can find to explain ... to understand ... to forgive (?)
The gravity of what he has done.
I thought about all the instances in which I found M's actions to be different.
When I saw him being judged by his peers.
When I had seen him respond to that judgment unpredictably.
When I had seen him in multiple therapy sessions.
Could his problem have been, you know,
    <you're being politically incorrect, Nandita>
        Could his problem have been in his head?
Thinking of M's actions as having stemmed from a psychological differ-

ence made it easy for me to reconcile the crime with the child. The violence with the innocence. The grit with the beauty.

    Perhaps he hadn't received enough attention from his family?

        Or perhaps he had been bullied to the point of being anxious and paranoid all the time?

           Anxiety and paranoia that had resulted in his crime?

              Perhaps…

My looking at "psychology" for an answer probably says more about me than it does about M.

I found myself trying to excuse or justify M's crime.

To somehow understand it.

    To understand it so that I could reconcile the child I knew with the intensity of the action that the criminal had executed.

And when I embarked on that task,

    when I found my ability to inhabit "grey zones" shoved off kilter,

        that's when the challenge became real.

Would I be able to still see M as the lively and participatory young man I had grown accustomed to interacting with?

Would I be able to know his crime and yet, see beyond it?

M remains a "model" prisoner.

M remains a "model" participant.

M remains a "model" collaborator.

M remains the boy who committed a heinous crime.

There is one image of M that I recall more than any other.

When, after my first workshop at the detention center,

M looked at me through the narrow pane of glass in his metallic cell door.

His eyes bright.

His curly hair sticking out in all different directions.

M waved as the door closed, locking him in for the night. For the next week. For the next little while.

That image of the young man smiling and waving at me from behind a closing cell door made my heart skip a beat.

Perhaps it was the juxtaposition between the warmth of M's smile and the metallic clanking of the door.

> Between the sparkle in his eyes and the narrowness of the glass window.
>> Between him and me.

I waved back.

Of course, I waved back.

Till I realized that the door that had locked me in with the boys for two hours was opening.

I could go home.

…

   …

      …

Unlike M's "model" behavior, Z jumped every time I went near him.

At first I thought it was a physical marker of past abuse.

> Of some invisible trauma.

Until, one time after he jumped yet again when I came near him, I asked:

>> "What am I doing wrong, Z? Am I scaring you?"

He smirked.

The others around him laughed.

>> "He's just fucking with you, miss."

Pause.

"Oh."

Z would hardly ever speak during our Friday sessions.

He would hardly ever contribute to *Lives*.

Some days he would be lively and full of energy in his interactions with his peers.

> But even then, even when he was energetic, he would not look me in the eye.
>> I don't think Z ever said one word to me that wasn't initiated by my asking him a question about something or the other.
>>> And even then, the responses were monosyllabic.
>>> Monotonic.
>>> Like my questions were an invasion of his privacy.

Perhaps predictably, Z eventually decided not to perform his role as Tishia Jackson, despite his enjoyment at crafting that character for himself.

I just couldn't connect with Z in the way that I could with the others.

So, like any educator would do (I suppose), I asked the prison officials about him.

About what I could do to engage with him better.

And then I found out:

I found out that Z's mother had died while he was in prison.

I found out that soon after his mother's death, Z's father had started living with someone new.

I found out that he was on medication for something.

"Z's only 14 and he's done every drug in the book,"

T said to me one day...

Maybe that had something to do with it too.

When I think about Z though, there are certain moments that stand out.

For instance, when we were doing out initial brainstorming for the content of *Lives*, Z was the only one who—from the outset—wanted the piece to be about the lives of young people in a detention center. He was one of the few contributors who wanted to make the piece about the young men's present circumstances, rather than being based on stimuli from elsewhere.

For instance, in an exercise during the weeklong program between the young people at the detention center and the students from my college, I gave the participants a particular writing task. In this task I divided the young people into smaller groups that contained two or three individuals; mixed groups with individuals from the two different institutions. Then, I asked each young person to write down one line (a quotation, lyrics from a song, anything) that was particularly important/relevant to him. And once the lines were written down, I asked each individual to cut up their line/phrase into individual words. So, for example, if one person's favorite line was "Where did I go wrong?" from the song by Twin Beredaz (2008), that person would cut up the sentence so as to end up with five separate words "Where," "did," "I," "go," and "wrong" (and with one punctuation i.e., the question mark). Then, when each youth had his individual word "bank," the young men in each small group were asked to contribute their words to a central pile and thus create a new text by mixing and matching the different words that had emerged from their respective texts. Each group of two/three youth was asked to use its collaborative word bank as a starting point and was invited to add new words/punctuation marks as and when they needed to. Z's group was composed of three people: Z, one more young man from the detention center, and one college student. They began with these three lines:

"The main character of the story lives in the USA. Slowly, his life worsens as he gets dementia."—The first contributor

"My only love springeth from my only hate."—Z's favorite line from Romeo and Juliet

"You would not be the person that you are without going through what you've been through."—The third contributor

By mixing and matching the individual words that came each of these contributions, this is what Z's group came up with:

> You would not love my life.
> The story slowly worsens without you.
> The lives in the USA have gone,
> More intense through hate.
> You would not love my life.
> I've hurt and stolen,
> Killed and tricked.
> Without you, life slows down until it stops.
> The story slowly worsens without you,
> And the lives in the USA get more intense through hate.
> The hate that moves me,
> That moved me away from you.

It turned out to be the piece of "mixing and matching" that everyone in the room found to be most powerful. I think it was followed by a round of applause.

While I could never really find a way to connect with Z, not in the way that I was able to connect with the other young men, it was obvious that he was a creative young man.

That his proclivity for making random sounds, for not making eye contact, and for "fucking with me" were juxtaposed with interests that ranged from creative writing, to Shakespeare. And to twinkies.

....

...

...

One of the counselors at the detention center—the person who informed me about Z's past—had her office next to the common room in which I conducted my sessions. So, sometimes, this counselor attended my theatre workshops and participated in the exercises. When she was not called somewhere for an emergency, that is.

        "A client in one of the other units cut himself,"

    she told me one day when she was unable to attend a session.

I understood from her tone that,

Somehow,

This was par for the course

… for her.

There was something about the mental health counselors at that detention center that seemed "different" within the detention center.

    Different from the guards.

        Different from the administrators.

            Different from the teachers.

While I will speak more to the teachers in the next chapter, I think this difference is highlighted in looking at the composition of the detention center staff who attended the performance of *Lives:*

    Not one of their teachers from school

    Certainly not the headmistress who disapproved of me

    Only the volunteer-teachers who taught dance

    Only a couple of prison administration staff

    But a healthy sprinkle of counselors

    Counselors who not only came to the performance

    But who stayed after

    And insisted on having a talkback with the actors, so that they could ask the young men questions about their process creating/performing *Lives.*

    "How did you all put the performance together?"

    "How long have you been working on this?"

    "What did you enjoy about working with your teacher?"

    "How many of you would like to work on theater again?"

    Questions that gave the young men the opportunity to present themselves as actors and writers.

And what was particularly striking was that the actors did not seem to be pressured by these questions

> They did not seem to feel the need to give the "right answers" to their counselors.
>
> They spoke, honestly, about what they had enjoyed about working with me,
>
> What they had enjoyed about working on theater.
>
> They admitted, honestly, that some of them didn't want to ever do theater again.

Watching the young men interact with their counselor's questions was an indicator of their comfort with these staff members.

> Their knowledge that they would not be judged for what they said.
>
> Their desire to share what they had experienced.

My interactions with M and Z; my interactions with the mental health counselors at the detention center.

Fragmented, yet interweaving puzzle pieces from Lives.

How would I find a place for these reflections in my attempts to autoethnodramatically recreate William and Tishia's scene?

Mystery Part Two: The Popular Narratives

The rewrites of William and Tishia's scene at the end of this chapter are framed by placing the personal narratives above in conversation with existing popular viewpoints around how persons with psychological differences are both perceived by, and often represented in, by media:

> "Psycho." "Freak." "Jason from the horror movie." These are the answers that counselor Habsi Kaba gets from Miami police officers when asked to describe people with mental illness. Such stereotypes are surprisingly common, says Kaba, and not just within law enforcement. But these misconceptions are especially dangerous when they're held by police, who are often forced to make split-second, life-or-death decisions about mentally ill suspects […] More Americans receive mental health treatment in prisons and jails than hospitals or treatment centers. In fact, the country's largest psychiatric facility isn't even a hospital, it's a prison—New York City's Rikers Island, which holds an estimated 3,000 mentally ill inmates at any given time. Fifty years ago, the U.S. had nearly 600,000 state hospital beds for people suffering from mental illness. Today, because of federal and state funding cuts, that number has dwindled to 40,000. When the government began closing state-run hospitals in the 1980s, people suffering from mental illness had nowhere

to go. Without proper treatment and care, many ended up in the last place anyone wants to be. "The one institution that can never say no to anybody is jail," Leifman says. "And what's worse, now we've given [the mentally ill] a criminal record" [Stephey, 2007].

Marlene Murillo's 31-year-old son with schizophrenia has been jailed as a result of his mental illness more often than he has been hospitalized to receive treatment, according to the Durango Herald. Murillo's story illustrates the level of failure in our mental health system but also highlights why some minorities are overrepresented in all stages of the criminal justice system. One reason for this is the disparity that exists in the use of mental health services—even though African Americans and Hispanics living in poverty are almost three times more likely to suffer from psychological distress. In fact, African American and Hispanic youth receive 60–50 percent less attention to their mental health care, according to data reviewed by Benjamin Le' Cook Ph.D., senior scientist at the Center for Multicultural Mental Health research at Cambridge Health Alliance. Even more tragic than the lack of access to mental health care is what happens as a result [Brooks, n.d.].

How Mental Illness Is Portrayed in the Media

- 10 percent of the programs involve mental illness, and 2 percent of the major characters (4 percent in late evening) are identified as having mentally illness
- 40 percent of all prime-time "normal" characters are violent, but 73 percent of characters with mental illness are violent.
- Almost twice as many of characters with mental illness on TV are victims of violence.
- A female character with mental illness has a 71 percent chance of being portrayed as violent

According to the article, "The vast majority of mentally ill characters on TV are not only dangerous, but also are touched with a sense of evil that justifies mistrust and eventual victimization. In short, Gerbner believes that the media set the norms for society as well as the price for deviance " [Gleason, 2015].

In speaking about the particular positioning of minority populations within mental health structures and systems, it becomes necessary to consider narratives about the intersections between mental health and cultural heritage; between mental health and the cultural frameworks that shape its design and execution; the impact of culture both on the patient and the doctor's contentions with mental health—especially within a total institution like a prison.

With a seemingly endless range of subgroups and individual variations, culture is important because it bears upon what *all* people bring to the clinical setting. It can account for minor variations in how people communicate their symptoms and which ones they report. Some aspects of culture may also underlie *culture-bound syndromes*–sets of symptoms much more common in some societies than in others. More often, culture bears on whether people even seek help in the first place, what types of help they seek, what types of coping styles and social supports they have, and how much stigma they attach to mental illness. Culture also influences the *meanings* that people impart to their illness. Consumers of mental health services, whose cultures vary both between and within groups, naturally carry this diversity directly to the service setting. The cultures of the clinician and the service system also factor into the clinical equation. Health and mental health care in the United States are embedded in Western science and medicine, which emphasize scientific inquiry and objective evidence.

- One way in which culture affects mental illness is through how patients describe (or present) their symptoms to their clinicians. Cultures also vary with respect to the *meaning* they impart to illness, their way of making sense of the subjective experience of illness and distress. Cultural and social factors contribute to the causation of mental illness, yet that contribution varies by disorder. Mental illness is considered the product of a complex interaction among biological, psychological, social, and cultural factors. The role of any one of these major factors can be stronger or weaker depending on the disorder.
- Many features of family life have a bearing on mental health and mental illness. Family risk and protective factors for mental illness vary across ethnic groups. But research has not yet reached the point of identifying whether the variation across ethnic groups is a result of that group's culture, its social class and relationship to the broader society, or individual features of family members.
- Culture relates to how people cope with everyday problems and more extreme types of adversity.
- It is well documented that racial and ethnic minorities in the United States are less likely than whites to seek mental health treatment, which largely accounts for their under-representation in most mental health services.
- Migration, a stressful life event, can influence mental health. Often called acculturative stress, it occurs during the process of adapting to a new culture.

To say that physicians or mental health professionals have their own culture does not detract from the universal truths discovered by their fields. Rather, it means that most clinicians share a worldview about the interrelationship among body, mind, and environment, informed by knowledge acquired through the scientific method. It also means that clinicians view symptoms, diagnoses, and treatments in a manner that sometimes diverges from their patients. "[Clinicians'] conceptions of disease and [their] responses to it unquestionably show the imprint of [a] particular culture, especially its individualist and activist therapeutic mentality," writes sociologist of medicine Paul Starr (1982). [Ultimately] Misdiagnosis also can arise from clinician bias and stereotyping of ethnic and racial minorities. Clinicians often reflect the attitudes and discriminatory practices of their society [U.S. Department of Health and Human Services, 2001].

Mental illness is complex subject matter whether we are discussing perceptions, portrayals, and/or diagnoses within or outside of the prison system. The rewritten scene at the end of this chapter therefore, attempts to problematize and nuance how mental illness is enmeshed within the juvenile justice system.

How can I, autoethnodramatically, represent some of the complexities around mental health in prisons?

What aesthetic strategies would invite audiences to think about—not only the issue of mental illness—but the cultural hegemonies that shape how diagnoses are made?

> How could I implicate some of the systemic inequities that are at play in any mental health system—inequities that define how/if treatment is sought, how symptoms are articulated, how diagnoses are made, and how medication is prescribed?
>
>> How do we contend with the criminalization of mental illness?
>>
>> How do we counter stereotypes about what mental illness in delinquency/criminality looks like?

It is these complicated questions, underscored by my interactions with Z and M, which inform the rewritten scene at the end of this chapter.

Mystory Part Three: The Expert Narratives

In his seminal work on asylums, Erving Goffman (1961) puts forward four ways in which inmates adapt to complete and total institutions: their coping mechanisms, if I might call them that. The first coping mechanism that Goffman (1961:61) puts forward is that of "situation withdrawal" where an "inmate withdraws apparent attention from everything" and curtails their involvement in any activity that requires interaction with others. This type of withdrawal is termed as "prison psychosis" or "going stir simple" in prisons and is categorized by the ways in which inmates distance themselves from their setting and from those around them. The second coping mechanism that Goffman (1961:62) proposes, is the "intransigent line" where "the inmate intentionally challenges the institution by flagrantly refusing to co-operate with staff." Resonating with what was discussed about N's masculine protests in the previous chapter, the refusal to cooperate is seen as potentially allowing the inmate a sense of agency—empowerment, even—within a context that is often designed to decimate those sentiments. The third mechanism of coping within total institutions, Goffman says (1961:62), is that of "colonization" where the world of the establishment is accepted wholly by the inmate, and where s/he builds a "relatively contented existence" within the surrounding structures. While all these modes of adaptation offer insights into how young people in detention centers might cope with incarceration, it is Goffman's (1961:63) fourth proposed mode of adaptation that I find particularly relevant to

M—and to this chapter—and that is the notion of "conversion." In this coping mechanism, the inmate takes over "the official or staff view of himself and tries to act out the role of the perfect inmate" (Goffman, 1961: 63) and while similar in some ways to the "colonized" inmate, "the convert takes a more disciplined, moralistic, monochromatic line, presenting himself as someone whose institutional enthusiasm is always at the disposal of the staff" (Goffman, 1961:63).

While a consideration of Goffman's proposals vis-à-vis the youth in *Lives* is informative to how I rewrite William and Tishia's scene at the end of this chapter, what is also interesting to me is how today's detention centers function as *two* kinds of total institutions: both a prison and a mental health facility. I say this because "[u]p to 65% of youths in detention meet criteria for a psychiatric disorder" and that while other youth "may not meet criteria for formal diagnoses," the remaining 35 percent are also said to be "markedly impaired by suicidal ideation, psychotic thinking, reliving trauma, or explosive anger" (Pajer et al., 2007:1661). Furthermore "three recent factors [are said to] have exacerbated the difficulties in administering health care to this population" (Pajer et al., 2007:1661). The first challenge lies in the roadblocks to providing health care to a changing demographic within the detention center population, "with larger proportions of younger children, violent youths, and girls" (Pajer et al., 2007:1661). The second challenge that makes mental health administration in detention centers challenging is the growing number of youth who are admitted with severe psychological differences, many of whom might be in detention "not for antisocial behavior, but because families have given them up to obtain psychiatric care" (Pajer et al., 2007:1661). Finally, in addition to the challenges posed by a shifting demographic and a view of prisons as "treatment centers," the final challenge facing mental health provision lies in "public attitudes toward youths in juvenile justice"; attitudes that see adolescents as "little adults" who need punishment, rather than as children who need help (Pajer et al., 2007:1661). To complicate matters even further, the challenges surrounding mental health treatment are not limited to the tenure of a young person's incarceration. While widely available figures indicate that "only a fraction of ex-prisoners are successfully restored to society," what these figures do not always highlight is that recidivism rates are significantly higher for prisoners with severe mental illnesses—approximately 80 percent of mentally ill prisoners are likely to recommit offences upon their release and as a consequence, return to prison (*Berkeley Journal of Criminal Law*, 2009:279). The challenges surrounding the provision of mental health care therefore are not only isolated within the walls of a prison; they also spill over in to the formerly incarcerated individual's reintegration to life outside those prison walls.

Reflecting on this information then leads me to ask a number of related questions: How are young people diagnosed as having particular kinds of mental illnesses? Does the diagnosis depend on the nature of the crime that was committed by the youth, or does the diagnosis depend on the inmate's state of mind during period leading up to the commitment of the crime, or does the diagnosis dependent on the prisoner's psychological well being while incarcerated? Are there different protocols that govern the use of medication within mental health structures in juvenile detention centers versus adult prisons? What checks and balances are in place to mitigate cultural hegemonies of diagnosis and treatment when dealing with inmate populations that come from a variety of backgrounds? When looking to answer these questions, research suggests that as "youths are adjudicated and move deeper into the juvenile justice system, factors other than offense become more salient in the decision making process" (Rogers et al., 2006:27); factors like gender, race, a history of "maltreatment, dysfunctional families, family substance abuse, and brain injury" (Teplin et al., 2012:1031). Furthermore, it has also been suggested that "for one-third of incarcerated youth diagnosed with depression, the onset of the depression occurred *after* they began their incarceration" (Holman & Ziedenberg, 2006:2; emphasis mine), i.e., that the experience of imprisonment was itself responsible for the occurrence of a mental illness. Although "some researchers have found that the rate of suicide in juvenile institutions is about the same as the community at large" other studies suggest that "incarcerated youth experience from double to four times the suicide rate of youth in community" and the Office of Juvenile Justice and Delinquency Prevention "reports that 11,000 youth engage in more than 17,000 acts of suicidal behavior in the juvenile justice system annually" (Holman & Ziedenberg, 2006:9): behaviors that are only heightened, ironically, by placing the punishment that is them meted out to these youth (like placing them in isolation). So if the processes of incarceration themselves can give rise to, or exacerbate, existing mental health conditions—mental health conditions that then increase the likelihood that these young people will re-offend upon their release—what can be done to address the dangerous interplay of cause and effect that might be at work?

Questions about *when* incarcerated youth develop/externalize symptoms of psychological differences—i.e., before, during, after incarceration—becomes important to consider so as to identify the role of the prison in the propagation of particular kinds of mental health risks. In considering this role, a study from the Center for the Study of the Prevention of Violence "has shown that as many as a third of young people will engage in delinquent behavior before they grow up but will naturally 'age out' of the delinquent behavior of their younger years" (Holman & Ziedenberg, 2006:6): an aging out that has been correlated to the establishment of significant relationships with a peer or adult mentor, and also to the availability of employment opportunities that are available to the youth in question. So, given this information, could we speculate that the high rate of mental illness among detained youth in the United States might be caused (largely) because of these youth being imprisoned *before* they have the chance to age out of their problems? And if it is indeed the case, if there is an (unwarranted) criminalization of what could simply be quotidian displays of juvenile "acting out," how do these occurrences link to discourse surrounding the race-based inequities that are perpetuated by the U.S. Criminal Justice system? This is to say: if youth are more likely to develop mental health issues because of incarceration, and if youth of color are more likely to be incarcerated, can we not extrapolate that it will be communities of color that will carry the burden of these crises?

Further complicating the issue of who is diagnosed and when they are diagnosed is the question of treatment, especially medication. For example, it has been documented that "[a]lmost all juvenile detention facilities have become dispensaries of psychoactive medications for youth" and "there have been growing concerns about the use of psychoactive medications for children and youth in out-of-home settings" (Cohen, Pfeifer & Wallace, 2014:738). A recent review of data from a national survey "showed that many more children and youth in child welfare placements have been prescribed these medications compared to children living informally with kin" (Cohen, Pfeifer & Wallace, 2014:738). Through the potentially excessive use of medication, therefore, begins another cycle where cause and effect start blurring their boundaries: a cycle in which the young incarcerated person who develops mental illness because of his/her imprisonment becomes dependent on medication; medication that s/he might not be able to afford or access upon their release; medication that—based on the racial/cultural background of the young person—might further contribute to how they are viewed in/by their homes and communities in reintegration efforts.

These varied expert narratives about coping mechanisms, diagnoses, and treatment of psychological differences frame my rewriting of William and Tishia's scene. M and Z's depictions (and descriptions) of William and Tishia's psychological status have remained important in my choice of language and imagery in the rewritten scene; the cultural subjectivity of mental health diagnoses and the stigma carried by particular labels are the central popular narratives that have been integrated. And from the expert narratives, I focus on the flooding of the juvenile justice system with youth who come in with and/or develop mental health issues in the prison setting. Through the integration of these different viewpoints, the rewritten scene additionally brings in the voice of the Outsider and the (auto) biographies of its audience members, so as to catalyze a more collaborative conversations about emotional, mental, and psychological within contexts of juvenile incarceration. How can I autoethnodramatically showcase the subjective ways in which mental health diagnoses are made? How can I autoethnodramatically ask my readers/spectators to think about the controversial usage of medication within the juvenile justice system? How can I theatrically showcase the incredibly difficult questions that mental health professionals in the juvenile justice system have to contend with? What are aesthetic strategies that I can use to allude to the modes of adaptation that Goffman suggests, for categorizing inmates' strategies when coping with life in total institutions?

In exploring these questions, given how difficult it is to represent psychological wellbeing in a nuanced, and ethical way that does not stereotype, there are parts of the rewritten scene in which I integrate excerpts from British playwright Sarah Kane's (1998) play *4.48 Psychosis*. I chose this particular play because of its own embodiment of mystory characteristics, particularly through its usage of techniques that allow spectators to bring in their own biographies into the performance. While *4.48 Psychosis* "does not clearly specify a setting, stage directions, or character names, there are approximately fifty 'silences,' 'long silences,' or 'very long silences,' [...] minimalism emerges as one of the play's strengths, offering readers and audience members opportunities to include their own experiences in the text and/or performance" (Tycer, 2008:26). Furthermore, there is no denying that Kane's work has come to be seen as being particularly relevant in dramatically representing the fragmentation of trauma in the theatrical arena. Ellen Kaplan (in Tycer, 2008:28) "uses trauma theory to analyze 4.48 when she reflects that 'trauma is taproot for Kane: the inability to feel, the feelings of disembodiment and dissolution of self ... are traces of inexpressible and hidden strain'"—a texture that I have come to see as essential in bettering my understanding about the manifestations of mental health in the context of a juvenile detention center. "Most explicitly, 4.48 can be interpreted politically as indicting a society that ostracizes people who are determined to be mentally ill" (Tycer, 2008:33)—thus leading to a "dumping" of these kinds of people in detention centers. Furthermore, in order to force her spectators to question the role of medication within the mental health establishment "Kane provides a long list of symptoms, diagnoses, and failed medications" where "tongue-twisting medical names and fluctuating dosages manifest more extreme side effects than cures" (Tycer, 2008:34). While Kane's list of medication "builds inexorably until the patient cuts off the flow with a clipped rejection of the medical establishment," using this list in the context of rewriting *Lives* forced me to also wonder how "minors" (as compared to adult prisoners) have/do not have a say in the medical treatment that is meted out to them in a total institution like a prison. All this having been said, it is important to clarify, before moving on to the rewritten scene, that there are many aspects to the text below that are fictional—fictional qualities that I make sure to underscore since, while I did have some interactions with mental health professionals in the juvenile justice system in New Mexico, the brevity of our interactions has led to my only being able to extrapolate larger ideas from statements that were often ambiguous.

Rewriting William Jones and Tishia Jackson

TRANSITION

This passageway is set up with tables and chairs. There are as many tables as there are audience members. Each table has two chairs.

Lining up the spectators along different walls in a passageway, the GUARDs collect all the pieces of paper that are being held by the audience members. As earlier, if any of the audience members have forgotten their papers, a show is made of opening DAVID's cell door again and collecting whatever has been left behind.

GUARD 2: I think you are all ready for us to change things up even more.... But in order to do so, we have to get to know you a little bit better. So, please line up near the walls. Someone will ask to speak with each of you individually. Answer their questions as best you can and we'll take it from there.

As many actors as there are audience members come into the hallway, and sit on one of the chairs at each table. The GUARDs silently direct the audience members to the table at which they need to take a seat. At each table, the actor (playing the character of a mental health professional) has a writing pad in front of them and asks audience members the questions that are suggested below (or a variation of them). As the audience members answer the questions, the actors evaluating them take copious notes and at the end of the "interview," a small piece of paper is given to the spectator. The "diagnosis" given is at the discretion of the actor who is "evaluating" a particular spectator. If audience members try to ask for an explanation for the "diagnosis" that is finally given to them, they find that no reason is forthcoming. If some actors complete their evaluations of audience before others, the GUARDs line the spectators up against a wall until everyone has been "diagnosed."

Questions[2]

- How old are you?
- When is your birthday?
- Do you have any brothers or sisters?
- Did you go to school?
- Did you go to kindergarten?
- Did you go to college?
- Did you get into trouble as a child? If so what kind of trouble and what were the consequences?
- Do you have a job?
- How old were you when you had your first job?
- Have you always lived in the same house / apartment?
- Growing up, did you live with both your parents?
- What quality did you most admire in your mother/father/other parental figures?
- What quality did you dislike in your parental figures?
- What were you doing four weeks ago?
- What were you doing six months ago?
- What were you doing a year ago?
- Growing up, did you ever get into trouble because you stayed out at night past the time you were supposed to be home?
- Growing up, did you ever have trouble sitting still?
- As a teenager, did you often not listen when people spoke to you?
- As a teenager, were there certain noises or sounds that you couldn't keep yourself from making?
- In your childhood, did you ever threaten someone with a weapon?
- Have you been so afraid of seeing blood or cuts that you've tried not to look when someone has had a cut or there was blood?

Four. Psychological Differences, William Jone and Tishia Jackson 123

While directors and actors are free to be as creative as they like in the execution of these assessments and the "diagnosis" that is given, care must be taken to see that actors do not take the improvisation to extreme levels or that the "diagnosis" that is given is in fact a real psychological or emotional condition. Our goal is not to "traumatize" the audience in any way. We are seeking to expose them to a couple of things: how juveniles who are incarcerated are caught up within systems of mental health diagnosis and evaluation that many of them do not understand; that decisions that are ultimately made have repercussions on the young persons short, medium, or long-term future (as the case may be).

Once all the audience members are finished with their interviews:

GUARD 1: Please keep the pieces of paper that have been given to you very carefully. You will need them in the next space.

Scene Five

When the audience walks into William's space, there are four sections. One is labeled NO RISK; one is labeled LOW RISK; one is labeled MEDIUM RISK; one is labeled HIGH RISK. The GUARDs take a look at each spectator's piece of paper and directs him or her to the appropriate section. Whether or not the papers given to the audience members contain the name of one of the sections, or whether the notes include more "obscure" notations that are open to the GUARDs interpretation, is up to the director and the particular point that is being made vis-à-vis mental health protocols within prisons in that context.

As they walk in, WILLIAM is seated in silence. The OUTSIDER walks to WILLIAM and sits down beside him. WILLIAM watches the audience members. As he watches the GUARDs sending audience members to different sections, we see him get more agitated. His agitation starts subtly but builds through the text below.

While WILLIAM speaks, TISHIA keeps stuffing herself with twinkies

WILLIAM: My name is William. Will–I–Am. (*He starts to get agitated.*) You know, when I came in here, I was like this chair.... I was just there, just doing my own thing. And now, now I'm like... (*He picks up the chair and throws it across the room. He begins to pace up and down.*) I had everything as a child you know? My parents got me everything I wanted. That night, the night that stupid George started the fire, I was hanging out in the RV that my parents had given me. And then.... And then... (*He screams. He throws things around. He*

kicks things.) And then the police came; and then, and then. (He throws more things around. He kicks more things.) And now all I have to say is FUCK THE POLICE. FUCK THE POLICE. FUC-
GUARD 2: William.

Lights change. William walks over to the area of the room where the OUTSIDER is seated and sits in front of him/her. Silence.

OUTSIDER: So...
WILLIAM: I know.
OUTSIDER: What do you know, William?
WILLIAM: I've had a rough week. I know I... I know I misbehaved just now and I ... apologize.
OUTSIDER: Thank you for that; I appreciate that you understand that you misbehaved.
WILLIAM: ...
OUTSIDER: Do you know why you misbehaved?
WILLIAM: I was angry, I guess.
OUTSIDER: At what?
WILLIAM: I... I don't know.
OUTSIDER: You must have an idea?

Lights change.

GUARD 1: Do you know why you were classified as low risk? (*The question is directed to someone in the LOW RISK section*).

GUARD 1 and GUARD 2 alternate between questioning different members of the audience who are seated in different sections. In each instance, the audience members is given a few seconds to respond but a response is never forced. After a number of the spectators have been questioned—
Lights change.

OUTSIDER: Many of the two million children and adolescents arrested each year have a mental health disorder. As many as 70 per cent of youth in the system are affected with a mental disorder, and one in five suffer from a mental illness so severe as to impair their ability to function.[3]
WILLIAM[4]: A room of expressionless faces string blankly at my pain, so devoid of meaning there must be evil intent.
   Dr This and Dr That and Dr Whatsit who's just passing and thought he'd pop in to take the piss as well. Burning in a hot tunnel of dismay, my humiliation complete as I shake without reason and

stumble over words and have nothing to say about my 'illness,' which anyway amounts only to knowing that there's no point in anything because I'm going to die. And I am deadlocked by that smooth psychiatric voice of reason, which tells me there is an objective reality in which my body and mind are one. But I am not here and never have been. Dr This writes it down and Dr That attempts a sympathetic murmur. Watching me, judging me, smelling the crippling failure oozing from my skin, my desperation clawing and all-consuming panic drenching me as I gape in horror at the world and wonder why everyone is smiling and looking at me with secret knowledge of my aching shame.

Shame shame shame.

Drown in your fucking shame.

Inscrutable doctors, sensible doctors, way-out doctors, doctors you'd think were fucking patients if you weren't shown proof otherwise, ask the same questions, put words in my mouth, offer chemical cures for congenital anguish and cover each other's asses until I want to scream for you, the only doctor who ever touched me voluntarily, who looked me in the eye, who laughed at my gallows humor spoken in the voice from the newly-dug grave, who took the piss when I shaved my head, who lied and said it was nice to see me. Who lied. And said it was nice to see me. I trusted you, I loved you, and it's not losing you that hurts me, but your bare-faced fucking falsehoods that masquerade as medical notes.

Your truth, your lies, not mine.

And while I was believing that you were different and that you maybe even felt the distress that sometimes flickered across your face and threatened to erupt, you were covering your ass too. Like every other stupid mortal cunt.

To my mind that's betrayal. And my mind is the subject of these bewildered fragments.

Nothing can extinguish my anger.

And nothing can restore my faith.

Except maybe you.

He looks at TISHIA with tenderness. Pause.

TISHIA: My best friend in elementary school was this girl named Alice. We went everywhere together ... to school, to the park, to birthday parties. One day, Alice disappeared from my life. I couldn't find here anywhere. I was told that her parents wanted to move to a "better" neighborhood; they wanted to be around more people like them. They didn't want Alice to be around people like us. Like me. Eating twinkies calms me down. It makes me happy. Twinkies calmed me down when Alice left because her parents didn't want her around poor black kids. They calmed be down when my uncle came into my room and…. Eating twinkies calms me down. They make me happy.

She starts eating twinkies again, looking at William while she does so. They smile at each other. Lights change.

OUTSIDER[5]: Have you made any plans?
WILLIAM: Take an overdose, slash my wrists then hang myself.
OUTSIDER: All those things together?
WILLIAM: It couldn't possibly be misconstrued as a cry for help.

Silence.

OUTSIDER: It wouldn't work.
WILLIAM: Of course it would.
OUTSIDER: It wouldn't work. You'd start to feel sleepy from the overdose and wouldn't have the energy to cut your wrists.

Silence.

WILLIAM: I'd be standing on a chair with a noose around my neck.

Silence.

OUTSIDER: If you were alone do you think you might harm yourself?
WILLIAM: I'm scared I might.
OUTSIDER: Could that be protective?
WILLIAM: Yes. It's fear that keeps me away from the train tracks. I just hope to God that death is the fucking end. I feel like I'm eighty years old. I'm tired of life and my mind wants to die.
OUTSIDER: That's a metaphor, not reality.
WILLIAM: It's a simile.
OUTSIDER: That's not reality.
WILLIAM: It's not a metaphor, it's a simile, but even if it were, the defining feature of a metaphor is that it's real.

A long silence.

OUTSIDER: You are not eighty years old.

Silence.

WILLIAM: Are you?

A silence.

OUTSIDER: Are you?

A silence.

WILLIAM: Or are you?

A long silence.

WILLIAM: Do you despise all unhappy people or is it me specifically?
OUTSIDER: I don't despise you. It's not your fault. You're ill.
TISHIA: I don't think so.
OUTSIDER: No?
WILLIAM: No. I'm depressed. Depression is anger. It's what you did, who was there and who you're blaming.
OUTSIDER: And who are you blaming?
WILLIAM: Myself.

WILLIAM takes out a ball of wool from under his mattress. He gives one end of it to the OUTSIDER and gives different sections of the wool to different audience members. Sometimes he circles the chair of some audience members with the wool. This continues till the room looks like a web. While he is setting up and dismantling the web, he repeats these lines (either spoken or sung):

WILLIAM: Sertraline, 50mg. Insomnia worsened, severe anxiety, anorexia, (weight loss 17kgs,) increase in suicidal thoughts, plans and intention. Discontinued.

Zolpiclone, 7.5mg. Slept. Discontinued following rash. Patient threatening and uncooperative. Paranoid thoughts—believes staff are attempting to poison her.

Melleril, 50mg. Co-operative.

Lofepramine, 70mg, increased to 140mg, then 210mg. Weight gain 12kgs. Short term memory loss. No other reaction.

Citalopram, 20mg. Morning tremors. No other reaction.

Fluoxetine hydrochloride, trade name Prozac, 20mg, increased to 40mg. Insomnia, erratic appetite, (weight loss 14kgs,) severe anxiety. Discontinued.

Thorazine, 100mg. Slept. Calmer.

Venlafaxine, 75mg, increased to 150mg, then 225mg. Dizziness, low blood pressure, headaches. No other reaction. Discontinued.

At the same time, TISHIA is eating twinkies again. There is a disconcerting interplay between what WILLIAM says and the sounds that TISHIA makes as she eats.

Lights change.

WILLIAM continues creating his web during the following conversation.

OUTSIDER: I need your help.
TISHIA: That's new.
OUTSIDER: He's not responding to any of the medication.
TISHIA: Probably cos he doesn't need it.

Silence.

OUTSIDER: What do you think he needs?
TISHIA: Things and people that he can't get in here.

Pause.

OUTSIDER: You know what he did to bring him here, right?
TISHIA: Yes.
OUTSIDER: Someone who can do something like that needs…
TISHIA: Needs help?
OUTSIDER: Yes.
TISHIA: You think living like this is helping him?

Silence.

TISHIA: Why do you do this work?

Silence.

TISHIA: You see the worst of us.
OUTSIDER: Yes.
TISHIA: We know nothing of you.
OUTSDIER: No.
TISHIA: But I like you.
OUTSIDER: I like you.

Silence.

TISHIA: You're his last hope.

A long silence.

OUTSIDER: He doesn't need a friend he needs a doctor.

A long silence.

TISHIA: You are so wrong.

A very long silence.

OUTSIDER: But you have friends.

A long silence.

OUTSIDER: You have a lot of friends. What do you offer your friends to make them so supportive?

A long silence.

OUTSIDER: What do you offer your friends to make them so supportive?

A long silence.

TISHIA: What do you offer?

Silence.

OUTSIDER: We have a professional relationship. I think we have a good relationship. But it's professional.

Silence.

OUTSIDER: I feel his pain but I cannot hold his life in my hands.

Silence.

OUTSIDER: You'll be all right. You're strong. I know you'll be okay because I like you and you can't like someone who doesn't like themself. The people I fear for are the ones I don't like because they hate themselves so much they won't let anyone else like them either. But I do like you. And I know you'll be ok.

Silence.

OUTSIDER: Most of my clients want to kill me. When I walk out of here at the end of the day I need to go home to my lover and relax. I need to be with my friends and relax. I need my friends to be really together.

Silence.

OUTSIDER: I fucking hate this job and I need my friends to be sane.

Silence.

OUTSIDER: I'm sorry.
TISHIA: It's not my fault.

OUTSIDER: I'm sorry, that was a mistake.
TISHIA: It's not his fault.
OUTSIDER: No. It's not anyone's fault. I'm sorry.

Silence.

OUTSIDER: I was trying to explain—
TISHIA: I know. I'm angry because I understand, not because I don't.

Lights change.

GUARD 1: You know you're gonna have to clean this up?

WILLIAM stretches out his hand to the GUARD and is given a pair of prison-issue scissors. WILLIAM goes around the room and cuts the web randomly till the floor is covered with string. He squats on the floor and tries to collect the string with his hands. The OUTSIDER and TISHIA go to help him and ask audience members to join in if they would like. GUARD 1 helps; GUARD 2 doesn't.

GUARD 2: We're going to take these people elsewhere now. Can we leave you two alone with this till we come back or are you going to—
GUARD 1: We can't leave them alone with this.
GUARD 2: What do you want me to do then?
GUARD 1: You, you, you (*points to some members of the audience*). Please take some of that mess out with you, if you don't mind. Thank you.

WILLIAM is seated next to the string and watches morosely as the string is taken away from him. Tears roll down his face. TISHIA goes to him and they embrace.

GUARD 2: We need to leave, please.

The OUTSIDER and spectators are led outside and the door is locked. GUARDs advise the audience members that they can place the string outside the door and take them further down the passageway for TOBIAH's scene.

Chapter Five

Education and Tobiah Edwards

Tobiah Edwards: Tobiah plays basketball and is really athletic. He is 17 years old, from Kansas City. He lost his mother when he was really young and his father is an alcoholic; his family is extremely poor. Although he got involved with negative people who got him involved with a gang, Tobiah's basketball skills get him a college scholarship. He is crazy in prison: beating everyone, rushing staff, and yelling all the time. Because of this behavior, Tobiah is the first to get sentenced and is also the first to make a name for himself in the prison. Upon his release from prison, however, Tobiah is able to turn over a new leaf. He joins the NBA and becomes a successful basketball athlete.

Mystory Part One: The Personal Narratives

There are three experiences that have shaped my thoughts on education and learning in the detention center context:

EXPERIENCE #1

I expected hesitation.

Mistrust.

Hostility, even.

After all, these young women get do-gooders like me visiting them all the time.

Why would they want to engage with someone who they knew was going to be short-term; inconsistent?

Why would they even begin to trust a "do-gooder" (South Asian) Indian lady who had never been into a prison before?

Why should they even try?

I walked into the girls' unit that morning, with about twenty of my college students

The fluorescent lighting made me need to go to the bathroom. Constantly.

Maybe my nerves had something to do with that.

I noticed the shower stall and toilet that were conspicuously placed in the middle of the unit common room.

I observed the young women needing say "May I step out?" before stepping outside their cell doors into the common area where we were.

I saw the "curtains" that were hung on the glass windows in the cell doors. You know, for them to have privacy when they changed clothes.

Only when changed their clothes, though.

There was no reason for these young women to want to engage with someone who they knew was going to be short-term; inconsistent.

There was no reason for these young women to begin to trust a "do-gooder" (South Asian) Indian lady—and her "privileged" college students—who had never been into a prison before.

There was no reason for them to even try.

They greeted us with smiles.

Warmth.

Enthusiasm.

SMILES!

I did not expect that at all.

She's going to be paroled in a month. But in prison, she has been taking online classes on Theater Appreciation, she tells me. She now knows that this is what she wants to do. She wants to become an actress. While the three other units we met that day did not know what theater was, this one did. All because of the budding actress in their midst.

> She sat alone, almost sulking. It was a speed-dating type of exercise in which the two groups of young women rotated partners and had a couple of minutes to talk about a prompt. "Talk about something that excites you." She sulked for a while and then muttered under her breath, "I like the philosophy of Desmond Tutu."

I did a double take.

I certainly did not expect a young incarcerated person in a New Mexican prison to know who Desmond Tutu was.

And while my own ignorance and stereotyping are at play here, listening to this young woman's answer was the first spark of my thinking about education in the detention center setting.

The next time I returned to the detention center, I took in a podcast of one of Desmond Tutu's interviews with me.

I have no idea whether she listened to it or not.

...

Experience #2

L was the first to ask about whether or not the young men in *Lives* could get academic credit for their workshops with me. "I just need one more credit to finish my GED,"[1] he said, and seemed to be the most excited of the group when the school officials initially indicated that this would be a possibility. Of course, this happened before the issue of "swearing"-dependent credit was brought up on the day of my performance (that I've discussed in Chapter One); when my good intentions were thrown amuck…

L seemed determined. Absolutely determined.

To move on with his life.

To become a "success."

His creation of the character of Tobiah in *Lives* was created in this vein: a young man who wanted to become better; for himself; for his younger brothers and sisters.

L also spoke often of his love for poetry. He had published pieces of his poetry in newspapers and magazines and told me, from day one, that he enjoyed writing. When I once took in a video of Rafeef Ziadah's (2011) "We teach life, sir," to show him how an example of poetry might be performed, his eyes lit up.

While L never did seem to find the inspiration to write/perform poetry for *Lives*, he was a dependable (and indispensable) ensemble member. I recall very clearly when, on our last rehearsal the week before the performance, three of the young men said that they didn't want to perform any more. One of these young men was set to play the GUARD and just as I was about to lose my cool and cancel the show, L stepped up.

> "I'll play the guard's role, Nandita,"
> he said,
> "I know what needs to happen"
> "I'll improvise"
> "It'll be fine."

And it was.

Fine.

With no rehearsals under his belt for the character of the Guard, L took on that role while also playing the role of Tobiah.

I was impressed.

Floored.

Grateful.

I really hope L gets his GED.

I really hope he finds ways to do pursue his learning.

I saw L once after *Lives*, when I took my students from the college to the detention center.

Planning for the trip, I often thought of L

Since our goal was to put together a small creative writing magazine at the end of the week

I thought L would be the most enthusiastic contributor of them all.

After all, he was a writer!

As always though, things had changed.

And when I got the detention center for the project, I was told that L was no longer in that unit.

I missed him.

One day, though, as I sat under the shade of a tree while the youth were playing football or something else in an outdoor space,

> "Nandita"
> I heard a whisper.
> "Nandita"
> The voice whispered again.

I spun around, and there was L.

Walking in single file

With his new peers
Back to his new unit.

"Hey"

I think I shouted a little too loudly.

L glanced nervously at the guard who was escorting his unit back and before he could be disciplined for speaking out of turn to a woman sitting under a tree, L focused his attention on his shoes and kept walking.

Part of me wanted to go up to L. Stop the line. And catch up.

But I knew that would cause some upheaval.

I didn't know the guards in that unit.

I didn't know the other young people in that unit.

What if my going up to L to give him a hug or shake his hand actually ended up causing more problems for him?

So I didn't go up to L and had to content myself with our awkward and hushed exchange.

I listened to the other part of myself that told me to just shut up and sit down.

I wish I hadn't…

Experience #3

The first time I interacted with anyone other than the headmistress in the young men's school was during a rehearsal that occurred about three weeks before the performance. Given the promenade quality to the performance, the rehearsal was scheduled to happen in different classrooms within the school building (where the performance was ultimately showcased). One of the prison officials had told me that all permissions had been procured and that we were cleared to use the school building.

As it turned out,

we weren't.

While I had been told in advance that teachers had been informed of our rehearsals happening in their classrooms that day, either that message had not been communicated to the school staff or the announcement was selectively ignored. Whatever the case, instead of encountering relaxed and collaborative educators who might be open to sharing their space with a colleague—as I hope I would behave should a fellow educator who was working with my students wanted to use my classroom—I encountered hostile gazes.

    Confrontational body language.

        Worst of all, frustration being taken out on the young men.

            "You better not touch anything."

            "No, you cannot use my classroom."

            "Who gave you permission to do this?"

It was…

I lost my temper.

And while I tried to keep calm and not let my frustration show, I guess I failed.

Because a couple of the young men said,

            "Relax, Nandita. It'll be fine."

    I realize that I am in no position to judge those teachers.

        I realize that being educators within a prison system that is designed to limit creative and intellectual freedom might be juxtaposition in and of itself.

        I realize that I am in no position to judge those teachers.

           And yet, I can't help but do so.

The way their gazes seemed to dehumanize the young men.

    The way they tried to stare me down when I wouldn't simply smile in the face of their rebukes and walk away.

    The way in which they treated their classrooms as prized territory that was being invaded by an outsider who had a hoard of hooligans with her.

I was at a complete loss about how to engage with my fellow educators.

I knew I couldn't judge them.

And yet, I did.

…

The only teachers who came to the final performance of *Lives* were the young men's dance teachers. Not a single other teacher or administrator from the school seemed to even bother to attend. Some of the detention center's mental health counselors and social workers attended the performance. Members of the prison's administrative staff attended. But the teachers, not a single person came to show their support. Except for the part-time-contractor dance teachers.

Every educational institution has its issues and I cannot deny that all the schools that I've worked in have had theirs. And yet, I could not extend my imagination to grasp what is must be like to be en educator within a prison setting.

Why do people choose these jobs?

> Is it because they are looking to educate the crime out of criminals?
>> Is it because they realize the role that education can play in reducing recidivism rates?
>>> Are they trying to change the system by being part of it?
>>>> Are they doing it for the money and the pension?
>>>>> Are they here because there was nowhere else to go?

How does the psychology of an educator become affected by wires and surveillance cameras and criminal histories and the constant presence of guards and the sense of suffocation that can only be experienced in a total institution?

> Is it a profession for those who already have proclivities to exercise power and those who enjoy disciplining their students harshly?
>> Or is a career for well-meaning idealists who want to genuinely work with these young people, with the hope that the prison won't pervade their pedagogy?
>>> How can you "educate" when everything—from the content of your syllabi to how your students sit in your classes—is controlled and surveiled?

There is a part of me that admires the teachers who choose to work in contexts of incarceration. Those educators who believe in the potential of their craft to broaden the horizons of young people who are often cast off by the way side.

But there is also a part of me that does not understand how any kind of mind-freeing, avenue-generating, learning can be implemented in a context of incarceration.... I cannot fathom how the Ls of the world will find the kind of mentorship they need to go from where they are, to where they could be.

Between the young Desmond Tutu fan, and the aspiring actress, and L's dreams for himself there were/are many experiences in which I have been in awe of the young people I work with in New Mexico's detention centers.

Their desire to learn. Their desire to educate themselves. Their desire to move forward.

And then I look at the possibilities that they have around them. The exhausted and overworked staff. The stressed and (seemingly) angry teachers. The transient and "do-gooder" volunteers.

What does education even look like in a context like this?

It is this question that shapes my rewrites of Tobiah Edwards' scene.

Mystory Part Two: The Popular Narratives

My point of departure for the popular narrative component to Tobiah's rewrites comes from L's love for poetry and the potential for creative expression within prison settings.

As I prepared myself to get involved with the juvenile detention system in New Mexico, I realized the sheer number of arts-based (especially creative writing focused) initiatives that are ongoing in prisons across the United States (U.S.). Reflecting on L's love for poetry alongside the expert narratives that speak to the challenges facing formal educational environments within the juvenile justice system (in the next section of this chapter), it is perhaps only natural that my focus—as an arts based practitioner and researcher—would find its punctum in existing archives of creative projects in the juvenile justice system.

A brief search on poetry within prison walls reveals an entire realm of practice: organizations functioning as portals for incarcerated populations to contribute their own writing; long distance projects that pair prisoners and poets in writing to each other; workshops that are conducted by poets and other artists in various kinds of correctional facilities. To understand why and how such initiatives have been justified, I include below some of the diverse popular narratives that showcase the importance of poetry as a form of informal education in contexts of incarceration.

On why prisoners might want to write poetry (according to the Outsider):

> The sensitivity required to write poetry and the harsh atmosphere of prison might seem unsympathetic partners, but [...] therapeutic purpose makes for a fertile creative environment. "To write poetry, you have to have life experience, which they have here in spades; an active mind—well, they're doing therapy every morning; and time, and they're locked up from 7.30 at night. Most of them are writing to escape" [Tickle, 2007].

On why poets might want to work in prisons:

It has made me much more willing to accept other people. The first one I worked with was a murderer. He'd assisted in killing three people—three girls. I decided that my policy would be—what I saw written out in front of a church on a billboard said you have no past here, only a present or a future. And I thought as long as he treated me decently and I knew he was not involved in any ongoing crimes, I would treat him the same way. He turned out to be a very talented writer [NPR, 2015].

On why prisoners write poetry (according to a former prisoner):

Jimmy Santiago Baca grew up in rural New Mexico. At 21, he was in prison, serving five years in a maximum security facility in Arizona for narcotics possession. He learned to read and write in prison. A man described by Baca only as Harry, a good Samaritan, responded to Baca's request for English and Spanish books. With these books, Baca was able to teach himself to read and write. He says he was motivated to become literate for "love and hate: love for women (my grandma, my aunts, my friends) and hate for authority." Baca became more than just literate—he became a poet. Describing his time in prison, Baca says, "Most people never experience the miracle of raw emotion. They're too busy trying to win approval, but I was in the mouth of the volcano." Baca channeled his energy into poems. These poems helped Baca navigate the trials of prison life, including solitary confinement and a nearly deadly altercation with another inmate. "Everyone has their own twisted labyrinth journey," Baca says. "I almost feel lucky that I didn't have parents because I know people who have parents who are totally bonkers." Instead of leaving prison as a hardened criminal, Baca was released in 1979 as a poet. His first book, "Immigrants in Our Own Land," was published that same year. Baca wrote about injustice, life from Native American and Mexican decent and of overcoming hardship both in and out of prison. His work was met with high praise. Baca feels that in teaching himself to be literate rather than learning to write in school, he is able to truly create his own world in poetry—a world beyond traditional American institutions. When asked what inspires his writing now, Baca says, "The world intrigues me. I'm worried about people in general because something is missing in their spirits. I'm not sure what it is but they're taught and conditioned not to risk or explore their own beauty. Everyone is so caught up in their own prisons that they diminish themselves out of existence" [Merz, 2013].

On the possible role for art in prisons:

The good that art does for prison inmates seems self-evident—provides accomplishments, offers a different avenue for self-expression than violence, builds confidence, frequently leads to other areas of learning—but has not been studied and quantified, although the directors of several prison art programs offer anecdotes of former inmates who have left the path of crime. In part, the lack of research reflects the varying state definitions of recidivism (ex-convicts returning to criminal activities)—does it mean back to jail in six months or two years? Does a suspended sentence or parole count?—in addition to the fact that criminologists have not regarded the benefits of prison art programs as worthy of quantitative analysis [Grant, 2010].

Murals, for example, were painted in prison by the inmates on pieces of plywood and then reassembled by public work crews on site. In being able to create art for the public, inmates got "the sense that they were giving back to their community on their own terms," he said. "These were, for the most part, inmates who were ready to make a change in their lives" [Lee, 2014].

I think the volunteer experience has the advantage that your students are there because they want to be there. They are not just motivated by the end goal of the degree or the time cut (getting time knocked off their sentences). And you are there because you feel like you are doing something good. You are changing their lives and hopefully that gives back to society, because, eventually, most inmates will get out of prison. The teacher is there because he or she wants to be and the prisoners know that, so they have extra respect and appreciation. And you are going to get the best people in the program if they are there because they want to be there. So I think volunteer programs have a lot of advantages. Of course, it doesn't pay the bills, but hopefully you have a day job [Reed, 2013].

On why teachers in prison become teachers in prison

The majority of my students are incarcerated for 12–18 months, though there are some with sentences long enough that they will go on to the adult system once they are 18. Do I know what crimes they have committed? I can find out if I want to. Do I want to? I discovered the hard way that I definitely don't after seeing that one of my favorite students was charged with multiple counts of rape and incest. From that point on, I couldn't see or teach him the same. So, why do it? Why should I put myself in a dangerous, heartbreaking situation? From a teaching perspective, there are upsides. The maximum number of students I can have in my class at a time is 13, though the classes tend to be closer to an average of seven (and even then, those numbers fluctuate on a daily basis). I went from teaching almost 130 students in public school to less than 50—I haven't taken a single piece of paper home to grade in a year. If any of those seven students are not cooperating, I can have them removed from my classroom, no questions asked. While I still spend a fair amount of time redirecting behavior, I actually get to focus some one-on-one attention on the students who need it when they need it. And while my students take the same core classes and are expected to pass the same standardized tests as other high school students in the state, I don't feel anywhere near the pressure I did in public school to constantly improve my students' scores. There are also small, but incredibly meaningful, victories that are always popping up. I helped one of my students who just turned 18 and will be released by the election fill out his voter registration form. Our guidance counselor lets the students come to us to see their standardized test scores, and there is nothing better than seeing the face of a kid who has never once passed find out that he did [Shannon, 2012].

- "I have no textbooks, I try to follow the […] curriculum and make adaptations and modifications to it"
- "I teach basic reading skills"
- "I don't have full texts or even a teacher's edition, I pull information from the internet…"
- "My son is in high school now so I 'borrow' a lot from his school and teachers" [Steinberg & Jacobs, 2011]

On being an Outsider teacher in prison

On a typical day, I trade in my license for my ID and head to the classroom. I check the rosters to see who's in double-lock or which inmates have to be kept separated for the day and then I devise my class lists. Some classes might only have 2 students in them, while other classes can have up to 8 students [...] The other thing that is a bit frustrating is that I am an outside provider. Although the jail staff respects me and is cordial, I'm not "one of them." The other teachers and I don't feel as though we can hang out in the break room and we're never included in social functions. [...] Although I had to go through a six hour jail orientation and a three hour orientation this past year, there are some things that I had to discover on my own. No one prepared me for the emotional ups and downs of the inmates. A lot of these inmates are being forced to quit drugs, drinking, smoking, or a combination of these, cold turkey. I wasn't prepared that one day an inmate might be very withdrawn and the next day is down right ugly in his tone and words. [...] One of my favorite things to do when I meet someone new is to ask, "What's your story?" Asking that question in a jail setting usually results in a non-trusting glare from the inmate. However, when I further define the question by letting the inmate know he can tell me about his family, his hobbies, etc., he realizes that I'm not particularly interested in knowing why he's sitting in jail. It's amazing the stories that I hear. [...] Teaching in a jail setting requires flexibility. No two days are ever the same! Some days when I arrive, I'm told that certain pods are under "lockdown." This means that there are searches going on or that there has been a fight and everyone needs to cool down. I then need to revamp my schedule and see inmates from other pods or do paperwork. A few times I have been in the middle of teaching something, the inmates are into the lesson, and then BAM! The classroom is pushed open, officers charge in and immediately escort an inmate out of the class. I rarely get to know why the inmate needed to be removed. It obviously had nothing to do with his behavior in class. [...] If you're looking to teach in a jail setting because you think it sounds cool or you want to brag to your buddies about where you work, then this isn't for you! Each day when you enter the facility, you need to put your personal life behind you. If you're having a bad day, the inmates will pick up on it, and they'll play you. You need to be consistent each and every day! If you like teaching in a small group, and at times 1-on-1, then the jail setting is an awesome opportunity to do so [Just Jobs Academy, 2011].

On why education in prisons matters (from a study done in the United Kingdom)

Most states do have statutes that require juveniles to have at least 6.5 hours of schooling every day, and Ross said sometimes the instruction they receive within these facilities is the best education possible for them because the teachers are qualified to handle at-risk adolescents. But Ross feels the problem for many of the juveniles he spoke with lies in what he calls "the culture of expectations." "Their families have limited expectations of who they can be and they themselves have limited expectations," Ross said. "But when you get a teacher that's dedicated to these kids and they say, 'ladies and gentlemen I expect something of you,' they can amaze you" [Fritz & Brown, 2012].

Prison(er) Education is a powerful collection of "Tales of Change and Transformation" that demonstrates the huge diversity in prisoners as learners. Emma Hughes, a contributor, draws on prisoners' letters, written to the Prisoners' Education Trust, to highlight positive effects of education:

- "Having a meaningful course to study is a great help in coping with prison life"
- "Forms and tests have always frightened me, so I find this new experience really beneficial to me"
- "I just really wish more people were able to take education seriously in prison. It really is the only place you feel both human and confident. Achievement I believe is the best possible form of rehabilitation"
- "…the implications are quite profound if applied both in theory and practice. Prisoner education is about people learning in a particular setting—a prison setting—and once that distinction is made, education programmes in prisons can be seen as something that may offer benefits and opportunities to individual prisoners—as people"

But although no one actually said they had been taken off education as punishment, [this study] heard that prisoners, or others they knew, had been taken off classes for disruptive behaviour:

- "I got kicked off my other English class. I was asking her how to spell a word and she wouldn't tell me. She kicked me out and said I was bad"

One young offender spoke of penalties for non-attendance:

- "The thing I don't like is, if you don't feel like going [to classes] in this prison you get nicked. You might just feel depressed. You might have had a confrontation with your officer, or a phone call with your Mum. You might just want to rest on your bed. But you've got to go"

Another spoke of officers in his previous prison, who had adopted a punitive attitude to the whole enterprise:

- "If they [the prisoners] do education we'll make them do it instead of exercise"

Far more significant than pay, for some, were the other sacrifices called for if you came to classes. Gym was universally a casualty. But in one prison it was worse than that:

- "If you're on education you miss out on everything: exercise, showers, phone calls, kit change. You sacrifice a lot"
- "You can have showers at the weekend, but there's no hot water. Everyone wants one"
- "You know who's on education: they smell!"

For one woman, unable to read or write when she came into prison, art classes had done wonders for her self-esteem:

- "I want to do art college [on release]. I didn't think I could draw. I came to prison and I realised that I can draw. I used to think, 'Look at those hippies going to college'—and I can draw!"

One prisoner spoke with pride and satisfaction about the coursework for a sports course he had particularly enjoyed:

- "The homework gives us something to do behind the doors. … It keeps you occupied day and night. I was sat there a good three hours working on one assignment."

Positives, in prisoner-learners' eyes, included the fact that they were generally there of their own volition:
- "I've found it much better now because I want to do it."
- "In school it was compulsory. Here you can choose."

The positive differences between this and their own primary and secondary school education were recognised and appreciated:
- "Here you can work at your own pace."
- "At school you work as a class and you feel stupid if you can't keep up."
- "It's better in terms of teacher-student ratios."
- "In school I couldn't get a proper education. Here they want to help you more. They want to educate you more."

In four of the ten education groups, some prisoner-learners felt they were not being treated as adults, both by certain tutors, and by the teaching materials they used:
- "When you get here they treat you straight away as if you're dumb. There's no other problems: that's it. They treat you like you're children."
- "You're spoken down to: very patronising."

Underlying many of these complaints was a sense that they were lowest on the list for quality teaching staff. In one third of the groups we heard that some staff were perceived as below the standard they would expect, say, in school or college. Whilst most seemed to put this down to bad luck, poor selection, or the generally second-rate quality of everything about the prison experience, one young prisoner reflected on some of the difficulties faced by the department in getting staff:
- "There's a high staff turnover here and a lot of them have no experience of prison. They come from school. They're used to people obeying them."

A few also identified particular staff who they felt had abused their authority. In two prisons we heard of staff getting involved in the disciplinary system of the prison:
- "Some teachers like to get you going. If you disagree it's a written warning."

For many, the staff in prison education departments were outstanding. Prisoner-learners recognised the importance of a good tutor in opening up the joy of learning:
- "The courses I've enjoyed most, it's the tutor that's been the motivating factor."
- "[X] is phenomenal: he teaches English, sociology, general studies—everything. There's a certain academic structure as to how you do things and he takes a lot of time to help you. Nobody has a bad word to say about him."
- "I can think of three. It's as though they're on a mission to get people to realise their potential and build their self-esteem."
- "Staff buy things out of their own pockets. The art teacher hasn't got a budget, but she's getting T-shirts and postcards for us [to create art work]."
- "I prefer teachers who act like teachers. They don't really know what it's like for us."

Many group members told us that they valued being able to put a bit of physical distance between themselves and the rest of the prison, the wings, the staff, the routines.
- "It takes you off the wing and away from prison staff. You need to get away from them."
- "It's a better atmosphere down here than on the wing."

- "This is a pretty miserable prison. This is the only place, apart from the chapel, you get a release from the awful surroundings."

One put it this way:
- "For me, coming to education helps to pass the time. Time drags if you're doing nothing. I can't break out, I don't want to be crawling out, I want to be walking out."
- "Keeping your mind occupied was also seen as important: 'It stops you brooding about past mistakes."
- "Prison is a poor man's college." [Prison Reform Trust, 2003].

There are various viewpoints in the mainstream realm about education within the U.S. prison system. However, while popular narratives are available about the positive impacts of education or about the financial issues being faced by schools within detention centers, there are some huge gaps—it seems—in these voices. For instance, it is very difficult to find interviews with, accounts by, teachers who work within the prison system. There are some accounts from volunteer teachers and new teachers (as the reader can see above). But there is not much to be found in terms of reflecting a diversity of opinions.

It is also difficult to encounter narratives about formal versus informal learning opportunities within the prison system. There are volunteer accounts about informal experiences. There are academic analyses about the formal schools, as the reader will see in the next section. But there is not much to be encountered in terms of how the informal opportunities might complement the formal ones.

How volunteer-teachers might collaborate with, and learn from, and share with, their non-volunteer counterparts that have full time jobs in the prisons.

There seems, to me, the lack of a bigger picture of what education means in contexts of incarceration. To some prison officials/prisoners, it is the granting/gaining of a GED. To others, it is a means toward a better job post-release. To some it is entertainment from the dreariness of a cell. For some it is about reform. For others it is about subversion. With such a variety of ideologies within prison systems about what education in that context is supposed to accomplish ... well, what can happen?

Mystory Part Three: The Expert Narratives

The importance of correctional education can be articulated in many ways: as an avenue for prisoners to divert their minds from the monotony of their otherwise cell-confined lives; as the opportunity to earn a formal degree and thus heighten employment opportunities when inmates leave prison; as being a space in which the prison inmate can interact with their peers in ways that are different from what is permitted within units/cells/courtyards; as a place for prisoner-students to learn from/interact with mentors whose positions of power are framed differently than that of correctional officers. For all these reasons it seems obvious that young people in detention facilities should have access to both formal and informal learning opportunities—for their lives both behind and outside prison walls. However, despite the abovementioned reasons for the importance of education in prisons, it has been witnessed that "education programs in juvenile corrections have been underfunded and neglected" (Leone & Cutting, 2004:260) and that in addition to challenges with funding, the very structures that define the prison system both, do not allow the provision of a high quality education, and do not facilitate the provision of equal opportunities for incarcerated individuals with physical and/or psychological differences. Research into the correctional education system also points toward a more intrinsic challenge: that, very often, there exists a disconnect between students, teachers, school administrators, guards, and prison officials about the *purpose* of correctional education. Before speaking to some of the structural factors that inhibit the achievement of a clarity of purpose, though, I must inform the reader that much of the discussion below—elucidating why correctional educational programs maintain a "second-class" citizenship (Horvath, 1982:8)—has emerged from scholarship surrounding adult prisons. However, I would contend that the same factors that impede correctional education in adult prisons remain relevant when considering the positioning of education within juvenile justice systems; hence my seeing a place for these ideas in rewriting Tobiah Edwards' scene.

One of the primary factors that is said to result in a lower status for education in prisons lies in "the recognized function of prisons in American society," which is widely considered as being punitive rather than rehabilitative (Horvath, 1982:8). In this vein, correctional education's second class citizenship is heavily shaped by "the administrative organization of prisons" where the prison officials who administer the non-school-based lives of the inmates have much more power within the chain of command than their peers who work within the school system (Horvath, 1982: 8). This structural hierarchy that perpetuates U.S. prison's punitive tendencies thus results in constant conflicts between the objectives of each particular stakeholder:

> (1) the conflict between administrators within the prison; (2) the low priority of education in the prison setting; (3) the lack of adequate funding for educational

programs; (4) the lack of comprehensive planning that characterizes most correctional education programs; (5) the conflict between custody, treatment, and educational philosophies; and (6) the hostility of security staff toward educational programs. Each of these issues can be shown to be natural, and perhaps inevitable, outgrowths of attempting to effect educational objectives in a penal setting [Horvath, 1982:9].

Ultimately, prison schools "are institutions within larger institutions" and, as such, despite the individual successes of particular prison education programs, "the prison 'school' designation implicitly connotes goals, objectives, attitudes, values, and methods that are fundamentally at odds with the emphasis upon order, discipline, security, and expedience that characterizes the larger prison" (Horvath, 1982:9). Since the "freedom of thought and the 'intellectualization' of issues that higher education symbolizes" are "flatly contrary to the concept of control," there is a "degree of anti-intellectualism [that] is alive and well among prison superintendents" (Horvath, 1982:9). Furthermore, in addition to a core contradiction between what education seeks to manifest and what a punitive justice system seeks to perpetuate, questions surrounding correctional education get more muddled when we begin to think about how the value of correctional education might be measured. At the moment, the efficacy of correctional education, like rehabilitation, is "measured in terms of recidivism rates" i.e., the rate at which former offenders recommit crimes and renter prisons, (Horvath, 1982:11). However, as some researchers suggest, an "attempt to connect educational success to recidivism is unrealistic" (Horvath, 1982:11) and possibly, not useful. Surely there are other, intrinsic benefits to education that might be of value, regardless of whether or not a student recidivates? Since recidivism also hinges on the support structures that are present/absent for a former offender when they return to their communities, is re-incarceration really an effective measure about what correctional education can/cannot do? Ultimately, then, how might educational "success" be understood and framed in a detention center context?

The presence of education within the criminal justice system leads to conflicts between the various groups of prison stakeholders:

- First, correctional education catalyzes conflicts between students and the guards. It has been said "that many of the officers who supervise" inmates often lack educational backgrounds themselves and therefore, "the issue of the 'relative intelligence' of officers and inmates often becomes a persistent and sensitive one" (Horvath, 1982:14). Furthermore, since "many correctional educational programs provide no services to institutional staff, correctional officers are likely to perceive correctional education programs as the creator of, or a contributor to, [an] imbalance" between the opportunities that are afforded to the "criminal" rather than the "protector" (Horvath, 1982:14).

- Second, some prison school administrators tend to stereotype their students and express not wanting "any more criminals in their schools" (Hellriegel & Yates, 1999:62).
- Teachers have their own concerns as well and have sometimes documented their concern with statements like: "I don't see why they have to come to our school.... They aren't from our area, and we don't get any extra resources to teach them" (Hellriegel & Yates, 1999:62).

This multiplicity of conflicts between different prison stakeholders ultimately manifests, therefore, in lacks of professional collaborations: both between teachers in correctional education programs and their counterparts outside the prison, and between "treatment, security, and education staff within juvenile correction" (Leone & Cutting, 2004:262). For example, the "emphasis on security necessitated by the type of students placed in juvenile correctional education programs" requires the presence of armed correctional officers within the classroom context (Pasternack, Portillos & Hoff, 1988:157). Throughout *Lives* and in all the young men's classes at school, therefore, there had to be security guards present at all times, in addition to the teacher/facilitator. And predictably, this security presence often clashes with the pedagogy of individual teachers, resulting in the "hostility of security staff toward correctional education programs" (Horvath, 1982:13) and vice versa, in the hostility of educators toward security personnel.

In addition to conflicting ideologies surrounding imprisonment and education, the relationship between prison guards and prison educators is underpinned by a lack of clarity about organizational hierarchy. Although the "hierarchy of authority is clear within the security and treatment components of the institution, the relative authority between the two is not" (Horvath, 1982:14). This is to say that "while it is implicitly clear that the individual correctional officer has authority over the correctional educator in matters of security, the lines of authority regarding the daily operation of classes and other educational activities are not so clear" (Horvath, 1982:14). As a result, "[p]roblems over absent inmates, the dismissal of classes, and inmates who are 'out of place' within the school frequently bring the officer and educator together in situations in which the relative authority of each is unclear to both" and therefore, lead to "misunderstandings and 'hard feelings' as the net result" (Horvath, 1982:14). This lack of clarity, subsequently results in an explicit/implicit lack of collaboration between correctional officer and educator; in the worse case scenario, leading to direct/indirect instances of "sabotage" (Horvath, 1982:13). In one particular study, for example, teachers "ranked the problem of conflicts with security staff second only to the problem of student motivation" with reports stating, "that security regulations inhibited their effectiveness" as educators (Horvath, 1982:13). Since correctional education programs—with their "differing class schedules, cancelled classes, and special educational activities"—often inconvenience the duties of the guard, "correctional officers find themselves in the position of having to compromise their needs in an effort to accommodate the needs and wishes of correctional educators" (Horvath, 1982:13). This issue is one that I will return to in the next chapter, in terms of the detention center officers' responses to being inconvenienced by my work on *Lives*. So, if correctional officers, teachers, students, and school administrators often find their work to be at odds with each other's efforts, what can correctional education realistically accomplish?

While educators in institutions like the college that I teach at often choose to become teachers, it has been said that "many correctional educators find themselves teaching in jail and prison classrooms accidentally, rather than as a result of intentional professional decisions"—and when this accidental choice is compounded by the many dynamics discussed above, it creates an environment in which correctional educators often "feel isolated and removed from the educational process" (DelliCarpini, 2008:220–221). In this isolation, teachers in prisons "struggle with identifying best practices" for the unique needs of their students (DelliCarpini, 2008:221): a large number of whom "are marginally literate or illiterate and have experienced school failure and retention" (Leone & Cutting, 2004:261). The students tend to be "disproportionately male, poor, and members of minority groups" and additionally, is a demographic that has "significant learning and/or behavioral problems that entitle them to special education and related services" (Leone & Cutting, 2004:261). As a result, "the extensive nature of the academic difficulties in this population has led juvenile justice settings to be described as default systems for housing youth who cannot read, write, or relate with others" (Mathur & Schoenfeld, 2010:20)—creating an immediate bias amongst teachers, and the students themselves, about what might be possible within the correctional education paradigm. Instruction in a juvenile detention center's education arm therefore, needs to take into account a whole host of factors, "including students' perceptions of their academic competencies, their levels of motivation, background knowledge, and interests" (Mathur & Schoenfeld, 2010:21). And in addition to these more socially framed contextual factors, from "a cognitive perspective" there remains the challenge that "effective instruction should stimulate students' prior learning and employ strategies that unite prior knowledge with new learning objectives" (Mathur & Schoenfeld, 2010:21)—individualized learning plans and mentorship that teachers in correctional education might not have the resources to pursue. While in "traditional public schools, student assignments are organized by grade level," in correctional education settings "assignments are based on ability groups" (Leone & Cutting, 2004:263). It has been documented that in some "correctional classrooms, all instruction is individualized and there are no group activities" and as a result, students often work "independently in workbooks and [seek] assistance from the teacher when they encounter difficulties" (Leone & Cutting, 2004:263). In the detention center that I worked in during *Lives*, the classroom grouping was even more complex and was based on particular living units into which the youth had been divided based on age, seriousness of the crime, and whether or not other participants in that crime (codefendants in the same case, for instance) were incarcerated in the that unit. When the transient/variedly-abled demographic of the juvenile prisoner community is placed alongside the ideological dissonance between prison/education, and the constant shifts in prison administration that occur when politicians (under whom juvenile justice laws fall) change, we must wonder what—realistically—educational institutions within detention centers can bring about for their students.

These various complexities to correctional education ultimately manifest in problematic occurrences within the classroom setting. It has been recorded that "[c]riminal identities [are problematically] reinforced through expressions of humor between teachers and youth" where students joke about "needing [their] lawyers," or teachers make light of particular uses of vocabulary, or joke are made about student's crimes within the classroom (Young, Phillips & Nasir, 2010:212). As a personal example, during one of the first creative writing exercises that I conducted during the weeklong experiential education program between the young men at the detention center and my students at the college, at the end of a particularly chaotic exercise, I said—off-handedly—"Well, that was better than I expected!"; to which one of the young men replied, "Why, miss? 'Cos we're prisoners?" This young man started laughing when I spluttered: "No, no; that's not what I meant" and left me discomfited at how my off-the-cuff remark had led to a moment of dark humor that potentially revealed some of the biases this young man had encountered within his experiences of education. While I understand that the invocation of dark humor could function as a coping strategy, and while prison humor might be a benign manifestation of how teachers and students cope with the gravity of their setting, I do wonder when such coping mechanisms become indicators of more deep-seated biases.

I am aware that much of the discussion above paints a bleak picture about correctional education and I must say that this bleakness does *not* stem from the biases caused by my not-so-positive interactions with the teachers during *Lives*. Rather, in all the research that I undertook about correctional education in juvenile detention centers, I have found scarce instances that speak about positive learning experiences and environments within correctional education. These rare studies showcase teachers who are satisfied with "aspects of their working conditions": aspects like not having to deal with the parents of their students, and the job security that comes from these kinds of positions (King, Hendley, & Ray, 1979:12). Notably, even such documentation about teacher satisfaction does *not* include mention of the "intrinsic" rewards that make education appealing for teachers in non-prison contexts. From the student's perspective one of the only recorded instances that I was able to locate, which demonstrated optimism about correctional education, posits that "[p]ositive learning experiences [in prison education are] most often attributed to a constructive relationship with a teacher" (Young, Phillips & Nasir, 2010:217). Drawing from this study, one teacher's success in a correctional education setting was attributed to his dismissal of "some of the policies regarding safety and control, such as having students sit quietly at their desks without any interaction"—a dismissal that resulted in this specific educator being "to create a more learner centered classroom climate, as opposed to an institutionally centered classroom climate" (Young, Phillips & Nasir, 2010:218). Apart from such isolated instances that speak to one-off success stories of prison educators, existing research and my own personal observations paint a bleak picture about the status of formal educational opportunities within prison walls. While the realm of the popular/mainstream is sprinkled with success stories vis-à-vis informal learning programs within contexts of incarceration, expert narratives—it seems—are far more encompassing of the challenges that accompany formal education within correctional facilities.

The following rewrites of Tobiah's scene have, therefore, place education (formal and informal) at their core. My personal interactions with

L have influenced the developed characterization of Tobiah; the rewrites—especially the sections that invite audience members to become part of the performance event—draw from the popular narratives that showcase an array of opinions surrounding the role for creative expression within informal education in prisons. And finally, Tobiah Edwards' rewritten scene highlights—from the expert narratives—the vastly different ideologies that define the prison educator and the prison guard. Onward then, to the autoethnodramatic version of Tobiah's original scene in *Lives*.

Rewriting Tobiah Edwards

TRANSITION

This time, there is no long transition in the passage way and the audience members directly enter the next space.

SCENE SIX

No directions are given to the audience members about where to sit or stand. They can choose their positions. TOBIAH is dribbling a basketball on the ground till the audience members settle down.

TOBIAH: Mr. H, can we show them the pictures now?

GUARD 1 nods.

TOBIAH: Would you all please come sit in a circle with us?

Audience members go sit with TOBIAH in a circle. GUARDs encourage them to do so but if some spectators do not want to come any closer to the action, that is also fine.

As TOBIAH speaks of a picture to the audience, that picture is projected onto the walls or the ceiling of the space. GUARD 1 controls the projector. On occasion, TOBIAH rests his hand on GUARD 1's shoulder while describing the pictures. There are moments of some elusive form of "tenderness" between the two men.

TOBIAH: This is my mom. I took this picture right after she had the last big fight with my dad. She was sad but to me, that's the best thing that could have ever happened to her.

Next picture.

TOBIAH: This is my little brother. He's a football star. I'm going to make sure he goes to college.

Next picture.

TOBIAH: This is my hermanita. Isn't she beautiful? She's going to be so proud of me when I get out of here.

Next picture.

TOBIAH: This…. This is a picture that I took in photo class.

Next picture.

TOBIAH: This. This is the kind of basketball legend that I'm going to become.

Silence. Lights change.
TOBIAH wanders around the audience while speaking the poem below. The audience is not given directions as to whether to stand or sit. They can do as they please.

TOBIAH[2]: Restless, unable to sleep
Keys, bars, the guns being racked
Year after year
Endless echoes of steel kissing steel
Noise
Constant yelling
Nothing said
Vegetating faces, lost faces, dusted faces
There's no beauty in cellbars.

During TOBIAH's recitation of the poem, the OUTSIDER has become the TEACHER.

TEACHER: That's not what I asked you to do.
TOBIAH: You asked us to—
TEACHER: Follow Shakespeare's iambic pentameter and write a sonnet.
TOBIAH: But miss, I don't understand that shit.
TEACHER: Excuse me?
TOBIAH: This is more real, miss. This is—
TEACHER: This is not what I asked you to do.

Silence.

TOBIAH: I can rewrite it, miss.

TEACHER: I want it on my desk first thing tomorrow or you're not getting any credit for this. Do you understand me?

TOBIAH shakes his head in the affirmative and walks over to his mattress where he tears the poem up and starts writing something again. We see him struggle with the rewrites.

TEACHER: (*To GUIDE 1*) You disagree with me?
GUARD 1: Nope.
TEACHER: I can see it in the way you look at me.
GUARD 1: I have no problem with you.
TEACHER: Look, educating them is my job. You just do what you're supposed to do and control them.

GUARD 1 and TEACHER stare at each other. Lights change. There is "something" that happens to indicate that the scene is being rewound: a lighting cue; a sound cue; particular physical movements; it is up to the discretion of the director.

TOBIAH[3]: Restless, unable to sleep
    Keys, bars, the guns being racked
    Year after year
    Endless echoes of steel kissing steel
    Noise
    Constant yelling
    Nothing said
    Vegetating faces, lost faces, dusted faces
    There's no beauty in cell bars.

Pause.

TEACHER: That's not what I asked you to do, Tobiah.... But. I like it. Did you write that yourself?
TOBIAH: Not really, miss. I took it from this guy called Spoon Jackson.
TEACHER: Why not write your own poem? I know you have a lot to say.
TOBIAH: You think I can write a poem?
TEACHER: I think you can certainly try.

Pause. A huge smile comes across TOBIAH's face. He goes back to his mattress and begins to write excitedly.

TEACHER: (*To GUIDE* 1) You think I'm giving them too much freedom.
GUARD 1: Nope.
TEACHER: I can see it in the way you look at me.
GUARD 1: I have no problem with you.
TEACHER: Look, educating them is my job. You just do what you're supposed to do and control them.

GUARD 1 and TEACHER stare at each other. Lights change. There is "something" that happens to indicate that the scene is being rewound: a lighting cue; a sound cue; particular physical movements; it is up to the discretion of the director.

TOBIAH[4]: Restless, unable to sleep
Keys, bars, the guns being racked
Year after year
Endless echoes of steel kissing steel
Noise
Constant yelling
Nothing said
Vegetating faces, lost faces, dusted faces
There's no beauty in cell bars.

Pause. Lights change.

Lights come up on the walls, which have been set up to display poems and creative works by prisoners that are available on many online databases.

TOBIAH wanders around and look at the displayed pieces. The GUARDs indicate to the audience that they can also walk around. After the audience has had some time to look at the pieces, the lights on the wall turn out. Focus on TOBIAH and the OUTSIDER.

OUTSIDER: This could be you someday.

TOBIAH smiles.

OUTSIDER: Really. It could be.
TOBIAH: Will you help me?
OUTSIDER: Of course. Of course I will. Look what you need to do is come up with a concept for what you want to write about … and then, and then we need to discuss the form, you know? What kind of poem are you going to write. Then we write drafts and share it with the others in the unit. We get their feedback and keep reworking it. And then, once we have a draft that—
TOBIAH: Whoa slow down! Is this my future or yours?

Five. Education and Tobiah Edwards

Lights change. The OUTSIDER and TOBIAH do a mirror exercise. They stand in front of each other and move as mirror images of one another. It is difficult to tell who is leading and who is following. As the movements continue, the GUARDs talk to each other in lowered voices. They turn out the light on the OUTSIDER and TOBIAH (though the audience should still be able to see their silhouettes in motion).

GUARD 1: Time to move on, ladies and gentlemen.

GUARD 2: Can we just leave that one in here with him?

GUARD 1: I've raised the alarm. The boss needs to decide what to do about this one.

GUARD 1 goes outside and returns with a large blanket or sack. It is put on the OUTSIDER and covers the performer entirely. GUARD 1 and 2 carry TOBIAH and put him in his bed. They lead the audience out of the space and start locking the door. As they are locking the door, the "boss" comes by and the guards immediately open the door for him/her, close the door, and start to lead the audience to the next space. As the audience walk in their lines:

ACTOR in AUDIENCE: Excuse me. Excuse me—I, uh ... what was that about?

GUARD 1: What was what about?

ACTOR in AUDIENCE: Why was the boss called in?

GUARD 2: Just you know ... protocol.

ACTOR in AUDIENCE: Protocol for what?

GUARD 1: Look, when we let people from the outside in here, they have to play by certain rules. That person ... well, the rules were not being followed.

ACTOR in AUDIENCE: They weren't doing anything wrong, though. How were they breaking the rule?

GUARD 2: Look, answering those kinds of questions is above our pay grade. Just follow along quietly please.

They reach the next space.

Chapter Six

The Guards

In the original performance of *Lives*, the GUARD was used to chaperone the audience around the different spaces in which the monologues/scenes occurred. The character was not multidimensional and mostly functioned in an authoritarian manner. Furthermore, while the initial script was written to contain two GUARDs—as the reader will find in Appendix A—one of the actors deciding to pull out of the performance the week prior led to only one GUARD performing this function in the final showcasing of *Lives*.

Mystory Part One: The Personal Narratives

W rarely ever participated in the workshops. And even when he did, he seemed completely disinterested in what was going on. What kept him coming back, I think, was the fact that his friends seemed to like me. And because they liked me, he thought he would give me a chance.

W, I recall someone telling me, was also struggling with various "mental health" issues—I place the term in quotes because I remain unsure if that was a formal or informal diagnosis. And, as a result of these issues, whatever they were, W seemed to have become notorious for acting out against the guards and for getting in different kinds of trouble. In line with what the officials told me about W, I also often caught him saying or doing things that communicated his resentment of authority—that of the prison officials and my own.

One day though, I happened to look over at W in the midst of a session and to my surprise, there he was: standing in the corner of the room next to a guard, resting his head on the guard's shoulder. An image that lasted only a few seconds. But nonetheless, an image that blew me away for the way in which it contrasted mainstream narratives that I have encountered about how prisoners and their guards interact with each other. Especially when the prisoner in question is considered "troublesome," as W was.

How was it then, that despite his often getting into trouble with the prison officials, W seemed to have an almost tender relationship with a particular guard?

How was W able to look beyond his own resentment of authority in that moment and how often did these moments happen?

I saw W rest his head on the shoulder of the guard standing next to him and for those few seconds, I saw the child.

I saw a young man and an older potential role model.

I saw two people hanging out.

Just for those few seconds,

I did not see the prisoner and the guard.

Was this kind of ... intimacy—if I can call it that—made possible because of the setting? Do juvenile detention centers allow for kinder interactions to occur between inmate and corrections officer?

Or was it just this one particular guard and one particular inmate who had formed a bond with each other?

Or was it an unconscious occurrence; an "accidental" moment that I just happened to witness?

...

Mr. H decorated the unit for Thanksgiving, with materials that he had brought from his home. He also brought in home cooked food for the holiday, to share with the young men.

No one messed with Mr. M but the young men would often ask him to play music for them on his computer in the unit common room, and he would oblige.

The younger guards would get fist bumps and slaps on shoulders.

Guards from other units would pop in and exchange banter with some of the young men before returning to the units that they were supervising.

The unit supervisor went out of his way to ensure that there was enough food for the "Jailhouse Spread" when I took my students from the college on the weeklong project.

> Some guards played football with the inmates.
> They did all of these things
> But—
> They were still the police.
> They still told the boys
>> How to stand.
>> How to sit.
>> How to line up.
>> How to speak.
>> How to wear their pants.
>> When they could use the restroom.
>> When they could step out of their cell.
>> When they could watch television.
>> They were still the police.
>>> …

At one point the young men were intent on using N.W.A's (1988) "Fuck the police" in Lives. Furthermore, during rehearsals, they insisted on playing the song in the unit common room on the speakers that were attached to Mr. M and Mr. H's workstations. The first time that they asked the guards to play the song for them, I was sure that the officers would refuse to do so. Surprisingly though, they always agreed. Mr. M would look on Youtube for "Fuck the police" and play the song on his computer. And the young men would sing along. Enthusiastically. "FUCK THE POLICE," they would laugh and sing at the top of their lungs.

One day, I asked Mr. H
> "Does it bother you when something like this happens?"
>> "They are saying 'fuck the police' after all"
>>> "And you are the police!"

Mr. H shrugged.
"It's fine."
"We know what they say about us."

I don't know how the young men got away with doing this in the presence of the guards.... If I am to be honest, I myself was a little bit afraid of Mr. M. For instance, if I arrived for my workshop earlier than the time allocated to me—as I sometimes did because I needed to schedule a one and a half hour long train ride + a twenty minute bus ride + a twenty minute walk in order to get to the detention center on time and occasionally, I got my calculations wrong.... Anyway, sometimes I would arrive a bit early for my workshops and if/when that happened, Mr. M was not happy. He would barely look up from his paperwork to acknowledge my presence, only moving when it was exactly the time for my workshop to start.

Mr. M made me nervous. Another time, when I went into a classroom to get a prop with one of the actors, I was given a quiet talking to by Mr. M....

"You cannot go anywhere with a client without a guard present"

he said.

"But I just went into the room next door to get something"

I tried to justify.

Mr. M wouldn't have any of that.

As the sessions went on, Mr. M became a little less … intimidating. Just a little less. Once, when we were talking from the unit to the education building for a rehearsal, he told me quietly (and a little bit patronizingly):

"The boys should volunteer to do activities like this."

"It gets chaotic sometimes because not all of then want to be there.

"We shouldn't force them to be there"

"It was supposed to be optional, Mr. M"

I told him

"Only the young men who wanted to do theater were asked to participate"

"That's not what we were told."

He smirked.

Shrugged.

And walked on to the school.

Man, Mr. M knew how to make a person uncomfortable.

The only time I saw Mr. M show the hint of a smile was when I was talking to the young men about my issues with some of the hip hop numbers that they had chosen (as explained in Chapter Two), suggesting instead that we use less sexually explicit—but more politically striking—music by the likes of Tupac Shakur. That's when I saw Mr. M smile. When I mentioned Tupac Shakur. And then, while we listened to Tupac's (1998) "Changes":

"Shit, Mr. M's singing"
N said.
Mr. M smiled.
And continued singing along

It took Tupac Shakur to make Mr. M sing and smile.

I wish I had known that earlier...

As a theater practitioner-researcher in contexts of conflict, I have always been fascinated by "grey zones" between parties that are variously positioned in those settings: not considering a conflict in terms of binaries like "victim" and "perpetrator"; considering, instead, the space between the two. The in-between spaces. The murky areas. The grey zones. While all my prior exposure to mainstream popular culture suggested that I would encounter a violent binary between victimized inmates and aggressive prison guards, this particular detention center was surprising. Don't get me wrong. There was still a lot of control and discipline that was being directed at the young men from those who guarded them. But there were still these in-between spaces where one could see glimpses of something different … something almost friendly/intimate in the ways in which the prisoners and guards were interacting with each other. These glimpses … well, those were my grey zones in that detention center. And these grey zones—the spaces where stereotypical relationships between prisoners and guards seemed to break down—form the crux of how I have used the personal component to mystory so as to reconceptualize the Guards' presence in *Lives*.

Mystory Part Two: The Popular Narratives

"Corrections officer" or "correctional officer" seem to be the currently preferred terms when speaking about prison guards. While there are many histories that underscore this shift in terminology, I use the terms loosely in this book—the people who are in charge of watching inmates are sometimes referred to as corrections officers; sometimes as guards. I make this choice because the etymology of these specific terms falls outside the scope of this book and yet, I point this out so as to assure the reader that I am aware of the politics of language that are at play through my choice.

Given these reflections about my own interactions with corrections officers in New Mexico, when looking for narratives from the popular/mainstream realm, I had a couple of objectives. First, I wanted to better understand how guards become guards: the qualifications that are required of applicants and the way in which selection processes are carried out. Second, given how un-nuanced our characters of the Guards were in *Lives*, I looked through various archives so as to locate different perspectives about the benefits and challenges of working as a correctional officer: from inter/intrapersonal relationships between guards, inmates, and other prison administrators; to factors that make the job notably stressful (as research suggests); to initiatives that are in place—state sponsored and otherwise—to address the needs faced by the officers.

I began by looking into the qualifications that are required of correctional officers in the United States (U.S.):

> Although correctional officer jobs at the municipal, county and state levels typically require a high school diploma, correctional officers serving in federal penitentiaries are required to have a college degree. Even among the correctional officers that work in county jails and state prisons, a college education can contribute to a better starting salary, career longevity, and make it easier to ascend the ranks to a leadership position. A great many correctional officers complete their bachelor's degrees in criminal justice, psychology, sociology, counseling or another area of behavioral science [Correctional Officer Education, 2016).].

Correctional Officer Interview Questions (State of New Jersey, 2016)

1. Are you willing to work in a job where you are not free to discuss many of your daily activities with family and friends?
2. Are you willing to wear a uniform to work everyday?
3. Are you willing to be trained in the use of firearms?
4. Are you willing to attend a physically intensive [...] training program?
5. Are you willing to undergo a comprehensive psychological evaluation if this position is offered to you?
6. Are you willing to undergo an intensive physical examination if this position is offered to you?
7. Are you willing to work in a locked area of a building, supervising the activities of inmates who have been convicted of murder, rape, child molesting, armed robbery, etc?
8. Are you willing to work eight hours a day, with dangerous inmates in an area which can be unlocked only from the outside?
9. Are you willing to work a shift, which may be one the following: 6AM to 2PM; 2PM to 10PM, 10PM to 6AM?
10. Are you willing to work weekends with your regular days off during the week?
11. Are you willing to work ALL Holidays?
12. Are you willing to work double shifts (16 consecutive hours) and scheduled days off with little or no advance warning?

13. Are you willing to be confined to the institution for your entire tour of duty, including the meal break, and eat only the meal provided by the institution?
14. Are you willing to work alone for an entire eight-hour shift?
15. Are you willing to supervise the activities of inmates who might call you filthy names and / or threaten you and your family?
16. Are you willing to supervise the activities of inmates while they are in the bathroom or shower?
17. Are you willing to pat frisk inmates, visitors, other staff members and to conduct visual searches of inmates' body cavities?
18. Are you willing to testify in court concerning events that have occurred in the institution?
19. Are you willing to work in an infirmary with sick inmates who could have serious diseases such as AIDS or Tuberculosis?
20. Are you willing to work in building areas that smell of unpleasant odors such as body odor, body wastes, etc?
21. Are you willing to respond to life threatening incidents such as inmates and / or staff who have been stabbed, had heart attacks, attempted to hang themselves, etc.?
22. Are you willing to shoot an escaping inmate (possibly to death) should the need arise?
23. Are you willing to report a fellow officer who might be breaking prison rules or regulations?
24. Are you willing to risk your personal safety to rescue a fellow officer or an inmate from attack?

As you can see from the above Correction Officer has a challenging, difficult, stressful job that can sometimes be dangerous. **If you indicate an unwillingness to perform any of the above activities, and cannot answer "yes" to all of the above, you should not file an application to be a Corrections Officer** [emphasis in the original].

What are some of the highs and lows that come from being a corrections officer?

I like talking to people. Talking to prisoners and learning about their life was fascinating to me. Most of them just wanted someone to talk to [who'd] listen to them anyway. Least favorite was being stuck back there with them. When those gates closed behind you it was a horrible feeling because you knew if s—- went down, you wasn't getting out [Business Insider, 2012].

I heard a rape I couldn't do anything about. This was when I was working in the larger cell house with around 260 inmates. I heard the screaming coming from one of the cells but couldn't find it in time. When I finally did I knew something had happened but the inmate wouldn't talk [Business Insider, 2012].

The only hate we got from inmates were those trying to establish a reputation. None of them held us personally accountable for the reason they were there. They knew we weren't cops and we had nothing to do with their sentence. The only time we were tried up was as an attempt to gain some type of fear or control over the cell block. That never worked though [Business Insider, 2012].

> Gassing happens. I was gassed and one of the reasons I decided to leave. Not a pleasant experience. Mine was in the form of a "water balloon" though. Threw a bag of piss at me from a second story cell. It busted at my feet, getting all over my uniform. Thankfully he missed his target. That being the top of my head [Business Insider, 2012].
>
> We became corrections officers so we could go to work every day representing the good. We deal with criminals confined to constitutional walls, but it's us who chose a life sentence. Not a day goes by that we aren't only seen for the uniform we wear. Criminals do not see us as people: a father, a son, a mother, a daughter, a sister, a brother or a friend. They just see us as an enemy; the badge. I expect to be viewed this way by criminals, but I do not accept when our profession constantly is shown in a negative light by the media. […] The media does like drama, sensationalism and negativity. America thrives on drama. Bad is entertaining, while good is boring. How often do we hear about the good things corrections officers do on a daily basis in the media? We really don't. […] Media portrays corrections officers as lazy, crooked, overpaid, system-milking, power-hungry, hardened and desensitized. Media fails to show that we are dealing with the most irritating individuals in all society. Just because criminals are behind bars does not mean they give up their criminal ways. Corrections officers on a daily basis put their lives at risk, deal with constant verbal and physical abuse, catch new crimes being committed, and work in a world of absolute negativity. It seems that everyone forgets corrections officers are human too [Fox, 2013].

While the voices and opinions above counter more mainstream narratives that tend to demonize guards and paint a black and white victim/perpetrator binary between the oppressed inmate and oppressive guard, there is no denying that abuses of power within the prison structure also constitute a legitimate popular narrative that needs to be placed alongside those viewpoints in which the corrections officers' seek more acceptance by civilians and the media. Stories of abuse like:

> Beginning in March 2014, Thomas began supervising a female inmate at federal prison camp, according to the U.S. Attorney's Office for the Southern District of Texas. Soon after, it says, Thomas began making inappropriate comments to the inmate and began to hug, kiss and touch her inappropriately whenever they would be alone. Authorities say on July 19, 2014, Thomas told the woman to go into the back of the dry storage room behind several boxes where Thomas kissed her and then initiated sex. She says she resisted, but he had sex with her anyway, according to the attorney's office. Authorities add that Thomas told her that if she reported any of what happened he would "flag" her and that "it was his career and her good time" [abc13, 2016].

Apart from judgments about how guards negotiate their power and positioning within total institutions, there is one common condition that has been attributed to corrections officers across the spectrum: stress. While more theoretical analyses of stressors and coping mechanisms can be found in the third section of this chapter, below are less formal accounts of how stress manifests in law enforcement officers and the ways in which the larger institutions that employ these officers are attempting to assist the individuals for whom the stress often becomes overwhelming. The stresses of prison guards are hard to "turn off" and these narratives surrounding the experience of guarding—while less popular, at least in certain sections of mainstream culture—add important dimensions to understanding just how oppressive a prison might be. After all, if there are stressed out guards manning the ship, where else are they going to take out their frustration rather than on the prisoners themselves?

> As one officer who had worked 29 straight hours investigating a deadly arson scene said, "You'd think everybody would run right home, but we all just sat in the back room—just trying to compose [ourselves]… There's no switch you can just turn on, turn off: I'm going home—okay turn the emotion switch back on. It doesn't work like that. If anybody says so, they're mistaken" [Finn & Tomz, 1996:11].
>
> "My girlfriend is going to kill herself," the woman said. "I have a girlfriend who's a corrections officer, and she's talking about killing herself. I just don't know what to do." Norman Seabrook, president of the New York City Corrections Officers' Benevolent Association, is recounting a phone call he received two weeks ago from a distraught woman named Melanie. After almost 20 years working under the relentless stress of a New York City jail, Melanie's corrections officer girlfriend had had enough. […] "She lost it," says Seabrook. "Turns out we found a straight-edge razor in her car, she's threatening to commit suicide […] Nineteen years as a New York City corrections officer, and she says, 'I have nothing else left to live for. I'm going to cut my throat at lunchtime." […] The job is hard enough without what many officers describe as an inherent sense of shame about what they do, perpetuated by stereotypes of the big bad prison officer. Morale is so low […] that there is even embarrassment when it comes to the families of officers. "I realized that I had never in my entire career talked to my daughter about what I did for a living," [another officer] says. "If we have a public image problem with our children, then we have a real problem" [Lopez, 2014].

The stress of correctional officers is not limited to themselves though, and as indicated by the excerpt above, officers' stresses also—inevitably—affect those around them. For example:

> My husband came home more screwed up with department problems than with anything he ever encountered on the streets [Finn & Tomz, 1996:7].
>
> One officer's wife described the difficulty of coping with her husband's rotating shifts while she also worked a full-time job and they tried to raise three children. Friends stopped inviting her to social functions because (she felt) they were uncomfortable about the absence of her husband [Finn & Tomz, 1996:7].
>
> Another wife spoke of being constantly worried about her husband's safety: "I would hear reports of officers being shot and just have to wait to see if it was him. I even listened to the police scanner at night until he came home" [Finn & Tomz, 1996:7].

> A female officer said that her marriage had suffered because her difficult shift hours required her husband to do much of the child rearing, which he resented [Finn & Tomz, 1996:7].
>
> Another officer said that his eight-year-old daughter had witnessed one of his flashbacks to a shooting incident and had been frightened by her father "talking in tongues." "I never want to see my kids exposed to that again" [Finn & Tomz, 1996:16].

Furthermore, the stresses for prison guards are also influenced by personal characteristics like the race and/or gender and/or sexual orientation of the officer in question:

> One female officer went to investigate a neighborhood dispute in the countryside only to be told by the caller that he would not speak with her—that she should "go home and send a real cop." When the officer refused, the man called the department and was told to deal with the female officer; instead, the man went back inside his house and ignored her [Finn & Tomz, 1996:10].
>
> Another female officer experienced constant harassment from a male officer who kept telling her she wasn't up to the job. On the advice of another male officer, she finally dropped her belt at the stationhouse and told him, "OK! Let's go at it." They engaged in a tussle before the sergeant separated them. Later, the hostile officer changed his entire attitude toward the woman, becoming her friend [Finn & Tomz, 1996:10].
>
> In at least six states, guards have appeared in mock Klan attire in recent years, and guards have been accused of race-based threats, beatings and even shootings in 10 states. In addition, suits have been filed in at least 13 states by black guards alleging racist harassment or violence from their own colleagues [...] Instead of trying to contain the problems that rack our nation's prisons—like the race-based gangs into which many prisoners are organized—[some guards] conspire to make them worse [Southern Poverty Law Center, 2000].

So what efforts are in place to manage officers' mental, psychological wellbeing? How are institutions responding to the various ways in which their officers might be "losing the plot"? An investigation into existing state-sponsored initiatives reveals both the need for stress-management initiatives and the attitudes toward such programs by participating officers:

> Nationwide, state and local prisons are overseen by state departments of corrections. Most facilities have an Employee Assistance Program [EAP], which provides assessment and referral services for all types of difficulties related to health, family, marital, drug, alcohol, emotional, stress and financial problems. However, EAPs vary from state to state. For Susan Jones, a former warden in Colorado, the EAP program is "amazing," and Don Steele in Massachusetts says it can be "very helpful." But [in other places] the program is totally ineffective. Part of the problem is an innate sense of distrust for management and authority that is inherent in corrections culture. As Seabrook explains, "If the person has an addiction problem, you

don't go to your manager and say, 'I'm addicted to drugs, what do I do next week?' The guy fires you." Combine that with an endemic culture of machismo and you have what Spinaris calls "systemic, in-built cultural denial and minimizing" [Lopez, 2014].

Law enforcement administrators, union and association officials, and stress program directors cite several reasons [for the presence of stress management programs]:
- to provide a confidential, specialized approach to treating and reducing stress for officers and their families, and to improve their ability to cope with stress on their own (most officers do not trust—or use—city or county programs);
- to increase officer morale and productivity;
- to increase the agency's overall efficiency and effectiveness;
- to reduce the number of early retirements and workers' compensation claims due to stress-related disabilities;
- to reduce the number of on-the-job accidents;
- to reduce the potential for civil liability due to officers' stress-related inappropriate behavior;
- to reduce negative media attention, and
- to improve the general well-being of police families [Finn & Tomz, 1996:3].

Several police chiefs and other law enforcement administrators attest to the value of their agency's stress programs […] "We have a tremendous investment in cops, and if they leave after one traumatic incident, we have lost a tremendous amount. A dollar in psychological services now can save us hundreds of thousands down the road" [Finn & Tomz, 1996:3].

From my perspective of chief, I am obviously concerned about the well-being of the officers, but it goes beyond that. I also look at the financial end of it, and I look at the tremendous cost. We look at an officer at the end of one year and realize that we have probably over $1 million invested in that person. From the administrative perspective you don't want to lose that person. That is a little mercenary to look at it that way, but it is a reality…. I don't, quite frankly, think that departments can afford not to have psychological services for their officers [Finn & Tomz, 1996:3–4].

The management of stress, however, and the attitude toward programs that seek to target its manifestations, get varying responses:

Older officers, however, still frequently question the usefulness of stress services. "The biggest obstacle," one chief said, "is the old-timers who think officers should still tough it out. The older generation is derisive toward what the new generation wants." To be sure, even among younger officers the stigma—or fear of stigma—attached to psychological counseling remains strong in many agencies. As one officer said, "When you mention psychologists, everyone runs" [Finn & Tomz, 1996:4].

Another officer, for example, complained that "everything is becoming too sensitive" and that he always has to watch what he says because "people have forgotten how to laugh" and are offended too easily [Finn & Tomz, 1996:13].

While more information about state-sponsored efforts to address guards' wellbeing is spoken to in the next section on expert narratives, I include below a few examples of informal, non-state-sponsored initiatives that work toward similar goals. Before doing so, however, I must say that these particular narratives do not seem to be widespread. So, while the examples below are "popular" in their being encountered outside the realm of academic scholarship, such projects are not widely publicized or written about. Locating these particular initiatives required a lot of "digging around" and unlike the widely available archives about prison-based programs that work with inmates, there seems to be a relative dearth of information about the resources that are available to correctional officers…

Yoga & Meditation

International Association for Human Values (IAHV) is an international humanitarian and educational non-governmental organization that works in special consultative status with the Economic, Social and Cultural Council (ECOSOC) of the United Nations:

> It has long been my belief that all correctional personnel must find a creative way of limiting the effects of stress on their lives. Stress from day-to-day living, coupled with their workplace stress, takes an unrecognized toll on them. The breathing techniques have made my life better in ways you cannot imagine. Concentration is back; frustration is down. My home life has gotten better. I have recommended the program to everyone I come in contact with at work.
> —Correctional Officer IV, West Virginia Division
> of Corrections [IAHV, 2014]

Conflict Resolution

The Alternatives to Violence Project (AVP) with Correctional Officers

This work makes [correctional] organizations much more effective since it helps them work together as a cooperative, respectful community. That in turn helps them carry the skills of Transforming Power into their direct contact with prisoners in community situations [AVP, 2008].

Stress Management

The purpose of the course From Corrections Fatigue to Fulfillment™ (CF2F) is to educate corrections professionals on the nature of Corrections Fatigue, its facets and its precursors, and to present strategies for deterring it and for boosting staff well-being and professional growth, resulting in Corrections Fulfillment. The course includes the following components:

1. Definition and exploration of inherent wellness-related challenges of corrections work.
2. Examination of strategies to counter or prevent Corrections Fatigue and its effects both individually and organizationally.
3. Identification of individual and organizational strategies to pursue positive growth and professional satisfaction, and to increase resilience and even post-traumatic growth in the midst of often persistent adversity encountered in corrections work.

The CF2F course is now offered in **5 customized versions**, for: (a) staff who work in locked facilities (prisons/jails), (b) community supervision agents (probation and parole officers), (c) juvenile/youth community supervision staff, (d) juvenile/youth locked facility staff, and (e) new hires (in all settings) [Desert Waters, 2013].

Photography and Poetry

THIN BLUE LINES

PARTNER: Police Department

Challenges: improve morale and community relations

Strategy: increase departmental and public awareness of officers' experiences through poetry Thin Blue Lines, a project that partners police officers with poets and photographers, has been very successful. Engaging over 15% of the sworn officers, the project's outcomes include: a permanent exhibit of 60 photographs by officers and photographers at police headquarters; 5 police poetry readings attended by over 250 people; YouTube videos of officers and poets; 4 arts-based civic dialogues with the police and community; and the publishing of 2 internationally-acclaimed police poetry calendars. An evaluation funded by the Kellogg Foundation determined that Thin Blue Lines achieved its objectives by making the lives of police officers more visible and the challenges of their work more evident—to the public, to the department and to each other [Art at Work, n.d.].

Theater

FOREST CITYTIMES

PARTNERS: Portland Police Department, local high school students

Challenges: foster honest dialogue between police and youth; challenge stereotypes and judgments made on both sides; improve communication and overall relations between police and youth; increase city's awareness of necessity of these positive relationships

Strategy: create an original play from interviews with 25 officers, intentionally including officers who have an aggressive style of policing as identified by youth and other officers; bring police and student actors together to combine police play and student play into one performance followed by a civic dialogue; perform for over 50% Portland's high school students [Art at Work, n.d.].

It is corrections officers who spend the most time with inmates and as later discussions in this chapter will substantiate, the stresses of being a prison guard leads to lowered job satisfaction; lowered job satisfaction subsequently leads to officers having more negative and punitive interactions with inmates. So, why aren't enrichment programs for guards as widely available as they are for prisoners? If we must have justice systems that are structured as they are now, don't we also need interventions that would encourage the development of a less stressed, more satisfied, and less punitive correctional officer culture?

In the conversations with the young men leading up to *Lives*, very little thought or time was given to the characterization of the Guards—

both by the young men and myself. Somehow, I fell into the same trap that many mainstream representations seem to fall into: demonizing the prison guard as being nothing but an authoritarian figure. The characters did not include any of the intimacy that I saw glimpses of in the detention center; none of the humanizing qualities that are described in the popular viewpoints above; none of the complexities that come with being a corrections officer. In revisiting these characters by using the three mystory components then, my challenge was to find aesthetic strategies through which I could layer the characters of the prison officials in *Lives* while simultaneously honoring the young men's desire to highlight the Guards' authoritarian tendencies ... my challenge was to better showcase the grey zones.

Mystory Part Three: The Expert Narratives

> Jessica Mitford asks, "For after all, if we were to ask a small boy, 'What do you want to be when you grow up?' and he were to answer, 'A prison guard,' should we not find that a trifle worrying—cause, perhaps, to take him off to a child guidance clinic for observation and therapy?" Given her prescription for little boys, one can only imagine Mitford's treatment for a little girl who expressed the same aspiration.—Mitford in Britton, 2003:51

Prison scholarship "has tended to focus on prisoners, and by comparison correctional officers have largely been forgotten" (*Berkeley Journal of Criminal Law*, 2009:294). Furthermore, stereotypes "abound about how one comes to be a correctional officer" and of all of these stereotypes, possibly "the most common is the notion that those who seek out such employment do so because they possess authoritarian personalities and desire to indulge their taste for brutality" (Britton, 2003:80). Many existing studies that have been done with/about correctional officers suggest that most of these individuals have "'drifted' into the work" and there are very few (documented) instances where prison guards indicate "that they are now in the occupation to which they have always aspired" (Britton, 2003:80). Working as a prison guard seems to be tagged with numerous challenges: "low remuneration, difficult working conditions, and the ignominy that comes with doing society's 'dirty work'" (Britton, 2003:78); all of which combine to make this particular career choice one that is undesirable to many. Furthermore, looking at records of prison employment shows "both continuity and change" (Britton, 2003:78): for instance, while "[s]alaries have improved" they are still on the lower end of the spectrum, and while "[w]orking conditions have changed for the better during the past thirty years," these conditions continue to "vary widely across states and even from institution to institution within systems" (Britton, 2003:78). Because of this inconsistency, some "prisons are high-tech, climate-controlled facilities utilizing video monitoring of inmates and computerized access" while other prisons—sometimes in the same area— could be "un-air-conditioned in summer, are barely heated in winter, and rely on steel bars, gates, and razor ribbon wire for security" (Britton, 2003:79). A large number of correctional facilities are "located in remote, rural areas" and when the geographical location is added to other factors that influence career choice, the prison guard "marks the occupation as a working-class job, albeit one that offers a salary, job security, and all the benefits that accompany government employment" (Britton, 2003:79).

Apart from concerns about working conditions, one of the primary challenges that comes from being a prison guard is said to lie in the high levels of stress that occur for those who are in these positions. Certain studies "have estimated life expectancy of correctional officers at 59 years" when, by comparison, "non-police males have a life-expectancy of seventy three years" (*Berkeley Journal of Criminal Law*, 2009:294). In addition to shortened lives, given that many of these officers "spend more time with inmates than they do with members of their own families" (Britton, 2003:106), "the divorce rate for correctional officers is purportedly twice the national average, and high rates of alcoholism and suicide are found among line officers" (*Berkeley Journal of Criminal Law*, 2009:294). A comprehensive study about the stress of correction officers concluded that " illnesses related to stress at work, including hypertension, ulcers, and heart disease were abnormally high among correctional officer" (*Berkeley Journal of Criminal Law*, 2009:294). Furthermore, based on conversations with correctional officers, it has been said that many "officers recognized the changes that had taken place in themselves and spoke of those changes with sorrow and bitterness in the interviews" (*Berkeley Journal of Criminal Law*, 2009:295). Many of the officers who contribute their voices to studies about the psychology of correctional work speak of their "young marriages [being in] trouble or destroyed" and some "officers were so burnt out that they could not go into supermarkets or take their children to the zoo" (*Berkeley Journal of Criminal Law*, 2009:295). Other officers speak about becoming "so drug dependant that they had to get drunk before going to work on the 7 a.m. shift" (*Berkeley Journal of Criminal Law*, 2009:296).

This dependency was also said to be heightened by anger and frustration; so much so that many of guards spoke to punching holes in the walls of their home and abusing those that they loved (*Berkeley Journal of Criminal Law*, 2009:296). "They suffered severe headaches, hypertension, nightmares [and] they were desperately unhappy and despaired that life could ever seem good again" (*Berkeley Journal of Criminal Law*, 2009:296). Lucien X. Lombardo's *Guards Imprisoned*—"an investigation into the guard lifestyle and its bipolar mix of chaos and boredom"—presents similar conclusions and suggests that in being "[f]aced with danger and a sense of powerlessness" the prison guard becomes "a classic example of an alienated worker" (*Berkeley Journal of Criminal Law*, 2009:296). In order to cope with the frustrations of being alienated from his work, from his family, from his colleagues (as spoken to in the previous chapter about the relationship between prison guards and educators), and arguably even from himself, the alienated guard copes "with these frustrations [by] resign[ing] himself to the inevitability of forces beyond his control and finds alternatives to or strikes out against situations within his grasp" (*Berkeley Journal of Criminal Law*, 2009:296). Recent examples of these alienated workers can be seen in investigative projects done with prison guards at Guantanamo Bay who "have been reported to suffer psychological trauma as a result of the harsh environment, which is further testimony to the effects treatment of prisoners can have on their keepers" (*Berkeley Journal of Criminal Law*, 2009:295–296). When officers themselves are susceptible to the abovementioned issues and stresses, it is understandable why/how "the question of inmate rehabilitation begins to look like a purely theoretical construct" since "far from being able to manage inmates and contribute to rehabilitation, officers sometimes cannot even manage themselves" (*Berkeley Journal of Criminal Law*, 2009:296).

In addition to pressures within the job of interacting with prisoners, there are instances where correctional officers stress and alienation have been documented as stemming from frustrations with the criminal justice system; systemic challenges that lie outside the purview of the officers' control. For example, "[o]ne officer spoke for many when he expressed intense frustration with making arrests only to see cases dismissed or reduced through plea bargaining, adding that he felt powerless to reduce crime in his city" (Finn & Tomz, 1996:11). Similarly, "an officer whose partner had been killed in a shooting cited the court system as his primary source of frustration" (Finn & Tomz, 1996:11). In addition to being caught up within a system that many of them do not understand or agree with, "[s]everal others said that they do not receive the respect they deserve;

one was incredulous that a citizen had called his department supervisor to complain that he was driving too slowly while on patrol" (Finn & Tomz, 1996:11). And in speaking about the ways in which civilians view officers, it is also documented that a number of officers are "disturbed by the ramifications of negative press coverage of departments other than their own" (Finn & Tomz, 1996:11). Others observed that, "even if citizens are not necessarily critical of law enforcement, they do not understand what it is really like" (Finn & Tomz, 1996:11). As one officer says about her friends: "[they do not] want to hear the gruesome stories; they do not want to hear about the day-to-day pressures"; another said, "People don't realize cops have feelings, too" (Finn & Tomz, 1996:11).

The stress that dominates the correctional officer experience does not arise only from working with inmates and from the structural/perception related factors mentioned above. Rather, challenges for prison guards also include the stress that emerges from relationships and conflicts with "service staff, other officers, visitors, and administrative superiors" (*Berkeley Journal of Criminal Law*, 2009:296). Furthermore, as mentioned in Chapter Four, "officers today bear the added brunt of managing unprecedented numbers of mentally ill inmates"; a factor which adds to stress and alienation since mentally ill prisoners have different requirements of care than those who are deemed mentally well (*Berkeley Journal of Criminal Law*, 2009:296). Since "mentally ill prisoners are [documented as being] more difficult to manage and more violent than the general prison population," the increasing numbers of mentally ill prisoners leads to "more emotional strains for officers [...] including alcoholism, drug addiction, and domestic problems" (*Berkeley Journal of Criminal Law*, 2009:296). These observations and conclusions therefore, beg the question of the kinds of support mechanisms that are in place to support the mental and physical wellbeing of the guards. Literature about this particular dimension to the prison guard experience, i.e., if/how better cared for guards might in turn better care for the prisoners under their control, is surprisingly hard to encounter and when found, exhibit views that seem to be in need of further research. Studies document "the effects of the work environment on correctional staff job satisfaction": effects of work culture characteristics like "role stressors and job stress" which have negative impacts on job satisfaction; "job autonomy, participation in decision making, promotional opportunity, and quality supervision" that have positive effects on job satisfaction; "areas of pay, dangerousness, inmate population issues, and security level" that have "generally been found to have little or no impact on correctional staff job satisfaction" (Lambert, Hogan

& Barton, 2002:132). All of the abovementioned work environment related factors are said to "generally have a far larger effect than do personal characteristics" on the job satisfaction levels of correctional officers (Lambert, Hogan & Barton, 2002:132).

There are some documented studies of stress-relief programs that have been implemented to address the stress of correctional officers and it has been suggested that a law enforcement stress program can take many forms. Sometimes, these are implemented as "an employee assistance or psychological services program set up within the agency"; at other times "a group of officers [is] trained to provide support and referrals to other officers"; some institutions contract "a private mental health practice or independent practitioner who serves one or more law enforcement agencies"; or there are combination of these approaches (Finn & Tomz, 1996:2). Regardless of the diverse forms that these programs might take, "the common characteristics among these arrangements are that they have some kind of formal structure and are set up with the express purpose of preventing and reducing stress among law enforcement officers" (Finn & Tomz, 1996:2). While some law enforcement "administrators may be concerned that a stress program will be abused by some officers who will see the program as a way to escape discipline for substandard job performance," by and large, there seem to be more efforts to establish such stress relief programs than arguments to counter their need (Finn & Tomz, 1996:4). It seems to be generally acknowledged, within the corrections world, that stress programs can "educate officers about how to reduce and cope with stress, and it can provide needed services at critical moments (Finn & Tomz, 1996:4). That said, it is also widely accepted that a "stress program in and of itself cannot ensure that all officers will cope more effectively with stress" and that to "a great extent, coping depends on individual characteristics such as personality, physical condition, and spiritual and family support" (Finn & Tomz, 1996:4). Studies about the efficacy and manifestation of such programs in prisons across the country are careful to note that "[n]o single example of stress programming will be suitable for all types of law enforcement agencies" and that "departments need to tailor their services to the size of the organization, its geographic jurisdiction, available resources, officers' career levels and particular needs, and other agency characteristics" (Finn & Tomz, 1996:4).

In analyzing the programs that exist to support correctional officers, an unpublished report that was submitted to the U.S. Department of Justice underscores the fact that "programs and services that are provided by organizations seem to focus primarily on the officer" and that there is "little if any information available to identify the effectiveness and utilization of existing programs" (Delprino, 2002:2). This particular critique also suggests that "agencies have not recognized the resource that family members can be to assist in minimizing the potential negative consequences that a career as a correctional officer can have on the well-being of the officer, family and the organization"; resulting in less "attention and resources are given to addressing the officer's family members' concerns" (Delprino, 2002:2). Ultimately, this report suggests that "[c]orrectional agencies have not fully addressed the impact that a career as an officer can have on the family" (Delprino, 2002:2) and that more attention needs to be paid to the families of correctional officers since "they can play a crucial role by encouraging that officer to seek assistance before the problem becomes severe" (Finn & Tomz, 1996:5). And, of course, familial support "is more likely to occur if families have been properly trained regarding the signs of stress-related problems and the availability of services to treat these difficulties" (Finn & Tomz, 1996:5). I must mention here, however, that Delprino's critique about the lack of programming for officers' families seems to be contradicted by a National Institute of Justice report that speaks to how stress programs are in fact welcoming of family and go so far, sometimes, as "incorporating not only spouses and children but also parents, in-laws, siblings, significant others, and anyone else with whom an officer has a close relationship" (Finn & Tomz, 1996:5).

So given all of this, what can we say about the job satisfaction (or lack thereof) that might be experienced by prison guards across the United States? While "there has been an increase in research looking at correctional staff job satisfaction, it is unclear what the research tells correctional administrators and scholars" (Lambert, Hogan & Barton, 2002:116). For example, some research suggests that, "[a]lthough the results are far from conclusive, it would appear that education has a negative association with job satisfaction, especially among correctional officers" (Lambert, Hogan & Barton, 2002:121). Additionally, researchers have postulated that "race shapes an individual's job satisfaction in the field of corrections" (Lambert, Hogan & Barton, 2002:121); that "there is no relationship between gender and correctional staff job satisfaction" (Lambert, Hogan & Barton, 2002:123); that the "relationship between age and tenure on job satisfaction are mixed" (Lambert, Hogan & Barton, 2002:124). The influence of such personal characteristics on a prison guard's stressors are important to consider since prisons function as "gendered organizations"—where "organizations [seen] not as neutral organisms infected by the germs of workers' gender (and sexuality and race and class) identities but as sites in which these attributes are present in preexisting assumptions and constructed through ongoing practice" (Britton, 2003:3). And "just as prison administrators and penologists designed systems of discipline with inmates of specific gender, race, and class identities in mind," their designs were also influenced by what they imagined to be "the characteristics of the 'ideal' officer" (Britton, 2003:52). In so doing, it has been postulated that two "very different models of this officer accompanied the development of men's and women's institutions of incarceration" and these ideas "began to be challenged by forces that reshaped prisons, as well as the roles of those who work within them" (Britton, 2003:52). For instance, scholarship suggests that by "the mid–twentieth century, two different, and gendered, models of the job we now call 'correctional officer' had emerged" and in these models, the ideal guards "working in men's and women's prisons had very different orientations toward their work" (Britton, 2003:63). Adhering with mainstream societal "ideas about proper masculinity and femininity, men were to be officers in a paramilitary mold, and to serve primarily as enforcers, ready and able to use violence if necessary" (Britton, 2003:63). On the other hand, female guards in correctional institutions "were to be mentors and surrogate mothers, guiding their wayward charges toward rehabilitation" (Britton, 2003:63). As such it has been documented that some female and gay/minority officers might be subject to added stress because of:

- lack of acceptance by the predominantly white [heterosexual] male force and subsequent denial of needed information, alliances, protection, and sponsorship from supervisors and colleagues;
- lack of role models and mentors;
- pressure to prove oneself to colleagues and the public;
- exclusion from informal channels of support; and
- lack of influence on decision-making [Finn & Tomz, 1996:10].

I discuss the abovementioned aspects to job satisfaction here since, as Peter L. Nacci and Thomas R. Kane (in Lambert, Hogan & Barton, 2002:133) found, "when officers indicated greater job satisfaction, inmates were likely to say that their environment was more free from danger of sexual assault." Similarly Elyse W. Kerce, Paul Magnusson, and Amy Rudolph (in Lambert, Hogan & Barton, 2002:133) found among naval correctional staff that "those staff who reported higher levels of job satisfaction indicated a more positive view of incarcerated individuals and had a stronger attitude toward rehabilitation." Although there are a few studies that state the contrary—that there is no correlation between job satisfaction and officer orientation toward inmates—it seems to be that a larger number of investigations have "found a positive association between job satisfaction and support for a human-service orientation among Arizona correctional security staff. For example, one study concludes that "job satisfaction was negatively associated with a punitive orientation toward inmates" and "higher levels of job satisfaction were related to greater social distance from inmates" (Lambert, Hogan & Barton, 2002:133). Ultimately, "the literature suggests that higher levels of staff job satisfaction can lead to positive work outcomes that can benefit both staff and inmates through better staff-inmate relations, better correctional standards and conditions, and even safer environments" (Lambert, Hogan & Barton, 2002:133). And similarly, "low levels of job satisfaction are theorized to have significant effects on negative behaviors by employees" (Lambert, Hogan & Barton, 2002:133).

Guards and inmates share an intimate relationship and given the extended periods of time that they spend together, it has been seen that inmates sometimes speak to prison guards about "their own lives outside of prison, and officers sometimes reciprocate" (Britton, 2003:107). For instance, a corrections officer may "unburden things to an inmate that he would not tell his wife" (Britton, 2003:107). Additionally, the intense proximity between prisoners and their guards is said to have "a way of breaking down stereotypes and building relationships," where "officers may even come to view inmates as 'reasonable, responsible creatures who are fitting objects for emotional involvement'" (Goffman in Britton, 2003:107). This kind of involvement can become immensely problematic though, since it can place the officer "into a position to be hurt by what inmates do and what they suffer" and when this happens, it could lead to the officers "burnout" and/or "complete detachment" (Goffman in Britton, 2003:107). An inmate/guard involvement could also foster "the construction of unyielding boundaries between themselves and inmates" and the one common way for guards to manage the repercussions becoming emotionally involved with their prisoners has been said to be the "development of a kind of theory of human nature about inmates"—on the part of the guards—"a shared perspective that helps to [them] make sense of the duties officers are required to perform" and also "provides a subtle means of maintaining social distance from inmates and a stereotyped view of them, and justifies the treatment accorded them" (Goffman in Britton, 2003:107). As a result of such coping mechanisms, "staff in total institutions like the prison [could] participate in the construction and maintenance of an institutional perspective about their client population"—a perspective that "serves the functional purpose of rationalizing the divide between 'us' and 'them'" (Britton, 2003:164). Ironically therefore, the circumstances of confinement both "foster[s] more intimacy among officers and inmates than that which sometimes exists with their friends and families" while simultaneously producing "a contradictory set of notions": "[i]nmates are human, but not equal; they are too privileged, but not undeserving of rights" (Britton, 2003:164).

When looking at the expert narratives surrounding the experiences of correctional officers therefore, there is a lot of information that emerges through the lens of social psychology. And although I cannot claim that the scholarship above is in any way exhaustive, I believe that the studies and theories that have been highlighted provide more insights into the complexities of the profession—complexities that I did not pay enough attention to in *Lives*. By using personal, popular, and expert components that I find to be particular relevant to my experience in the detention center, therefore, the scene that ends this chapter is not so much rewritten as it is new; a new scene that I see as being an important autoethnodramatic effort in my project to rewrite *Lives*. From the personal narratives, I draw in the moments in which my understanding of the aggressive/authoritarian guard was challenged and nuanced. From the popular and expert narratives, I include dimensions of the stresses and stressors that surround the job of being a corrections officer. And finally, through these interwoven narratives, there is one important question I use to frame my analysis and reflections: if we could start over with a blank slate, with everything that we now know about the challenges of the current criminal justice system in the U.S., what would be the picture of an "ideal" guard?

Rewriting the Guards

Transition

An area in which the audience sees different kinds of prison officers—guards, bureaucrats, social workers.

OFFICIAL 1—a guard—is drinking at his office table.
OFFICIAL 2—an administrator—looks exhausted but carries on with work.
OFFICIAL 3—a social worker—is talking with a prisoner and seems to be in a really engaging conversation. Somehow, there is a sense that this person loves what they are doing.

When the audience first enters, they see each of these characters in silent images. They are given time to take in the images and interpret them how they will. After a few moments of silence, GUARD 1 clears his throat. When this happens, all the actors (except the prisoner, who leaves the room immediately) look at the GUARDs and the audience members.

GUARD 1: These people are here to listen to the young people's stories. Anything you all would like to say to them?

Lights change. Focus on OFFICAL 1. OFFICAL 1 is drinking, morose, staring off into space.

AUDIO RECORDING: I tried to make this work. I really tried to make this work. I can't do this anymore.

The same lines above are repeated but by different voices: male, female, old, young: voices that represent different people in the life of OFFICIAL 1, who are unable to take his lifestyle anymore. As the voices continue to speak, there is a transition that occurs on the face of OFFICAL 1. He drains the bottle. Opens another drawer in his desk. Opens it. And begins drinking again.

Lights change. Focus on OFFICIAL 2 who looks completely burnt out and is still working hard at his/her desk: it is important that this official is a minority, in some way.

OFFICALS 4 and 5 walk in and head to OFFICIAL 2's table.

OFFICIAL 4: You coming?
OFFICIAL 2: Where?
OFFICIAL 5: It's time for the workshop.
OFFICAL 2: What workshop?
OFFICIAL 4: Some stress management thing.... I don't know why they can't just tell people to toughen the hell up.

Pause.

OFFICIAL 2: I don't think I can go to the session today. Too much paperwork.
OFFICIAL 5: Suit yourself.

OFFICIAL 5 walks out of the room. OFFICIAL 4 lingers.

OFFICIAL 4: You can't keep acting like this.
OFFICIAL 2: Acting like what? I have tons of paperwork—
OFFICIAL 4: We both know what this is about.

Pause.

Six. The Guards

OFFICIAL 4: The longer you hide out the worse it's going to get.

OFFICIAL 2: It can't get any worse. They're never going to give me a seat at the table.

OFFICIAL 4: Not if you keep acting like this, they won't!

OFFICAL 2: You know what he called me, right?

Pause. They look at each other.

OFFICAL 4 walks out of the room. OFFICIAL 2 puts down his/her pen. Buries their head in their hands. S/he looks up at the audience, tears in her eyes. Just as she is about to say something to the audience, her phone rings.

Lights change. Focus on OFFICAL 3 who is happy and positive.

OFFICIAL 3: I hope you all have had an interesting time meeting our young people. I'm sure you will agree that many of them ... many of them are full of promise. They are just kids and ... we hope they'll get a second chan6ce. So, tell me. I've been working here for a few years now and would be happy to answer any questions you have from having met with our young people. Any questions?

This particular section is intentionally left to improvisation. Audience members are welcome to ask questions as they wish. The OFFICIAL is an actor who is particularly knowledgeable about juvenile/criminal justice in that context and can answer most questions that are thrown at him/her. Of course, if the OFFICIAL cannot answer a question they can honestly admit to not having a response or look to the GUARDs for help—at which point the GUARDs can shut the questions down.

After a few questions have been asked and answered, the lights turn off and there are projections on the walls and ceiling: headlines about police brutality; videos that talk about the ways in which law enforcement officers are losing control of themselves; something current; something that the audience members will immediately identify with. After a few minutes of these projected images and videos, the lights come back on—the three OFFICIALs are standing in front of different walls, each of them looking at what was being projected. They look at each other; they look at the GUARDs.

OFFICAL 1 walks back to his desk and begins drinking again.

OFFICIAL 2 walks back to their desk where the paperwork continues.

OFFICAL 3 looks at the audience.

OFFICIAL 3: I would love to chat more, but it's time for me to get back to work.

S/he returns to his/her desk. Lights change.

GUARD 1: Let me see a show of hands, ladies and gentlemen. How many of you here would like to become a corrections officer like us? Any takers?

If an audience member raises their hand or says yes, they are invited to step in front of their peers. If no audience member responds in the affirmative, an ACTOR in AUDIENCE steps forward.

GUARD 1: Let's see now. I'm going to ask you a series of questions and based on your responses, my colleague and I will decide whether or not we think you will make it.... Ok?

Lights change. Spotlight on the audience member who wants to be a corrections officer or the ACTOR in AUDIENCE.

GUARD 1 asks questions that take from those that are asked to applicants in formal corrections interviews; questions like those that have been included in Part 2 of this chapter. As the person in the spotlight answers the questions, the GUARDs do not show much of a reaction to the answers—however accurate or hilarious they might be. At the end of the interview, when the person goes back to the audience group, the spotlight turns off.

The two GUARDs begin laughing. Slowly at first. Building slowly into hysteria till they are both on the ground, laughing so hard that they have tears in their eyes.

A sound.

The GUARDs immediately stop laughing and stand up. Their expressions are neutral once again.

They unroll a huge roll of paper that covers a large part of the floor. They hand out markers to the audience. On the piece of paper, there are different questions that require the audience to draw/write down their responses:

1) Imagine that the juvenile justice system as we know it, does not exist. We are creating a system from scratch. Given what we know about the strengths and limitations of the system now:
    a. What would you change?
    b. What would stay the same?
2) Draw a picture of what you think a prison should look like architecturally.
3) How would you rate the behavior of the GUARDs who have accompanied you today?
    a. Poor
    b. Fair
    c. Good

  d. Very good
  e. Excellent
After a few minutes for the audience to work on this.

GUARD 2: All right, folks, thank you for doing that. Our supervisor wants your comments apparently. I hope you've said good things about us! Let's move on, shall we?

As the audience begins to walk out with the GUARDs, the three officials come over to the piece of paper and begin reading what the spectators have written.
The GUARDs close the door to this room too. And lock it.

Scene Seven

The GUARDs take the audience back to the waiting room in which they began their journey.

GUARD 1: I still don't understand why you all wanted to hear these stories.... But you're here, we're here; we all do as we're told, I guess.

GUARD 2: We've done this job for so many years now that we've learned how to tell which of these young ones will make it and which ones won't.

GUARD 1: That straight A student, George, I can tell that he's going to OD on heroin once he gets out of here.

GUARD 2: Carlos, well we all know what happens to him.... He'll get killed—probably by Marcos—who'll then get the chair. Those two aren't going to do so well.... The others though, may have a chance.

GUARD 1: The "savage" might actually change his life around when he gets out of here.

GUARD 2: William could become stable with more help.

GUARD 1: That young couple seem like they have a shot at making it work.

GUARD 2: We've gotten real good at telling what'll happen to these ones!

GUARD 1: Right then, our job here is done. You've watched, you've listened. Not much else for us to say, really.

GUARD 2: Please make sure you retrieve your items that you left on your entry. *(Points to the "check-in" location where audience members phones, wallets, and such were collected at the beginning of the show).* Good night and good luck.

The GUARDs leave and head back into the prison. There is one actor who mans the station where audience can retrieve their personal belongings and sign out. This actor also ensures that all the audience members leave the performance space.

No curtain call.

Conclusion

This concluding chapter is structured around evaluating the two primary mystory methodologies that have been implemented in this book: Gregory Ulmer's (1989) three-pronged approach that frames each chapter's central analyses; Norman K. Denzin's (1997) proposals that influence the autoethnodrama that has resulted from my attempt to rewrite *Lives* by incorporating the viewpoints of an Outsider. As such, the first part of this concluding discussion summarizes the main outcomes and questions that emerged in the preceding chapters. The second part evaluates my use of autoethnography in this book and highlights some areas in which it has succeeded; other areas in which it could benefit from further research and development. In the last part of this chapter, I look at the approach taken in this book and attempt to draw out the method that has arisen despite the intentional "messiness" of the approach.

The first chapter asks how popular narratives about volunteerism in prisons might tie in with personal and expert narratives about community and status. More importantly, the writing in this chapter asks how different dimensions to volunteers' impact on prison communities can be showcased autoethnodramatically. As a result, in rewriting George White's scene with the aforementioned ideas in mind, the new scene is not only about a young boy who gets thrown into prison for accidentally starting a fire at a party and who sees college as his way of escaping his overbearing father. Rather, the rewrites seek to address this young man's story for how it might be interpreted in the larger context of outsiders (like myself) engaging in prisons: what might outsiders read as subtext in George's story? How might all the multi-dimensionality that underscored the creative process be woven into one particular scene that was created by one specific young man? And in giving dramatic shape to the nuances and layers within the creation of George White's voice, how can the rewritten scene also do justice to what the young man who created this character wanted to say with/through his voice?

The second chapter's reflections and analyzes are underscored by questions and ideas surrounding language: the links between language, discipline, and surveillance; the connections between music, language, and criminality; the foreign-ness of artistic language; the nexus between culture, personal background, and the prison. In thinking about how to use these experiences in rewriting T and Q's scene therefore, I considered the following: how to include material about the complexities surrounding the young men's use of language—both personally and in terms of the languages they preferred in/of music; how to shape the dramatic narrative so that that attention might be to the participants' linguistic choices; how to nuance the characterization so as to allude to the politics surrounding the language that is spoken within prison settings. My personal encounters with miscommunication in the detention center, the popular narratives surrounding language and delinquency, and the scholarship about that speaks to larger disciplinary questions about language and criminality have come to shape the aesthetic choices that I have made in rewriting Carlos Sadaña and Marcos Gusmán's scene.

In rewriting David Villaseñor's scene, one of the central rewrites was the decision to bring in an interactive component that draws from the lived experience of each individual spectator through two questions for the spectators groups: What does it mean to be a man? What does it mean to be a real man? By using the integration of a question as a central strategy from which to revisit David's scene, I considered strategies through which I could bring in the stereotypes propagated by popular media representations of masculinity in prisons. Furthermore, I wanted to highlight the Outsider's voice in this scene by presenting layers to fear, power, protest, and the in-between spaces when discussing male-ness in prison contexts. As a result, the mystory analyses in this chapter investigate the ways in which existing voices in popular culture contribute to constructions of masculinity and additionally, these analyses consider how constructions of gender intersect with race, sexual orientation, class, and other sociopolitical and identity-based factors. Given that performativity of gender within the prison context is not any more or less complicated than the performances of masculinity/femininity/everything in between outside prison walls, David's rewritten scene takes fragmented personal, popular, and expert thoughts about gender and weaves them into an autoethnodramatic form. From the personal narratives I particularly highlight the ways in which my own preconceived notions of hyper masculinity in prisons was challenged, From the popular narratives, I am particularly interested in how to collaboratively—with audience members—engage in discussions about what it means to be a man; a real man. From the expert narratives, what interests me most in terms of the autoethnodrama is the notion of masculine protest; the forms of resistance and resilience that are adopted by those who are caught between being child and being man; the viewpoints of young people who might be considered man-subjects.

Mental health/psychological difference is the complex subject matter that is investigated in the fourth chapter and the three different kinds of narratives put forward the problematic perceptions, portrayals, and diagnoses of these forms of wellbeing within/outside of the prison system. William Jones and Tishia Jackson's rewritten scene attempts to problematize and nuance how mental illness is placed within the juvenile justice system. The rewritten scene also explores how aesthetic strategies might be used to invite audiences to think about—in addition to the broad notion of mental illness—*how* diagnoses are made and how medication might/ might not be implicated in deadline with "difficult" clients in the context of a total institution. Sarah Kane's *4.48 Psychosis* plays an important role in the rewriting of this scene, as does my desire to be responsible to the original characters and texts that were created for William and Tishia (as created by M and Z). It is important to clarify that there is an entire dimension in this particular chapter that is "fictional," that is built from my interpretation of interactions between the inmates at the detention center and the relationship that they seemed to have with their mental health professionals (in my presence). I make sure to underscore this clarification since, while I did have some interactions with mental health professionals in the juvenile justice system in New Mexico, the brevity of our interactions has led to my only being able to extrapolate from short chats and coded statements.

In the fifth chapter, Tobiah Edward's scene is rewritten by placing personal, popular, and expert narratives about (formal and informal) education at its core. Personal interactions with L influence the developed characterization of Tobiah; the popular narratives showcase an array of voices about the place for creative expression and/or informal learning in prisons; the expert narratives speak to different ideologies that define the prison educator and the intricate interactions between prison educators, inmates, prison administrators, and the prison guards. As an educator myself, my own conflicted interactions with educators in the detention center forced me to question the ideological juxtaposition between the supposed goals of education and the realities of incarceration. And just as the fifth chapter focuses on the prison educators and unpacks dimensions to their experience so as to autoethnographically develop the existing scene, the sixth and last chapter focuses on the prison guards—corrections officers, as I believe is the more acceptable term in present times—and asks how mainstream ideas about this particular kind of prison official might be nuanced and layered. As a result, not only have the characters of the guards been better fleshed out in the rewrites, but also a new scene (and new transitions) has been added so as to draw in some varied viewpoints and narratives. From the personal narratives, I attempt to draw in the moments where my understanding of the aggressive guard was challenged and nuanced. From the popular and expert narratives, I try to dramatically give shape to the stresses and stressors in the careers of corrections officer; stresses and stressors that are often to said to spill out from the job of the guard and flow into their homes and their families.

As I conclude this book, therefore, I ask myself how I might evaluate what this writing project has sought to do—a question that is (un)surprisingly difficult to answer given the nature of autoethnography. As Norman K. Denzin (1997:261) says in particular of "postmodern ethnographers," the lack "of criteria for evaluating their work" results in scholars being left "in a situation in which anything goes." As a result of this condition then, "[f]earful that others will not know how to handle this ambiguity, the critics then turn to their own criteria, offering the bewildered a way out of this postmodern madness" (Denzin, 1997:261). However, instead of devising my own evaluation criteria from scratch, I decided to look for an existing model of evaluating autoethnographic writing and in so doing, encountered distinctive possibilities that have been put forward by diverse researchers/practitioners of the methodology. For instance, Laurel Richardson (2000) suggests that "ethnography needs to be evaluated through two lenses: science and arts" and proposes five criteria to perform such evaluations: "substantive contribution, aesthetic merit, reflexivity, impact, and expression of a reality." For Carolyn Ellis (in Mendez, 2013:285), a good autoethnographic narrative should be able to "engage your feeling and thinking capacities at the same time as generating in the reader questions regarding the experience, the position of the author, how the reader may have experienced the event described, or what the reader may have learned." Pat Sikes (in Moriarty, 2014:68) offers the following criteria for judging powerful storytelling; criteria that Jess Moriarty adapts as a framework to assess and evaluate autoethnodrama. These criteria include: liminality, transgression, evocation, complexity, creativity and audience engagement. Ultimately, I think it is Tony E. Adams, Stacy H. Jones, & Carolyn Ellis' (2015:102) proposals that might best serve as a framework with which to evaluate the autoethnographic approach in this book:

- Making contributions to knowledge
- Valuing the personal and experiential
- Demonstrating the power, craft, and responsibilities of stories and storytelling
- Taking a relationally responsible approach to research practice and representation.

When beginning the process of writing this book, I must admit that I was worried: worried since this is perhaps the most "experimental" of my writings thus far; worried about whether or not the mystory methodology that I chose to adopt—of bring the personal, popular, and expert narratives in conversation with each other—would "work." Ultimately though, despite the worries that I still have about the "success" of this method, I have come to think that the application of the three-pronged (personal, popular, expert) conceptual framing of the mystory toward the creation of an autoethnodrama is precisely what contributes a new perspective and approach, especially to the fields of Theater & Performance Studies. Apart from what this approach might contribute to particular academic disciplines though, a more in-depth consideration of which would be immensely discomfiting for the arrogance it might purport, I have come to find the methodology in this book as being useful to the expansion of my own knowledge as a theater practitioner-researcher. For instance, I was aware from the outset that my work thus far in the detention centers has not been geared toward better understanding the experiences of corrections officers/prison guards. However, it was not until I began curating and analyzing material from the popular and expert arenas for Chapter Six that I realized just how complex this terrain is. It was one thing to know in theory that I did not have the whole picture about the guards' experiences; it was quite something else—from the standpoint of my own learning—to encounter facts, figures, and personal accounts about the role of stress in the life of the correctional officer. Apart from expanding my knowledge about facets of prison experience, while my past writing projects have involved a conversation between the expert and the personal, this was my first attempt to engage two more voices in addition: the mainstream/ the popular; the voices presented through the use of autoethnodrama. For all these reasons, in terms of the first criterion that Adams, Jones, & Ellis put forward of "making contributions to knowledge," I believe this writing project has achieved what it set out to explore.

In terms of the other three evaluation criteria that have been put forward by Adams, Jones, & Ellis (2015:102), the personal and the experiential are clearly highly valued in this book. In addition to the invocation of the personal as the first component of the mystory in every chapter and rewrite, the experiential and autoethnographical also served as the point of departure for the popular and expert narratives that were considered. This was an intentional order of operations that would have yielded different outcomes than if I had started with expert or popular narratives to frame my analyses and rewrites. It is for this reason that this book is autoethnography rather than ethnography: for the way in which it privileges the personal and the experiential. While I am content, for the most part, with the way in which the personal narratives have served as the central core from which the popular and expert considerations emerge, there is also a certain discomfort that arises from the centrality of subjectivity. While I have been using autoethnography as a way to write about my work over the last few years, in prior work the methodology served to complement the writing process rather than become integral to it. For example: in my doctoral project (Dinesh, 2015b) there was a central (more "traditional" research) project in place and autoethnography was implemented as one tool with which write about/ reflect on the work; in *Theatre & War* (Dinesh, 2016) my use of autoethnography was in conversation with more "conventional" analyses that drew from theater-in-war related scholarship. In comparison to these two efforts, autoethnography in this book has been the primary tool with which the writing has both been conceived and implemented. The discomfort that I experience, therefore, stems from battling my own academic conditioning that dictates what a scholarly work is supposed to look like; conditioning that (despite all my claims to enjoying the unconventional) still constrains my imagination.

In contending with my own academic conditioning, I realize that I am struggling with precisely the kind of discomfort that autoethnography considers as one of its central qualities: the vulnerability of the researcher/ writer. This vulnerability that becomes central in the writer/researcher/ practitioner taking on a relationally responsible approach to research, practice, and representation. In speaking to this relational responsibility though, there is one serious challenge that I must point out—the inability for me to contact the young men who participated in *Lives* and engage with their feedback and input as part of my own evaluation/creation/re-creation of the text that they remain an integral part of. The practical constraints of contacting the young men who have been released, and the ethical questions surrounding the discussion of this work with the young men who are still in the detention center, have led to the writing of this work being far more of a solo than a collaborative effort. And although I have tried, as best I can, to honor what happened in *Lives* and to honor the original characters and performances that were created by the young men—my attempts are ridden with the fallacies and weaknesses of memory. This inability to share the rewritten text with my co-creators, therefore, is one element that continues to irk me vis-à-vis how responsible this project might be. Clearly, this discomfort about being unable to re-engage with the young men was not strong enough to prevent my writing this book and yet, it is a discomfort that I do think I need to share with the reader.

Adams, Jones, & Ellis' final point of evaluation is one that, of course, is best left up to the reader and that is the way in which the writing in this book demonstrates "the power, craft, and responsibilities of stories and storytelling." I recall receiving a particularly harsh review from a reviewer at the first publishing house I sent the proposal for this book to: "she should stick to traditional modes of storytelling," the reviewer said; completely opposed to the fragmented and episodic strategies that I have adopted in rewriting *Lives*. To me though, it is precisely the fragmentation and discontinuity that makes for the stories being powerful in their representations of reality. Furthermore, I do not see the storytelling in this book as being limited to the personal narratives or the sections that have the autoethnodramatic rewrites; rather, I also see the popular and expert narratives that have been included in each chapter as also showcasing their own mode of storytelling. In so doing, then, it could be possible for this writing project to be performed in multiple ways. While the most obvious strategy would be to perform the rewritten scenes that end each chapter and to engage in a non-performance-based reading of the other sections, a reader/director might also choose to stage excerpts from the personal narratives or from the popular components or even from the expert analyses that precede the rewritten scenes in each chapter. The entire book could become the material for performative storytelling and while this particular theatrical aesthetic might not appeal to those who like linearity and realism in how stories are told and shared, it will appeal to those (like me) who revel in the post-modern and post-dramatic.

Each component to the storytelling in this book—the ways in which the personal, popular, and expert narratives/viewpoints have been curated—is clearly subjective and in each case, there were specific points of inspiration behind my choices. These stimuli were chosen in very specific circumstances—a specific time period in which this book was written; during specific events in my own life (and in the world around me); all of which led me to believe that certain themes would be more interesting to explore than others. However, it is entirely possible that in a different time/place—in a different state of mind—I would have made completely different choices about the particular narratives to focus on in each chapter; choices that would have ultimately re-shaped the autoethnodramatic, rewritten version of *Lives*. I include, below, the punctums behind the current analyses and rewrites in this book; but this time, I place these current choices alongside one alternative approach that each narrative could have taken in a different time/place. I do this so that the reader can immediately identify the "method to the madness" behind the messy texts in the preceding chapters and perhaps, by using this method, a similarly interested practitioner-researcher will be able to develop their own autoethnodrama simply by rearranging the puzzle pieces offered in this book.

The Current Analysis and Rewrite of George White's Scene

Personal Narrative Focus

The unpredictability that pervades the (supposedly) controlled setting of a prison

Popular Narrative Focus

The positioning of volunteers within the unpredictability of prisons

Expert Narrative Focus

Considering the notions of wispy communities and status

Autoethnodramatic Strategies

The OUTSIDER and GEORGE have a split scene in which there is no interaction between them. The GUARDS conduct how and when the audience interacts with the scene.

An Alternative Analysis and Rewrite of George White's Scene

Personal Narrative Focus

Observations about young people who are just about to be paroled from juvenile detention centers.

Popular Narrative Focus

Popular narratives about the challenges/successes of post-parole reintegration/rehabilitation programs in a particular region/context.

Expert Narrative Focus

Existing research conducted about post-parole reintegration programs and their impact on recidivism rates.

Autoethnodramatic Strategies

The OUTSIDER is someone who wants to start an education program for recently paroled youth. GUARDs ask audience members to talk about times in their lives when they have been in trouble with their parents/loved ones—times when their actions were being constantly monitored so as to determine the extent of a particular punishment (like being grounded or suspended).

The Current Analysis and Rewrite of Carlos Sadaña and Marcos Gusmán's Scene

Personal Narrative Focus

Miscommunications that occurred during *Lives* due to different uses/approaches to language.

Popular Narrative Focus

Different approaches to the use of language within the prison context.

Expert Narrative Focus

Different theoretical positions about the links between language and criminality.

Autoethnodramatic Strategies

The OUTSIDER and MARCOS have some interaction toward the end of the scene. The audience is still told how to interact but the GUARDS have less control over them than in the previous scene.

An Alternative Analysis and Rewrite of Carlos Sadaña and Marcs Gusmán's Scene

Personal Narrative Focus

The experiences of immigration that shape the characters' lives within and outside the detention center.

Popular Narrative Focus

Popular narratives about rates of incarceration among immigrant youth in the United States (U.S.). Including the voices of young people from immigrant communities.

Expert Narrative Focus

Studies that have been conducted with/about immigrant youth—speaking to their interactions with/in the justice system.

Autoethnodramatic Strategies

The OUTSIDER who is also an immigrant but had a very different lived experience of immigration than the young people in the detention center. Interactive components that ask audience members to trace their family lineage and consider their own status as migrants and immigrants, in one way or another.

The Current Analysis and Rewrite of David Villaseñor's Scene

Personal Narrative Focus

Coming to terms with my own biases vis-à-vis the performance of masculinity in prisons.

Popular Narrative Focus

Popular narratives what it might mean to be a "real" man, especially in relation to the intersections between gender and racial/ethnic identity in the United States.

Expert Narrative Focus

Exploring existing scholarship about constructions of hegemonic masculinities/adulthood and these concepts' subsequent manifestations within juvenile detention centers.

Autoethnodramatic Strategies

The OUTSIDER and DAVID interact almost from the beginning of the scene, but there is a visible distance between them. The audience members are given the opportunity to write down their own contributions about gender—thus bringing in more of their own voices than in previous scenes—but are still told by the GUARDs when they can add their voices.

An Alternative Analysis and Rewrite of David Villaseñor's Scene

Personal Narrative Focus

Interviews with the young man's gang member friends and with his family, about their knowledge of/attitude toward his gang affiliation.

Popular Narrative Focus

Popular narratives of how gangs are simultaneously glamorized and demonized in mainstream representations of gang culture.

Expert Narrative Focus

Existing scholarship about gang culture: why young people

join gangs; risk factors for joining gangs; observable patterns in terms of the demographic composition of different types of gangs.

Autoethnodramatic Strategies

The OUTSIDER is a former gang member, looking to connect with young people who are incarcerated for their having been/being involved in gangs. The audience is asked to interact by providing avenues for individual spectators to recount if/when they ever felt like they were part of a gang or clique (in school, for instance) and what they might have gained/lost through that experience.

The Current Analysis and Rewrite of William Jones and Tishia Edwards' Scene

Personal Narrative Focus

My reflections about the manifestation of mental health in the prison context.

Popular Narrative Focus

Representations of the mentally ill in popular culture.

Expert Narrative Focus

Analyzing literature that looks at how/why the presence of the mentally ill in America's prisons is increasing.

Autoethnodramatic Strategies

The OUTSIDER, WILLIAM, and TISHIA interact closely from the beginning of the scene. The audience is invited to contribute as they see fit, but there is a framework for interaction that is provided by the GUARDs.

An Alternative Analysis and Rewrite of William Jones and Tishia Edwards' Scene

Personal Narrative Focus

Encountering class-based politics among the young men who are incarcerated.

Popular Narrative Focus

Popular narratives about how members of different socio-economic classes view the Other in whatever location the play is being written/performed.

Expert Narrative Focus

Research about the hierarchies (the caste/class system) that manifests in prisons within/between inmates themselves, and within/between the inmates, guards, and prison officials.

Autoethnodramatic Strategies

The OUTSIDER is someone from a particular class and brings in that identity affiliation into their interactions with the young inmates. Audience interaction could manifest by separating audience members (spatially) based on the socio-economic class that they are perceived as belonging to.

The Current Analysis and Rewrite of Tobiah Edwards' Scene

Personal Narrative Focus

My confrontations/misunderstanding with teachers at the detention center.

Popular Narrative Focus

Different opinions on why people choose to teach in prison schools and examples of creativity-based informal learning opportunities for inmates.

Expert Narrative Focus

Discussions that stem from studies that have been done about prison educators' motivation and job satisfaction.

Autoethnodramatic Strategies

The OUTSIDER and TOBIAH interact in different ways throughout the scene and the audience members can interact however they like with the performance—much more open ended and less directed by the GUARDs than in the other scenes.

An Alternative Analysis and Rewrite of Tobiah Edwards' Scene

Personal Narrative Focus

Firsthand accounts by the young man about the domestic violence that he saw growing up in his home.

Popular Narrative Focus

Popular narratives of victimhood and perpetration surrounding domestic abuse.

Expert Narrative Focus

Analyses of theories surrounding why/how people become

abusers and how experiences of abuse in childhood link to delinquency/criminality in adulthood.

Autoethnodramatic Strategies

The OUTSIDER is someone who used to be a perpetrator/victim of domestic abuse. The audience members are asked to interact with the performance by defining the terms "victim" and "perpetrator" and consider what constitutes "abuse" in a general/specific sense—based on what would be less of a trigger in a particular performance setting.

The Current Analysis and Rewrite of the Guards

Personal Narrative Focus

My glimpses into interactions between the young men and the correctional officers during *Lives*, which nuanced my own popular culture-influenced opinions about prison guards.

Popular Narrative Focus

Voices of guards themselves—why do individuals choose these careers? What do they see as its benefits and pitfalls?

Expert Narrative Focus

Literature from existing studies that have been done with/about the psychology of prison guards.

Autoethnodramatic Strategies

The creation of a new scene—that did not exist in *Lives*—which seeks to show various perspectives of guards and other kinds of prison officials.

An Alternative Analysis and Rewrite of the Guards

Personal Narrative Focus

Personal/first-hand accounts from different prison officials.

Popular Narrative Focus

Popular narratives that focus on the voices of different kinds prison employees: doctors, janitors, nurses, and so on.

Expert Narrative Focus

Comparing and contrasting the outcomes of studies that have considered different types of prison employees (not only the guards as is the case in this book).

Autoethnodramatic Strategies
Adding more dimensions to the GUARDs by including different kinds of GUIDEs throughout the piece: guards, administrators, educators, counselors, and so on.

Ultimately, by tweaking the focus of one/more parts of the sections to each chapter, the rewritten scene from *Lives* can be further edited and adapted based on the interests of the reader/director, the context in which they seek to perform the piece, and their intentions for the work. Much of the writing in this book has involved an "organic" process that evolved from my personal narratives and from *Lives*. I realize now though, that a methodology like the mystory allows for innumerable permutations and combinations of the same material and should I have started with a slightly different point of focus in my personal narratives, the popular and expert narratives could have been differently curated; ultimately changing the nature of *Lives*' rewrites. This could be an argument made for any piece of writing of course, that a writing project could just as easily become something else with the slightest shift in focus. I remember realizing this at the end of my doctoral dissertation, that if had slightly tweaked one of research questions or a particular conceptual frameworks, I would have ended up with an entirely different thesis. So perhaps it is not too surprising that the mystory methodology retains the same properties as many (dare I say, all) writing projects: of containing stories within stories; of encompassing ideas within ideas. What does seem different in a mystory method though, is the way in which the approach chosen in this book became an incredibly useful tool in creating an autoethnodrama. As I mentioned in the Introduction, I have been/am in the process of creating an autoethnodramatic piece of work in Kashmir and in creating *IFF Kashmir* as an episodic promenade performance like *Lives*, I have—until now—added scenes in a more random fashion, i.e., I write a new scene when a particular idea strikes me. What this book has enabled me to think about is how the process of writing *IFF Kashmir* might benefit from a more structured methodology that weaves in the personal, the popular, and the expert. A methodology that takes care to mention and highlight—especially in contexts of conflict where the theater practitioner-researcher is an outsider—that the outsider in question has done their homework; that they have consulted different kinds of sources that hold different points of view before deciding on the narratives to include and exclude. I am hopeful that this methodology will be useful to other theater research-practitioners looking to generate alternative texts; I am hopeful, also, that the form of this book has been successful at "doing"—at "performing"—its resistance to more traditional forms of representation that do not always do justice to complicated, tenuous, and fragmented contexts like prisons.

The potential of this three-pronged approach to generating mystories therefore, is what I am most intrigued by as I conclude this project. When I began this book, the mystery and the autoethnodrama (as the reader might have realized in the Introduction) were seen as working in a somewhat linear sequence: where the mystory analyses would be used so as to explain the material that I sought to recreate for an autoethnodramatic rewriting of *Lives*. I did not necessarily see the two concepts as being in conversation with each other: where the mystery analyses would feed into ideas for the form and content of the autoethnodrama; where the autoethnodrama would feedback into refining what I wanted to curate within the personal, popular, and expert components to the mystery. Let me give a concrete example of what I mean here. Initially, when I set out on writing this book, the idea was to use the mystery analysis that would interweave the voice of an Outsider—an Outsider that was primarily intended at showcasing my own experiences within the prison context; the Outsider was supposed to be based only on my own lived experience. However, as the analyses progressed, and as the popular and the expert narratives came into conversation with my personal insights, the dramatic choice was made for the Outsider to manifest in various avatars in the rewrites of *Lives*. In the rewritten autoethnodrama therefore, the Outsider contains elements of my voice, yes; but it is also *not* only my voice. The Outsider, through the process of mystery analyses has become more amorphous than I initially imagined, representing different viewpoints, all of which resonate with my own experience but are also different enough so as to not just be a regurgitation of my Self. Given the symbiotic relationship that has emerged between the elements of the mystery and the autoethnodramatic (re)writing in this book, it is perhaps only appropriate that I end with mystery analyses of another occurrence. The difference with the following segment though, lies in its *not* being about the rewriting of a scene from *Lives;* it is simply the writing of a scene that the reader of this book is free to use however they see fit. The reader can integrate the material below somewhere in *Lives;* they can choose to see it as being a separate piece of writing that might/might not be performed; they could also decide that the writing below is nothing more or less than an evocative conclusion to this book.

* * *

Yesterday, a letter from Q arrived in my mailbox.
It was post-marked in March.
I received the letter in early August.
Between my being out of the country and whatever caused the letter to be delayed
It has taken five months for me to receive a letter that was mailed from a city that is only a two-hour drive away from where I live.
I hope Q does not think I've forgotten him.
That I've somehow lost interest.
I want to write back to Q, you see.
But in his letter, Q tells me that he is going to be released soon.
He asks if he can come visit us at the college once he's released.
I cannot tell him to come though
That I would love to see him
Because he's left the prison now.
And try as I might,
No one can give me an address with which to reach him.
I'm still trying.
If I could have written that letter, I would tell Q that we would love to see him
That he is welcome here any time that he wants to come.
But then, there is that tiny voice at the back of my head
What if he comes with some of his buddies, you know, the ones who were a "bad influence" on him
What then?
What if those buddies…
It's a completely unproductive and unnecessary line of thought.
One that I am ashamed of.
But I have to consider it because of all the other young people that I teach
The other young people that are here and who would be affected if—
I have to consider it.
Don't I?

* * *

Like every other aspect to prison life, the act of sending/receiving mail is just as regulated and controlled.

> Inmates may send and receive mail to whomever they wish but may not correspond with individuals who are incarcerated in a juvenile or adult correctional or detention facility.

Inmates who may have immediate family incarcerated must require written authorization to correspond by Director or designee of both facilities in writing.

There shall be no limit on the amount of incoming mail an inmate is allowed; however there is a limit to the amount of mail that may be store in the inmates tote box.

[M says in his letter that he is only allowed to send 2 letters a month]

Mail shall be inspected for contraband and distributed to inmates with (48) hours of its delivery to the facility, excluding weekends and holidays, or emergency situations, unless it is being withheld for review and/or secured for evidence.

Mail is sorted and subject to censorship along with searches for contraband if there is reasonable suspicion to suggest correspondence may contain information of criminal activity, contraband, risk of safety and security of persons, orderly management of the facility, or any violation of the facility rules.

All letters must be mailed through the United States Postal Service into the facility.

Packages (anything over 9 × 13 envelope is considered a package) and will not be accepted. The only exception will be if the package was pre-approved [Otero County Detention Center, 2016].

[Prohibitions]

Envelopes with additional writing other than addresses, drawings, stickers, gang related symbols or drawings are prohibited

Lipstick marks, any type of make-up, letters or envelopes doused in cologne or perfume

Letters containing pornographic and/or sexually explicit photos or publications

Any materials that depict or describe the use or manufacture of drugs, alcoholic substance, firearms, explosives and/or other weapons

Materials that promote hate, violence, or bias

Correspondence written in code or untranslatable

No downloaded or photocopied e-mail, newspaper, magazines articles, newsletters, or computer documents

Un-returnable mail (due to missing or incomplete return address) will be destroyed. Inmates will receive return notification when mail is refused and/or returned to sender.

Bibles and items necessary to practice a religion will be authorized. Additional materials will be pre-authorized by Director or designee. All materials must fit in the inmate tote box and excessive materials the inmate must release excess to a friend or family member [Otero County Detention Center, 2016].

* * *

On the one hand, there are many sources that speak to why and how the activity of letter writing is beneficial to both prisoners and to their senders/receivers of mail outside prison walls:

> Mail to every prisoner is the high point of their day. It's word from the outside, proof that someone cares and remembers you. It's also something to get you out of here, even if it's only in your mind [Barton & Hall, 2000:157–158].
>
>> I write daily to keep up with everybody, two or three letters a day"[Barton & Hall, 2000:158].
>
> Prisoners who do not receive letters and packages are, from my personal observation, grumpier and lack life and hope [Barton & Hall, 2000:158].
>
>> I started writing when I realized I had lost every one of my so called friends [Barton & Hall, 2000:158].
>
> After twenty one years my family is dead, in bad health or never showed any interest in me, I needed to adopt a family [Barton & Hall, 2000:158].
>
>>> Our libidos are still fully active as prisoners so its expression and unfolding is sometimes a big part of writing. Until my mid twenties my main expectations were sex and money; I've had about fifty correspondents over time, it was mostly about sex and my expectations were all met [Barton & Hall, 2000:158].
>
>>> I've found myself being an adviser, counsellor, marriage consultant, religious instructor, brother, friend, lover, editor, writer, poet [Barton & Hall, 2000:159].
>
> The only writing I did in the free world was school work but when I got locked up at age 17 I learned immediately it (letter writing) was my connection to the world and how I was going to get whatever I wanted out of it.... Most of our time, our life is the correspondence, we love, we cry, get upset, hurt, angry, share sexual experiences and fantasies, we grow, we learn and we live. I want to live and have the human experience and all the emotions that come with it [Barton & Hall, 2000:159].
>
>>> The relationships developed are far more significant and two-way than I ever imagined [Barton & Hall, 2000:164].
>
> I hoped it would make a change to a prisoner's life, and had no idea how much difference it would make to mine [Barton & Hall, 2000:164].

* * *

On the other hand, letter writing is not all about possibilities and connections; letters are also about hate; about retribution; about different kinds of blame:

> Some of my death row pals have mentioned that they have gotten some hate mail over the years. I've read that others have gotten some too. Apparently people read up on their crimes, then send them hate mail containing anything from ethnic slurs to "I hope you Fry!" and so on [Prison Mail, 2006].

I found out that someone who bullied me when I was younger is a child molester and I want to send him hate mail when he gets to prison (from what I found it looks like he's still awaiting trial). I know that prisons read mail so I was wondering this [Reddit, 2016].

> Man who's serving a five- to seven-year prison sentence for beating and threatening to kill a woman in June 2010 is accused of sending threatening letters to her and her sister [Amelinckx, 2012].

> The director general of the prison service [...] revealed yesterday that he had become a target of "extremely offensive" hate mail from prison staff after declaring that the service was "institutionally racist" [Travis, 2001].

Islamic terrorists in UK prisons are able to read hate messages from behind bars, it has been reported. Convicts linked to al Qaida can log on to a website and access inflammatory letters, despite tight government controls. The Sunday Times said inmates were able to access MuslimPrisoners.com, which contains notes written by some of the world's most dangerous terrorists [*Huffington Post*, 2012].

* * *

Lights come up on center stage. A disembodied voice. Or a person reading. Or a projection.

Dear Q,

I want to write back to you, but I can't.

You've been released, they tell me. They tell me they don't have an address for you. And so, I cannot write back. Even though that might mean you think I have forgotten you. That I have … simply forgotten.

Getting your last letter was the highlight of my day. You see, it had been a not so great day until then. I'd spent the night tossing and turning. Probably got about three hours of fitful sleep. My mind was racing with thoughts of … well, so many things. Things that seemed so important and stressful in those hours.

Before I got your letter, I was sitting in an early morning meeting and was drinking my fourth cup of coffee before noon, just to keep my mind and eyes working. When I couldn't sit still anymore, I went to check the box in the corner of the room where they sort the mail. And there it was, the letter.

Thank you for telling me that you miss me.

Thank you for telling me that you want to come visit.

Thank you for telling me that you're writing to me even though you hate writing.

Lights change.

> I hate that you are free.
> When they told me that you were going to come back to school… I couldn't breathe.
> What you did … it didn't change only your life.
> It ripped apart mine.

> The thought of seeing you again. Every day…
> I don't know if I can handle it.
> I don't know if I want to handle it.
> I hate that you are free.

Lights change.

I hope you are well, wherever you are. Being as charming and friendly and creative as you were when we worked together. I hope you don't have to join the army just to escape the home you don't want to go back to. I hope you join the army only if that is something you really think you want to do. I hope you feel like you have a choice.

Un abrazote.[1]

Lights change.

> They tell me that you have changed.
> They tell me that you are sorry for what you did.
> All I have to say:
> Fuck you, man.
> I hate that you are free.

Lights change.

Gracias por todo, guey. Por siempre haber estado sonriendo durante nuestras charlas. Por tu manera de ser. Por tratándome como una hermanita, pues. Te extraño y nunca sabrás cuanto me cuesta no poder mandarte una carta. Ojala, algún día, en este país o en otras tierras, nuestros caminos cruzaran. Seria mi honor conocerte en un mundo por este lado de los paredes.[2]

Pieces of paper float down from the ceiling. The voice that is appreciative of Q grabs the papers as they fall, and writes: notes of hope; of support. As the notes are written, they are also projected for spectators to read.

Just as this voice writes new notes though, the other voice tears them apart: with hate; with outrage. The tearing is not projected in the same way.

They keep writing and tearing. Writing and tearing. Writing and tearing.

No curtain call.

* * *

Epilogue

As I prepare this manuscript for publication, my work at the detention center remains in motion. I continue mentoring my college students on weeklong trips and twice a month visits to the facilities in Albuquerque. The group has jumped in size: from 25 college students who were part of the program last year, there are now close to 60. Which is mostly a good thing.

One of the young men from *Lives*, the only one who remains in the same unit, wants to start a Drama Club. He and I are talking to prison officials to make that happen.

Two other young men from *Lives*—N and L—were still at the detention center as of October 2016. I bumped into L once more since writing the narratives in Chapter Five. This time, I did say hello. This time, he told me he'd be released soon. This time, he said he would come visit when he's out.

N gave me a hug, much to his new unit's surprise. Said he has saved all the material from *Lives* in his new "room."

The prison officials and I share more of a rapport. The new superintendent says, with a mischievous twinkle in his eye, that I bother them too much. The unit supervisor says he wants to develop a joint curriculum for our weeklong trips. The new unit guards "shoot the shit" with me every now and again: one of them tells me about his weight loss program; the other about his discomfort with the systemic inequalities that are perpetuated by particular conflict resolution methodologies.

I am trying to set up a more formal Prison Education program at the detention center. One that offers rigorous accredited courses through the college, particularly in the arts and humanities. Maybe this could eventually become a post-release program too. Maybe the college could become a "learning hub" for the youth, during/after their lives behind the walls.

It's early days yet and I don't know if these ideas will come to pass.

Even if they don't though, even if I "fail" in formalizing my efforts and all that remains are informal spaces to work with these young people, I hope to do so as long as I can.

I hope that many of these young people will stay in my life.

I hope that the letters I receive every week are proof of relationships that might endure.

I hope.

Appendix A

The Original Script of *Lives Behind the Walls*

Characters

GUARD #1
GUARD #2
GEORGE WHITE
CARLOS SADAÑA
DAVID VILLASEÑOR
WILLIAM JONES
TOBIAH EDWARDS
TISHIA JACKSON
MARCOS GUSMÁN

Scene One

GUARD #1: So, you're the people who want to listen to the kids' stories, huh? All right; but before you come in you've got to know something. This is my show. You follow my instructions. I will tell you what to do. I will tell you where to go. If you don't want to listen to me, you can leave right now? Anyone want to leave?

A pause to see if any of the audience members want to leave.

GUARD #1: Ok, then. Today you will witness the stories of some young people; what brought them here; what they do now that they are here. They will tell you things, things about me, even. Whether or not you choose to believe them, well, that's up to you. This is my show. I guard this place. I also play some characters in the young people's stories—you know, I'm a nice guy and just want to make sure that these young ones' stories are told. This is my show.

Scene Two

Tupac Shakur's "Changes" plays in the background while the party goes on. The lines are fairly inaudible but the actions are self-explanatory. After establishing the nature of the party, the soundtrack changes to the sounds of a blazing fire. The characters respond to the change in sound that, after a few seconds, becomes the sound of police sirens. The sound of the sirens rises to a crescendo and stops abruptly. When the sound stops, the characters freeze in place.

GUARD #1: Follow me.

Scene Three

The audience walks into a classroom.

GUARD #1: Ah yes, I'm supposed to play the father in this one.

GUARD #1 puts on a costume piece to show that he has changed character. GEORGE is in the center of the room, sitting on the floor. There is a piece of paper on the floor beside him. GUARD #1 (FATHER) walks around GEORGE in silence. Then,

GUARD #1
(FATHER): B. You've brought home a B? I've given my life to serve this country and you've brought home a B? Answer me.

GUARD #1 (FATHER) repeats these lines over and over till he is screaming at the top of his voice until...

GEORGE: SHUT UP.

GUARD #1 (FATHER) freezes in position.

GEORGE: College was supposed to be my salvation. It was supposed to be my escape ... from him. I was going to college and thought I would become a doctor or a lawyer. Well, he thought I should become a doctor or a lawyer. He's my dad, man. He has given his life to serve this country.... I thought I owed him.... He told me once that when he was off fighting, he saved the lives of one of the men in his company. The guy couldn't hold a gun, my dad said, and in the middle of gunfire he—this guy in my father's squad—froze. So my dad leapt into action and saved that kid's life. He saved his life, man, and to this day, my dad speaks about this guy he saved. How he's like a son to him. A son. A son who froze in the heat of battle. A son he saved and forgave and loved. I wish I was that son.... College was supposed to be my salvation, man. That party, all I wanted was to go there and meet someone nice. I'd never been on a date before then.... I just wanted to meet someone nice. And then, I set that fire.

GUARD #1: All right, sir, that's enough. I think they've heard enough of your story. It's time for us to move on.

GUARD #1 goes back to his old costume and leads the audience to the next space (possibly the hallway right outside the classroom in which GEORGE's scene happens).

Scene Four

All the young people are lying on the floor in the hallway, their hands behind their backs. Each one is reacting to the invisible officers in their own way. Sirens in the background. At a certain point, the young people stand up and begin to walk out in a line. As they start to walk, the GUARD takes the audience to the next classroom, for CARLOS' monologue.

Scene Five

CARLOS is sitting on a chair in the middle of the room. When the audience walks in, GUARD #1 goes up to Carlos, shakes his hand and we see them whispering about something. We don't know what they are talking about but the implication is that GUARD #1 is doing "business" with CARLOS. When the audience has settled, GUARD #1 walks back and stands with the audience. A long silence while CARLOS looks at each of the audience members in the eye.

CARLOS: You all want to hear my story, huh? It's not going to be what you expect. It's not a story about a helpless boy who needs your pity. It's not the story about a boy whose family did him wrong. Far from it.... I think I want to tell you the story of Maria. My first love. Maria sat next to me in Spanish class and man, that girl was fine. Hair like … like brown silk. Eyes that could see right through you.... The first time Maria looked at me, man, I couldn't speak. I just couldn't find the words.... The first person I talked to about Maria, was my mother. My mother is a cool lady, man. Yeah she yelled at me sometimes when she caught me drunk or stoned or something, but she was a cool lady. You know the coolest thing about her? She was my friend. Not many people can talk to their moms about being in love but for me, my mother was the first person I went to.... I tried to stay under the radar when I first came to this joint. I tried to stay to myself. But if people mess with you, you got to stand up for yourself. That's what my mom taught me. I tried to stay to myself in here, man. But, hell … things changed. And now....

CARLOS looks at GUARD #1 and smiles.

CARLOS: And now, I run this bitch.

Q added his piece at a later date.

GUARD #1: Why you looking at me, inmate? You trying to imply something?

GUARD #1 turns to the audience while CARLOS smirks.

GUARD #1: I don't what he's trying to imply, ladies and gentlemen. As I said, these young people say things. We can't always believe them. Let's move on.

Scene Six

As the audience is led out the young people are all lined up against a wall in the hallway with their backs to the audience. GUARD #2 sits at one table.

GUARD #1: Ah yes, they need me in this one.

GUARD #1 seats himself at another table. He turns to GUARD #2 and nods. The lines below are said simultaneously. The prisoners and guards coordinate their actions.

GUARD #1: Inmate number 23456.
GUARD #2: Inmate number 23457

GEORGE and WILLIAM step forward.

GUARD #1: Squat and cough.
GUARD #2: Squat and cough.

GEORGE and WILLIAM face their backs to the audience, squat and cough. The guards pat them down (in sync). GEORGE and WILLIAM walk back to the wall and stand facing forward.

GUARD #1: Inmate number 23458.
GUARD #2: Inmate number 23459

CARLOS and DAVID step forward.

GUARD #1: Squat and cough.
GUARD #2: Squat and cough.

CARLOS and DAVID face their backs to the audience, squat and cough.

The guards pat them down (in sync). CARLOS and DAVID walk back to the wall. As they do, they exchange glances and it is obvious that there is some animosity between them. They stand against the wall, facing forward.

GUARD #1: Inmate number 234510.
GUARD #2: Inmate number 234511.

TOBIAH and TISHIA step forward.

GUARD #2: Hey man, we got a female here. Do we need to get someone else in here to check her?
GUARD #1: I won't tell anyone if you don't. Just follow the procedure and send her along. We can't have any more delays here.
GUARD #1: Squat and cough.
GUARD #2: Squat and cough.

TOBIAH and TISHIA face their backs to the audience, squat and cough. The guards pat them down (in sync). TOBIAH and TISHIA walk back to the wall and stand facing forward. GUARD #1 turns to the audience.

GUARD #1: Did I play the part well? I did, yeah? I'm good at this acting thing, I got to say. I got it down. You, David, you're up next—go in there, please. Ladies and gentlemen, follow me.

Scene Seven

David is a smooth talker. As the audience walks into the classroom, he makes small talk with each of them, walking around, shaking hands; being extremely charming. After a few seconds of this,

GUARD #1: All right all right, that's enough. Get on with what you have to tell them.... This one's a smooth talker ... got to be careful with the likes of him.
DAVID: What do you mean, man? They got to be careful with the likes of me. The LIKES OF ME? What the hell is that supposed to mean? They got to be careful with the likes of me. You certainly weren't being careful when...
GUARD #1: THAT'S ENOUGH. Get on with what you have to say or I'm taking them to the next place.

Silence. DAVID and the GUARD stare at each other; DAVID eventually looks away.

DAVID: He talks about me like I'm a savage or something.... Maybe I am though. Maybe he's right. I used to run my streets, man. I knew people. People knew me. I used to run my streets, man. Let me show you all something.

DAVID does a martial arts sequence for the audience.

DAVID: You all know what that is? That's martial arts, man. I had to learn that shit real young. Got to be able to defend yourself when you're running the streets.

GUARD #1: You've said that already. Tell them why you were running the streets.

DAVID: Oh now you want me to speak? …Why does anyone run the streets, man? I needed the cash. You've heard the story before. Boy's father abandons his family. Mom has to work ridiculous hours to make ends meet but she still can't of course. She still can barely bring home any money. So young boy has to do what he can to take care of things at home. You all have heard that story before. Ain't nothing different about mine.

GUARD #1: All right then, I'll just have these nice people move—

DAVID: I'm not done. Just because my story ain't different, it doesn't mean it shouldn't be heard…. When I get out of here, I'm gonna change things up. I'm going to have the kind of life where I never have to come to a place like this again. I'm going to change my life. I'M GOING TO CHANGE MY LIFE…

GUARD #1: All right. That's it. Let's move on, ladies and gentlemen. This one's a savage.

Scene Eight

As the audience walks outside, all the young people are in the hallway. Public Enemy's Fight the power *plays in the background. DAVID and CAR-LOS walk to each other, they stare at each other. They point to people, like they are picking teams for a game. CARLOS picks MARCOS and TOBIAH; DAVID picks WILLIAM and TISHIA. The two groups stare at each other. As the music gets louder, the two groups circle each other, almost like a dance. The speed of their walking gets faster, as the music gets louder. When the music reaches a crescendo, GUARD #1 turns off the music. As soon as the music is off, the young people freeze in position.*

GUARD #1: That was getting a bit intense, wasn't it. Better to stop this before it gets out of control. Follow me, please.

The Original Script of Lives Behind the Walls

Scene Nine

WILLIAM shares his flashback while TISHIA keeps stuffing herself with twinkies. After WILLIAM's monologue ends, there is a moment of silence when attention is turned to TISHIA.

GUARD #1: You gonna put those twinkies down long enough to talk to these people, young lady?

TISHIA: What do they wanna know?

GUARD #1: Seeing as how you've been stuffing your face with twinkies for the last few minutes, maybe a good place to start would be why you eat so many of them!

TISHIA: My best friend in elementary school was this girl named Alice. We went everywhere together … to school, to the park, to birthday parties. One day, Alice disappeared from my life. I couldn't find here anywhere. I was told that her parents wanted to move to a "better" neighborhood; they wanted to be around more people like them. They didn't want Alice to be around people like us. Like me. Eating twinkies calms me down. It makes me happy. Twinkies calmed me down when Alice left because her parents didn't want her around poor black kids. They calmed be down when my uncle came into my room and…. Eating twinkies calms me down. They make me happy. I don't have to explain any more than that.

GUARD #1: Ok, then. Now that we've covered that, ladies and gentlemen, onward we go.

Scene Ten

The audience is led out into the hallway, where we see the young people on the floor in different levels of pain.

GUARD #1: What happened here?

GUARD #2: They've been fighting again. You two. Step forward.

DAVID and CARLOS step forward.

GUARD #2: Tell him about this mess?

Silence.

GUARD #2: You know the kind of trouble you can get into for this?

Silence.

GUARD #2: They've lost their tongues. These guys are hopeless, sir.

Haven't learned anything from being in here. They're all going to self-destruct. Just like all those before them.

Tupac Shakur's "Self-destruction" begins to play again. As CARLOS and DAVID listen to the song, something changes in their body language. We don't know what it is, but the two men step forward and shake each other's hands. We see a reconciliation happen between them and once this has been established, DAVID and CARLOS return to their gangs. We see DAVID talking to his gang about why he decided to reconcile with CARLOS—his gang members nod and agree with him. At the same time, we also see CARLOS talking to his gang but things don't go so well for him. MARCOS and CARLOS get into an argument. MARCOS shoves something in CARLOS' stomach and CARLOS falls to the floor. The actors freeze in position.

GUARD #1: Right, well, it didn't quite happen that way, of course. But we've had to be a little … careful in how we showed you this part of the story. We don't want you all having nightmares! Don't worry about that one on the floor. He's only playing dead here. Well, he does really die… just not right now. No need for you all to think about that though. Let's move on. One more story left.

Scene Eleven
(Tobiah's Flashback)

L added his improvised piece at a later date.

Scene Twelve

GUARD #1 takes the audience to the exit. As he speaks the lines below, Tupac Shakur's "Changes" plays softly in the background.

GUARD #1: I still don't understand why you all wanted to hear these stories…. But you're here, I'm here; we all do as we're told, I guess. I've done this job for so many years now that I've learned to pick my battles carefully. I've also learned how to tell which of these young ones will make it and which ones won't. That straight A student, George, I can tell that he's going to OD on heroin once he gets out of here. Carlos, well we all know what happens to him…. He'll get killed by a childhood friend and henchman who will no doubt get the electric chair. Those three aren't going to do so well…. The others though, may have a chance. The 'savage' might actually change his life around when he gets out of here. That young couple seem like they have a shot at making it work. And that last one ... the basketball star ... who knows, maybe he'll join the NBA someday. That's my guess.... As I said, I've done this job for many years and I've gotten real good at telling what'll happen to these ones. Right then, my job here is done. You've watched, you've listened. Not much else to say, really. Good night and good luck.

Appendix B

Extracts from the Script of *IFF Kashmir*

> This play and its title were inspired by Griselda Gamboro's *Information for Foreigners* (1992).

As the audience enters, they walk into a room that is set up like a lecture hall. Audience members are asked to wear some kind of ID as they walk in: a label with their name; a badge saying 'Visitor'; a hat; something like that. The design is one that conveys to the audience that they are attending a formal event. An audio recording plays: "Please take a seat. The event will commence shortly."

There are two GUIDES who take the audience around the spaces in this play. GUIDE #1 is Kashmiri; GUIDE #2 is an Outsider. It is intentionally left unclear as to where exactly this Outsider is from.

The GUIDES enter.

GUIDE #1: Welcome to this event, ladies and gentlemen; an event entitled "Information for/from Outsiders: Chronicles from Kashmir." It is a special event because, today, you will witness a conversation between an ordinary Kashmiri and an ordinary non–Kashmiri—not diplomats; not agencies; not NGOs—just two people from the inside and the outside; two people who have chosen to come together to explore if and how they might be able to walk together. What is the place for an outsider in the face of our struggles in Kashmir today? This is the question that lies at the heart of today's event.

GUIDE #2: My colleague here is from Kashmir. As for me, I am an outsider to this place. I look at Kashmir through the eyes of a … guest; a foreigner; an outsider. Today, with the support of my colleague, I will be sharing with you some of the stories that I have encountered in Kashmir. Maybe you will find resonances in what I share with you. Maybe you won't. After all, this is one outsider's entanglement with a place that many of you get to call home.

Extracts from the Script of IFF Kashmir   215

GUIDE #1: Today, my colleague will take us to different rooms in this building. In each space, he will share a perspective or a voice that he has come across in Kashmir. I have heard him speak of these experiences before but it is the first time that I will be witnessing the stories in this form—this event is as new for me as it is for you.... As someone who has grown up here, who has witnessed the highs and lows of Kashmir's struggles, I have always wondered what outsiders see when they come to my home. Do they simply see the beauty of the land? Or do they only see the curfews and the strikes and the voices of dissent? Do they speak to the common man and woman and get a sense of what is actually happening here? Or do they only sit on houseboats and drink copious amounts of Kashmiri tea, oblivious to what's happening around them? I have always wondered what outsiders see when they come to Kashmir and when my guest here offered to do an event like this, how could I refuse?

GUIDE #2: Today, I will be your guide and take you to different rooms in this building. You will walk around these spaces with me. In some of them, you will be asked to watch and listen. In others, you will be invited to participate. In all of them, you have a choice to be involved as much as you wish. Please, follow me.

GUIDE #2 leads the audience to another room where Scene 1 takes place.

[Scene 1 is a dramatic rendition of Stanley Milgram's obedience experiments—based on a similar scene in Gambaro's original text. At the end of Scene 1]

GUIDE #1: So, you said at the beginning that you were going to show us an outsider's perspective of Kashmir, yes?

GUIDE #2: Yes.

GUIDE #1: So, this story that you've shown us, you've witnessed this in Kashmir?

GUIDE #2: No, no. Not all the stories that I'm showing you are direct, necessarily. Something about this story reminds me of things that I've seen and heard here.

GUIDE #1: I see.... I think I understand what you're saying. I think you are asking: how do ordinary people become each other's torturers and murderers? How do ordinary people, like this teacher, like you and me, like the others here, become part of something dangerous and violent? How do we become complicit within acts of violence even though we are not the masterminds like Hitler? How does this happen?

GUIDE #2: Exactly. That's exactly what being here has made me think about.

GUIDE #1: Right ... so let me ask you something. What kind of teacher would you have been in that situation?

GUIDE #2: I would like to think that I would have said no from the beginning.

GUIDE #1: And if they had threatened to kill you if you refused?

GUIDE #2: I would have still said no.

GUIDE #1: What if they had threatened to kill the student if you didn't do what you were told?

GUIDE #2: It depends, I suppose. If I thought the experiment was going to kill him any way, would it make a difference if they killed him before I did? I mean, at least he would know that I refused...

GUIDE #1: What good would that do when he's dead?

Pause.

GUIDE #2: Yes, there is that.

GUIDE #1: Now imagine if they threatened one of your loved ones if you didn't participate in the experiment.... Then would you refuse? To make a statement?

GUIDE #2: I would want to protect the person I loved.

GUIDE #1 smiles.

GUIDE #1: So, Kashmir has taught you...

GUIDE #2: That it is not always easy to understand why people do what they do. Sometimes, it's hard to understand the psychology behind our own actions. Our own acts of complicity that—

GUIDE #1: —that are powerful and powerless at the same time?

GUIDE #2: Yes.

GUIDE #1: Yes. I agree with you.... What are you going to share with us next?

GUIDE #2: Please, follow me.

GUIDE #2 takes the audience to another room where Scene 2 takes place.

[Scene 2 showcases the emigration/forced migration of Kashmiri Hindus from the region. At the end of Scene 2]

GUIDE #1: So your time in Kashmir has taught you about the history of the Kashmiri Pandits?

GUIDE #2: A little bit, yes.

GUIDE #1: Why only a little?

GUIDE #2: It's a narrative that has been difficult for me to unravel. I met some Pandits in Jammu once ... when they heard that I was coming to Kashmir, this lady, her eyes filled with tears and she said, "You get to go back, and we don't."

GUIDE #1: And you think this is the story of all the Pandits who left?

GUIDE #2: No, of course not. I realize it's one story, one perspective.

GUIDE #1: Because some will tell you that the Pandits were safe and should have stayed in Kashmir.

GUIDE #2: And others have told me that the risks were real; that they had to leave because there was no one here to protect them.

GUIDE #1: Whom do you believe?

GUIDE #2: You think I should pick a side?

GUIDE #1: Don't you?

GUIDE #2: As an outsider, *janab*,[1] there are limits to what I can see and what I can know.

GUIDE #1: So?

GUIDE #2: So, all I can do is keep trying to learn, right? About the many different dimensions to Kashmir's stories?

GUIDE #1: I don't know about that. What's the point of hearing our stories if you don't do something with that knowledge?

GUIDE #2: Isn't there some value to acquiring knowledge even if you don't know what to do with what you learn?

GUIDE #1: I shall respectfully agree to disagree with you on that point. We are in the midst of a war here—many wars. In wartime, knowledge without action is useless.

GUIDE #2: What do you think I should do in response to something like this story though?

GUIDE #1: That's for you to figure out, no? I'm just sharing my thoughts here.... So many people, so many outsiders, come to Kashmir and ask for our stories. They listen to our stories, they leave, and nothing ever gets done about the injustices they have witnessed. It's a form of tourism ... a form of dark tourism—outsiders who come here to listen to our pain.

GUIDE #2: I can certainly understand that, sir. But in a story like this one or the one before, when there are so many parties involved in the mix, it is hard for me—as someone who hasn't lived through this—to see which side is actually telling the truth. It is impossible for me to know what to do because every voice I listen to claims its legitimacy; claims its truth.

GUIDE #1: Yes but ... look, I think we could discuss this for a long time but I don't want to delay things for these people. Please, let's continue with what you have to share with us and we shall continue to discuss this point later.

The GUIDE leads the audience to the next room, where Scene 3 takes place.

[Scene 3 depicts various challenges that Kashmir's artists confront. At the end of Scene 3]

GUIDE #1: It's a complex situation isn't it, *janab*? Tell me, you've met artists from outside Kashmir too—what do you think of the struggles that have been shared with us today?

GUIDE #2: I think that the struggles that these artists are facing are not limited to Kashmir. These are struggles that are being faced by artists across the world. How does one make a living through the arts? How does one balance the richness of tradition with the joys that come with experimentation? Where is the line between making art that sells and selling one's voice as an artist? These are important questions that artists have faced, still face, and will continue to face, across time and space.

GUIDE #1: But isn't there something about a place like Kashmir that makes the struggles different?

GUIDE #2: What do mean, *janab*?

GUIDE #1: Well, I've never met artists from outside Kashmir so I can't be sure. But it seems to me that artists here, they have to have a fire; a burning inside them to commit to their art in the face of violence and family obligation and censorship and fear. They need to find a way for their unique Kashmiri identities to come out through their work … that isn't easy.

GUIDE #2: I don't imagine that it's easy at all. Being caught between all these struggles can be exhausting, I'm sure. Do you see any particular solutions that might address what these actors are facing though?

GUIDE #1: I don't have any solutions but seeing this group's experience has made me want to think about it more.… In one sense, it begins with our children, doesn't it? When we tell them that they should become doctors and engineers and lawyers but very rarely do we tell them to become artists. So it starts there, and because we've created a culture where the arts are not valued as much as other things—when the people who do want to become artists go out into the world, they are faced with nothing but challenges. Add to that the fear of censorship … where artists become afraid to say what they're thinking because of fear of repercussions not only from expected sources like the government and other armed agencies, but also from the harsh criticism from their peers and neighbors and families.... I honestly don't know how some of Kashmir's artists have found the strength to keep going.

GUIDE #2: I must say though that despite all these challenges, I have been amazed by the number of creative and artistic people I have met in Kashmir. There seems to be a growing spirit of entrepreneurship and creativity here; people who are writing poems and articles and movies and songs and plays.... It's admirable. I don't know where they find the fight...

GUIDE #1: Well, they probably find it in their art, don't you think? *Chalo, janab*.² This has given us a lot to think about but perhaps we should keep moving?

GUIDE #2: Yes, let's go on.

The GUIDE takes the audience to the next room, where the next scene takes place.

[These conversations between Kashmiri GUIDE #1 and the outsider GUIDE #2 continue in this way after each scene that showcases a different dimension to the conflicts in the region. Finally, after the last scene]

They all return to the first room, where the audience members had entered the performance.

GUIDE #1: First, I want to thank our visitor here for sharing with us what he has encountered in Kashmir. But having seen some of your experiences and hearing some of your responses, I must say that you seem to be quire confused in your role as an outsider here, *janab*.

GUIDE #2: Yes, I think that's right. Confused is probably the best way to describe how I feel about being in Kashmir...

GUIDE #1: What is this confusion though? From where I stand, you understand the larger issues facing Kashmir quite well. Surely it is clear to you how you can best support Kashmiris?

GUIDE #2: That's the thing, *janab*. It's not clear to me at all. There are so many different points of view here that as someone who ... who hasn't lived through all of this myself, I feel impotent. Like whatever I do—in the grand scheme of things—will not matter. The more people I speak to, the more sides I listen to, the more confused I become about the role of the outsider in all of this. Sometimes I think there is no role for outsiders in Kashmir's affairs. But then I think, how can outsiders not want to learn and become aware of what's happening here, so that we can be better global citizens? I don't know ... confusion is accurate in describing how I feel about what my role is in Kashmir.

GUIDE #1: Do you think you will return to Kashmir?

GUIDE #2: Yes, yes I believe I will. As you say, Insha'Allah I will return.

GUIDE #1: So maybe next time, you will be less confused?

GUIDE #2: Maybe (*Smiles*)

GUIDE #1: Maybe (*Smiles*). On that note, we thank you all for attending this event. As I told you in the beginning, we organized this event because we believe it is important to consider how outsiders see and understand our home ... so that we can consider what the outsider's place might be in Kashmir's future ... if there is a place for them in our future at all...

The term outsider is one that we've used a lot in this event and as we get ready to leave, I shall leave you with a question: Who is an outsider in Kashmir? Is it only the person like this visitor who was not born or brought up here? Or can an outsider also be found in those Kashmiris who do not conform to what others want/expect from them? Can an outsider be found within each one of us, in one-way or another?

With that question, I thank you all for coming and we hope you will join us at our next event.

The GUIDES gesture the audience toward the exit. No curtain call.

At the exit, there is a large blackboard with pieces of chalk around it. The board has a question written in large letters: "Who else should the outsider speak to/learn from in Kashmir?" The audience members can choose to write on it/or not as they exit the space.

Chapter Notes

Chapter One

1. Volunteers of America, 2016.
2. Volunteers of America, 2016.
3. Volunteers of America, 2016.
4. Kushner, 2016.
5. Federal Bureau of Prisons, n.d.
6. Prison Fellowship, 2016.
7. National Council on Crime and Delinquency, 1992.

Chapter Two

1. My mother is … my mother is incredible. She is my best friend and she has taught me how to overcome circumstances that seem impossible. She has taught me how to think for myself—clearly my decisions haven't been perfect and that's why I'm in this shithole but the situation I'm in is not her fault.
2. All screen projections below take from a transcript of Rajneesh Osho's (infamous) talk about the various uses of the word "fuck" (Spiritual Satya, 2016).
3. This was an actual response during the exercise—by one of the young men in the group (X)—when I used it during one of my workshops in the detention center.

Chapter Three

1. The phrases in quotation marks are used to indicate verbatim instances from N's characterization of David.
2. The subsequent images and explanations can be found at (CorrectionsOne, 2014).

Chapter Four

1. Wherever possible, I use the term "psychological differences" rather than "mental illness": it is a personal preference; an ethical choice.
2. Columbia University, 2006.
3. National Conference, 2007.
4. Adapted extracts (Kane, 1998).
5. Adapted extracts from *4.48 Psychosis* (Kane, 1998) till the end of the scene, with the exception of stage directions that specify William and/or Tishia specifically. The extracts continue till the line "I'm angry because I understand, not because I don't."

Chapter Five

1. GED is an acronym for the General Education Diploma: the accreditation that is most often offered prisoners within state-sponsored prison education programs.
2. Excerpts from *No Beauty in Cell Bars* (Jackson, n.d.).
3. Excerpts from *No Beauty in Cell Bars* (Jackson, n.d.).
4. Excerpts from *No Beauty in Cell Bars* (Jackson, n.d.).

Conclusions

1. A big hug.
2. Thank you for everything, man. For always smiling in our chats. For being you. For treating me like a sister. I miss you and you will never know how much it gets to me that I cannot send you a letter. I hope, some day, in this country or in other lands, our paths will cross. It would be my honor to know you in a world on this side of the walls.

Appendix B

1. The Urdu word for "sir."
2. All right, sir.

Bibliography

abc13. 2016. Ex-prison guard faces up to 15 years for having sex with inmates. Available: http://abc13.com/news/ex-prison-guard-faces-up-to-15-years-for-having-sex-with-inmates/1150156/ [2016, August 23].

Adams, T.E., Jones, S.H., & Ellis, C. 2015. *Autoethnography*. Oxford: Oxford University Press.

Alexander, M. 2012. *The new Jim Crow: Mass incarceration in the age of colorblindness*. New York City: New Press.

Amelinckx, A. 2012. Man in prison allegedly sent victim hate mail. Available: http://www.correctionsone.com/corrections/articles/5882007-Man-in-prison-allegedly-sent-victim-hate-mail/ [2016, August 23].

American Civil Liberties Union. 2016. School to prison pipeline. Available: https://www.aclu.org/issues/juvenile-justice/school-prison-pipeline [2016, August 23].

Anderson, B. 1983. *Imagined communities*. London: Verso Books.

Appalachian State University. n.d. Music and crime. Available: http://gjs.appstate.edu/media-coverage-crime-and-criminal-justice/music-and-crime [2016, August 23].

Arbogast, E.L. 2013. What I learned volunteering in prison for 6 months. Available: https://byrslf.co/what-i-learned-volunteering-in-prison-for-6-months-e748e0c82589#.fivuqsjdz [2016, August 23].

Art at Work. n.d. Art at work: A city of Portland and Terra Moto initiative. Available: http://www.artatwork.us/about/intro_and_past_projects.pdf [2016, August 23].

AVP. 2008. Alternatives to violence Project International Gathering. Available: http://aglifpt.org/publications/articles/avp/pdf/ingathering.pdf [2016, August 23].

Balfour, M. Ed. 2004. *Theatre in prison: Theory and practice*. Bristol: Intellect Books.

Barton, D., & Hall, N. 2000. *Letter writing as a social practice*. Amsterdam: John Benjamins Publishing Company.

Berkeley Journal of Criminal Law. 2009. Mental illness in prison: Inmate rehabilitation & correctional officers in crisis. *Berkeley Journal of Criminal Law*. 14(1): 277–301. DOI: http://dx.doi.org/doi:10.15779/Z38JP6M

Boal, A. 1985. *Theatre of the oppressed*. New York: Theatre Communications Group.

Borreli, L. 2013. Parents who scream and swear at teens increase child's risk of depression, bad behavior. Available: http://www.medicaldaily.com/parents-who-scream-and-swear-teens-increase-childs-risk-depression-bad-behavior-255455 [2016, August 23].

Britton, D.M. 2003. *At work in the iron cage: The prison as gendered organization*. New York: New York University Press.

Brooks, C. n.d. System stacked against minorities with mental illness. Available: http://www.treatmentadvocacycenter.org/home-page/71-featured-articles/2593-system-stacked-against-minorities-with-mental-illness [2016, August 23].

Brown, C. 2013. Capturing the transient. *Journal of Applied Arts & Health*. (4)1:117–124.

Buchleitner, K. 2010. *Glimpses of freedom: The art and soul of theatre of the oppressed in prison*. London: LIT Verlag.

Business Insider, 2012. A former prison guard reveals what its like to work on death row. Available: http://www.businessinsider.com/a-former-prison-guard-reveals-what-its-like-to-work-on-death-row-2012-8#q-what-was-your-favorite-and-least-favorite-part-about-your-job-3 [2016, August 23].

Caldwell, M.G. 1956. Group dynamics in the prison community. *Journal of Criminal Law and Criminology*. 46(5): 648–657.

Clemmer, D. 1938. Leadership phenomena in a prison community. *Journal of Criminal Law and Criminology.* 28(6): 861–872.

Cohen, E., Pfeifer, J.E., & Wallace, N. 2014. Use of psychiatric medications in juvenile detention facilities and the impact of state placement policy. *Journal of Children and Family Studies.* 23: 738–744. DOI 10.1007/s10826-012-9655-4.

Columbia University. 2006. Interviewer manual. Available: https://www.cdc.gov/nchs/data/nhanes/limited_access/interviewer_manual.pdf [2016, September 1].

Correctional Officer Education. 2016. How to become a corrections officer. Available: http://www.correctionalofficeredu.org/ [2016, August 23].

CorrectionsOne. 2014. Prison tattoos and their meanings. Available: http://www.corrections one.com/prison-gangs/articles/7527475-15-prison-tattoos-and-their-meanings/ [2016, August 23].

Cowburn, A. 2015. People who are really good at swearing have an important advantage. Available: http://www.independent.co.uk/news/uk/people-who-are-really-good-at-swearing-have-an-important-advantage-a6770486.html [2016, August 23].

Darwish, A. 2009. Masculinity in the Muslim world. Available: http://www.altmuslimah.com/2011/12/masculinity_in_the_muslim_world/ [2016, August 23].

DelliCarpini, M. 2008. Creating communities of professional practice in the correctional education classroom. *Journal of Correctional Education.* 59(3): 219–230.

Delprino, R.P. 2002. *Work and family support services for correctional officers and their family members: A national survey.* National Criminal Justice Reference Service.

Denshire, S. 2014. On auto-ethnography. *Current Sociology Review.* 62(6) 831–850. DOI: 10.1177/0011392114533339

Denzin, N.K. 1997. *Interpretive ethnography: Ethnographic practices for the 21st century.* Thousand Oaks: SAGE Publications.

Denzin, N.K. 2003. Performance ethnography: The call to performance. SAGE Research Methods Online edition: SAGE.

Desert Waters. 2013. From corrections fatigue to fulfillment. Available: http://desertwaters.com/?page_id=749 [2016, August 23].

Dinesh, N. 2015a. Delusions of singularity: aesthetics, discomfort and bewilderment in Kashmir. Research in Drama Education: *The Journal of Applied Theatre and Performance.* 20(1):62–73. DOI:10.1080/13569783.2014.975111.

Dinesh, N. 2015b. Grey zones: Performances, perspectives, and possibilities in Kashmir. Ph.D. Dissertation: University of Cape Town, South Africa.

Dinesh, N. 2016. *Theatre & war: Notes from the field.* Cambridge: Open Book Publishers.

Drybread, K. 2014. Murder and the making of man-subjects in a Brazilian juvenile prison. *American Anthropologist.* 116(4): 752–764. DOI: 10.1111/aman.12147.

Espejo, R. 2002. America's prisons: Viewpoints. Available:http://www.dikseo.teimes.gr/spoudastirio/ENOTES/A/Americas_Prisons_Viewpoints.pdf [2016, July 20].

Fahy, T., & King, K. Eds. 2003. *Captive audience: Prison and captivity in contemporary theater.* New York: Routledge

Federal Bureau of Prisons. n.d. You can make a difference. Available: https://www.bop.gov/jobs/volunteer.jsp [2016, August 23].

Fine, G.A., & Scott, L-J van den. 2011. Wispy communities: Transient Gatherings and imagined micro-communities. *American Behavioral Scientist.* 55(10): 1319–1335. DOI: 10.1177/0002764211409379.

Finn, P., & Tomz, J.E. 1996. *Developing a law enforcement stress program for officers and their families.* National Institute of Justice.

Fox, H. 2013. How did we become the bad guys? Available: http://www.corrections one.com/women-in-corrections/articles/6463916-Orange-uncorked-How-did-we-become-the-bad-guys/ [2016, August 23].

Fritz, M., & Brown, A. 2012. Juvenile education: Inside a confined world. Available: http://www.pbs.org/newshour/updates/american-graduate-jan-june12-richardross_02-02/ [2016, August 23].

Funk, J.B., Elliott, R., Urman, M.L., Flores, G.T., Mock, R.M. 1999. Violence scale: A measure for adolescents. *Journal of Interpersonal Violence.* 14(11): 1123–1136.

Gambaro, G. 1992. *Information for foreigners: Three plays.* Northwestern University Press.

Gardstrom, S.C.1999. Music exposure and criminal behavior: Perceptions of juvenile offenders. *Journal of Music Therapy,* 36(3): 207–221.

Gleason, M. 2015. How pop culture portrays mental illness. Available: http://mhaok.org/how-pop-culture-portrays-mental-illness/ [2016, August 23].

Goffman, E. 1961. *Asylums: Essays on the social*

situation of mental patients and other inmates. New York: Anchor Books.

Goodey, J. 1997. Boys don't cry: Masculinities, fear of crime and fearlessness. *The British Journal of Criminology*. 37(3): 401–418.

Grant, D. 2010. Artists as teachers in prisons. Available: http://www.huffingtonpost.com/daniel-grant/artists-as-teachers-in-pr_b_565695.html [2016, August 23].

Hellriegel, K.L., & Yates, J.R. 1999. Collaboration between correctional and public school systems serving juvenile offenders: A case study. *Education and Treatment of Children*. 22(1): 55–83.

Holman, B., & Ziedenberg, J. 2006. *The dangers of detention: The impact of incarcerating youth in detention and other secure facilities*. Justice Policy Institute Report.

Horvath, G.J. 1982. Issues in correctional education: A conundrum of conflict. *Journal of Correctional Education*. 33(3): 8–15.

Huffington Post. 2012. Terror inmates can read hate mail. Available: http://www.huffingtonpost.co.uk/2012/02/19/terror-inmates-can-read-hate-mail_n_1287273.html [2016, August 23].

IAHV. 2014. Prison S.M.A.R.T.: Stress management and rehabilitation. Available: http://www.prisonsmart.org/images/contentPages/PrisonSmartBooklet_2014.pdf [2016, August 23].

Illich, I. 1968. To hell with good intentions. Available: http://www.swaraj.org/illich_hell.htm [2016, August 23].

Jackson, S. n.d. No beauty in cell bars. Available: http://www.prisonerexpress.org/?mode=poetry&file=Jackson_NoBeauty.xml [2016, August 26].

Jenn. 2014. Masculinity vs. "misogylinity": what Asian Americans can learn from #UCSB shooting. Available: http://reappropriate.co/2014/05/masculinity-vs-misogylinity-what-asian-americans-can-learn-from-ucsb-shooting-yesallwomen/ [2016, August 23].

Just Jobs Academy. 2011. Despite inmate threats jailhouse teacher continues to change lives. Available: http://academy.justjobs.com/jail-teacher/ [2016, August 23].

Kane, S. 1998. *4.48 psychosis*. London: Bloomsbury Methuen.

Kansas Children's Service League. n.d. Facts about juvenile delinquency. Available: https://www.kcsl.org/PDFs/TipCards2014/Half_Facts%20About%20Juvenile%20Delinquency.pdf [2016, August 23].

King, R.A., Hendley, A,J., & Ray, J.L. 1979. Exploring job satisfaction: Working conditions and salaries in corrections teaching. *Journal of Correctional Education*. 30(4): 12–16.

Kushner, J. 2016. The voluntourists dilemma. Available: http://www.nytimes.com/2016/03/22/magazine/the-voluntourists-dilemma.html [2016, August 23].

Lambert, E.G., Hogan, N.L., & Barton, S.M. 2002. Satisfied correctional staff: A review of the literature on the correlates of correctional staff job satisfaction. Available: http://scholarworks.gvsu.edu/scjpeerpubs/13. [2016, August 23].

Lawston, J. E., & Lucas, A. M. 2011. *Razor wire women: Prisoners, activists, scholars, and artists*. New York: State University of New York.

Lee, C. 2014. Class on arts in prison a hit with students and inmates. Available: http://newsroom.ucla.edu/stories/class-on-arts-in-prison-a-hit-with-students-and-inmates [2016, August 23].

Leone, P.E., & Cutting, C.A. 2004. Appropriate education, juvenile corrections, and No Child Left Behind. *Behavioral Disorders*. 29(3): 260–265.

Lil Cuete. 2010. So you wanna be a gangster [Song].

Lopez, O. 2014. Prison officers need help but they won't ask for it. Available: http://www.newsweek.com/2014/06/06/prison-officers-need-help-they-wont-ask-it-252439.html [2016, August 23].

Markham, A.N. 2005. "Go ugly early": Fragmented narrative and bricolage as interpretive method. *Qualitative Inquiry*. 11(6): 813–839.

The Marshall Project. 2015. Preying on prisoners. Available: https://www.themarshallproject.org/2015/06/17/preying-on-prisoners#.4YVvyJUP4 [2016, August 23].

Mathur, S.R., & Schoenfeld, N. 2010. Effective instructional practices in juvenile justice facilities. *Behavioral Disorders*. 36(1): 20–27.

McAvinchey, C. 2011. *Theatre & prison*. London: Palgrave Macmillan.

Mendez, M. 2013. Autoethnography as a research method: Advantages, limitations and criticisms. Available: http://www.scielo.org.co/pdf/calj/v15n2/v15n2a10.pdf [2016, August 23].

Merz, J. 2013. Jimmy Santiago Baca: From prison to poetry. Available: http://articles.mcall.com/2013-04-06/features/mc-jimmy-santiago-baca-northampton-college-20130406_1_martin-meditations-jimmy-santiago-baca-prison [2016, August 23].

Mitchell, K. 2011. *Five truths* [Performance]. London.

Moriarty, J. 2014. *Analytical autoethnodrama: Autobiographed and researched experiences with academic writing*. Rotterdam/Boston/Taipei: Sense Publishers.

NAACP. 2016. Criminal justice fact sheet. Available: http://www.naacp.org/pages/criminal-justice-fact-sheet [2016, August 23].

National Conference. 2007. Mental health needs of juvenile offenders. Available: https://www.ncsl.org/print/cj/mentaljjneeds.pdf [2016, September 1].

National Council on Crime and Delinquency. 1992. Does involvement in religion help prisoners adjust to prison? Available: http://www.nccdglobal.org/sites/default/files/publication_pdf/religion-and-prisoners.pdf [2016, August 23].

National Education Association. n.d. Swearing at school: What's your policy? Available: http://www.nea.org/tools/16342.htm [2016, August 23].

Nedhari, A. 2009. What does it mean to be a real man? Available: http://learning.blogs.nytimes.com/2015/09/10/what-does-it-mean-to-be-a-real-man/ [2016, August 23].

Newman, N. n.d. Machismo: A cultural barrier to learning. Available: http://cronkitezine.asu.edu/latinomales/machismo.html [2016, August 23].

NPR. 2015. Reforming prisoners through poetry. Available: http://www.npr.org/2015/02/07/384589764/reforming-prisoners-through-poetry [2016, August 23].

N.W.A. 1988. Fuck the police [Song].

Otero County Detention Center. 2016. Inmate correspondence. Available:http://ocwebserver7.co.otero.nm.us/Main_Page.php?Dept=detention&Page=correspondence [2016, August 23].

Pajer, K.A., Kelleher, K., Gupta, R.A., Rolls, J., & Gardner, W. 2007. Psychiatric and medical health care policies in juvenile detention facilities. *American Academy of Child and Adolescent Psychiatry*. 1660–1667. DOI: 10.1097/chi.0b013e318157d2da.

Pasternack, R., Portillos, R., & Hoff, H. 1988. Providing an Appropriate education to adjudicated and incarcerated juvenile delinquents: The challenge to correctional education administrators. *Journal of Correctional Education*. 39(4): 154–159.

PBS. n.d. Hip hop: Beyond beats & rhymes. Available: http://www.pbs.org/independentlens/hiphop/masculinity.htm [2016, August 23].

Prison Fellowship. 2016. Would you like to volunteer with prison fellowship? Available: https://www.prisonfellowship.org/action/ [2016, August 23].

Prison Mail. 2006. Hate mail questions—Why would the mailroom let it in and why would anyone send it? Available: http://www.prisontalk.com/forums/archive/index.php/t-198344.html [2016, August 23].

Prison Performing Arts. 2015. PPA youth programs. Available: http://prisonartsstl.org/youth-program/ [2016, August 23].

Prison Reform Trust. 2003. Time to learn. Available: http://www.prisonreformtrust.org.uk/uploads/documents/Time_to_LearnBook.pdf [2016, August 23].

Reddit. 2016. Will prisons give a prisoner hate mail that is sent to them? Available:https://www.reddit.com/r/Prison/comments/4a8bo3/will_prisons_give_a_prisoner_hate_mail_that_is/ [2016, August 23].

Reed, C. 2013. Breaking into prison: An interview with prison educator Laura Bates. Available: http://www.triquarterly.org/interviews/breaking-prison-interview-prison-educator-laura-bates [2016, August 23].

Richardson, L. 2000. New writing practices in qualitative research. *Sociology of Sport Journal*. 17: 5–20.

Rogers, K.M., Pumariega, A. J., Atkins, D.L., & Cuffe, S.P. 2006. Conditions associated with identification of mentally ill youths in juvenile detention. *Community Mental Health Journal*. 42(1): 25–40. DOI: 10.1007/s10597-005-9001-z.

Roy, A. 1999. *The cost of living*. Modern Library.

Saldaña, J. 2011. *Ethnotheatre: Research from page to stage*. Walnut Creek: Left Coast Press.

Schlosser, E. 1998. The prison industrial complex. Available: http://www.theatlantic.com/magazine/archive/1998/12/the-prison-industrial-complex/304669/ [2016, August 23].

Schulten, K. 2015. What does it mean to be "a real man"? Available: http://learning.blogs.nytimes.com/2015/09/10/what-does-it-mean-to-be-a-real-man/ [2016, August 23].

Selfhout, M.H.W., Delsing, M.J.M., ter Bogt, T.F.M, & Meeus, W.H.J. 2008. Heavy metal and hip-hop style preferences and externalizing problem behavior: A two-wave longitudinal study. *Youth & Society*. 39(4): 435–452. DOI: 10.1177/0044118X07308069

Sermjin, J., Devlieger, P. & Loots, G. 2008. The narrative construction of the self: Selfhood as a rhizomatic story. *Qualitative Inquiry*. 14: 632–650.

Shailor, J. Ed. 2011. *Performing new lives: Prison theatre*. London: Jessica Kingsley Publishers.

Shannon. 2012. It happened to me: I teach in a juvenile correctional center. Available: http://www.xojane.com/it-happened-to-me/it-happened-to-me-i-teach-in-a-juvenile-correctional-center [2016, August 23].

Shelton, R. 2007. *Crossing the yard: Thirty years as a prison volunteer*. University of Arizona Press.

Sher-Censor, E., Parke, R.D., & Coltrane, S. 2011. Perceptions of Mexican American adolescents and parents regarding parental autonomy promoting: Divergent Views and adolescents' adjustment. *Journal of Early Adolescence*. 31(5): 671–693. DOI: 10.1177/0272431610373099.

Sommers, J. 2015. Masculinity in prison: The "mask" men have to wear behind bars. Available: http://www.huffingtonpost.co.uk/2015/11/21/masculinity-in-prison_n_8472628.html [2016, August 23].

Southern Poverty Law Center. 2000. Allegations of racist guards are plaguing the corrections industry. Available: https://www.splcenter.org/fighting-hate/intelligence-report/2000/allegations-racist-guards-are-plaguing-corrections-industry [2016, August 23].

Spiritual Satya. 2016. OSHO: meaning and versatility of the word "FUCK." Available: http://www.spiritualsatya.com/osho-meaning-and-versatility-of-the-word-fuck/ [2016, August 25].

State of New Jersey. 2016. Department of corrections application questionnaire. Available:http://www.state.nj.us/corrections/pdf/careers/DEPARTMENT_OF_CORRECTIONS_APP_QUESTIONNAIRE.pdf [2016, August 23].

Steinberg, M.A. & Jacobs, E. 2011. Curriculum in juvenile schools. Available: https://education.ufl.edu/project-liberate/files/2011/01/Curriculum_Juv_Correctional_Sch.pdf [2016, August 23].

Stephey, M.J. 2007. De-criminalizing mental illness. Available: http://content.time.com/time/health/article/0,8599,1651002,00.html [2016, August 23].

Teplin, L.A., Welty, L.J., Abram, K.M., Dulcan, M.K., & Washburn, J.J. 2012. Prevalence and persistence of psychiatric disorders in youth after detention: A prospective longitudinal study. *Arch Gen Psychiatry*. 69(10): 1031–1043.

Thangaraj, S.I. 2015. Desi hoop dreams: Pickup basketball and the making of Asian American masculinity. Available: http://nyupress.org/books/9780814760932/ [2016, August 23].

Thompson, J. Ed.1998. *Prison theatre: Practices and perspectives*. London: Jessica Kingsley Publishers.

Tickle, L. 2007. The voice inside. Available: https://www.theguardian.com/uk/2007/aug/21/ukcrime.poetry [2016, August 23].

Tocci, L. 2007. *The proscenium cage: Critical case studies in U.S. prison theatre programs*. Amherst: Cambria Press.

Travis. 2001. Prisons boss received hate mail. Available: https://www.theguardian.com/society/crimeandpunishment/story/0,,437828,00.html [2016, August 23].

Trounstine, J. 2004. *Shakespeare behind bars: One teacher's story of the power of drama in a women's prison*. Ann Arbor: University of Michigan Press.

Twin Beredaz. 2008. Where did I go wrong? [Song].

Tupac Shakur. 1998. Changes [Song].

Tycer, A. 2008. Victim. Perpetrator. Bystander: Melancholic witnessing of Sarah Kane's "4.48 psychosis." *Theatre Journal*. 60(1): 23–36.

Ulmer, G. 1989. *Teletheory*. New York: Routledge.

U.S. Department of Health and Human Services. 2001. Mental health: Culture, Race, and ethnicity: A supplement to mental health: A report of the surgeon general. Available: http://www.ncbi.nlm.nih.gov/books/NBK44249/ [2016, August 23].

Volunteers of America. 2016. Our ministry of service. Available: https://www.voa.org/our-ministry-of-service [2016, August 23].

Wikipedia. 2016. Hip hop activism. Available: https://en.wikipedia.org/wiki/Hip_hop_activism [2016, August 23].

Young, M.V., Phillips, R.S., & Nasir, N.S. 2010. Schooling in a youth prison. *Journal of Correctional Education*. 61(3): 203–222.

Ziadah, R. 2011. *We teach life, sir* [Performance]. UK/Canada/Palestine.

Index

Adams, T.E. 6, 8–10, 186–187, 189
autoethnodrama 2, 4–5, 10, 16–17, 183, 185–187, 190, 196–197
autoethnography 1–10, 16–17, 183, 186, 188

Barton, D. 173–176
Berkeley Journal of Criminal Law 117, 169–172
Bochner, Arthur P. 5
Britton, D.M. 84, 93, 169–170, 175–177
Brown, Corinna 5–6

Coltrane, Scott 61–63
Cutting, Candace A. 145, 147–149

Denzin, Norman K. 6, 10–11, 17, 183, 186
Drybread 92, 96

Ellis, Carolyn 5–6, 8–10, 186–187, 189

Fine, G.A. 32–34
Finn, P. 164–166, 171–174

Gambaro, Griselda 1, 215
Goffman, Erving 116–117, 120, 176
Goodey, J. 93–96

IFF Kashmir 1, 3, 196

Jones, S.H. 6, 8–10, 186–187, 189

Kane, Sarah 120–121, 175, 185, 221

Lambert, E.G. 172–176
Leone, P.E. 145, 147–149
Lil Cuete 53, 64
Lopez, O. 164, 166

Mathur, S.R. 148–149
Moriarty, J. 4–5, 186
mystory: approach 5, 7, 10–12; expert narratives 30, 58, 92, 116, 144, 169; personal narratives 12, 19, 48, 74, 103, 131, 156; popular narratives 15, 27, 54, 88, 113, 138, 160; rewritten scenes 36, 63, 97, 121, 151, 177

Nasir, N.S. 149–150

Parke, Ross D. 61–62
Phillips, R.S. 149–150

Saldaña, J. 4–5
Schoenfeld, N. 148–149
Scott, Lisa-Jo van den 32–34
Sher-Censor, Efrat 61–62

Tomz, J.E. 164–166, 171–174
Tupac Shakur 160, 205, 212
Twin Beredaz 53, 110

Ulmer, Gregory 10–12, 183

Young, M.V. 149–150

www.ingramcontent.com/pod-product-compliance
Ingram Content Group UK Ltd.
Pitfield, Milton Keynes, MK11 3LW, UK
UKHW041949140426
5217IPUK00014B/711